PROFILES OF POWER
HOW THE GOVERNORS RUN OUR 50 STATES

ALLEN H. NEUHARTH
WITH KEN PAULSON AND PHIL PRUITT

GANNETT CO. INC.

WASHINGTON, DC 20044

❛ *Being governor was the best training school for this job.* **❜**

Ronald Reagan
Elected president 1980, 1984
California governor 1967-74

Interviewed Sept. 10, 1987

❛ *The states are the original repository of authority and power.* **❜**

Jimmy Carter
Elected president 1976
Georgia governor 1971-75

Interviewed June 10, 1988

ISBN 0-944347-14-2

C O N T E N T S

HAWAII
GOV. JOHN D. WAIHEE III

63

MAINE
GOV. JOHN R. McKERNAN JR.

95

IDAHO
GOV. CECIL D. ANDRUS

67

MARYLAND
GOV. WILLIAM DONALD SCHAEFER

99

ILLINOIS
GOV. JAMES R. THOMPSON

71

MASSACHUSETTS
GOV. MICHAEL S. DUKAKIS

103

INDIANA
GOV. ROBERT D. ORR

75

MICHIGAN
GOV. JAMES J. BLANCHARD

107

IOWA
GOV. TERRY E. BRANSTAD

79

MINNESOTA
GOV. RUDY PERPICH

111

KANSAS
GOV. MIKE HAYDEN

83

MISSISSIPPI
GOV. RAY MABUS

115

KENTUCKY
GOV. WALLACE G. WILKINSON

87

MISSOURI
GOV. JOHN ASHCROFT

119

LOUISIANA
GOV. CHARLES E. "BUDDY" ROEMER III

91

MONTANA
GOV. TED SCHWINDEN

123

NEBRASKA
GOV. KAY A. ORR

127

NEVADA
GOV. RICHARD H. BRYAN

131

NEW HAMPSHIRE
GOV. JOHN H. SUNUNU

135

NEW JERSEY
GOV. THOMAS H. KEAN

139

NEW MEXICO
GOV. GARREY CARRUTHERS

143

NEW YORK
GOV. MARIO CUOMO

147

NORTH CAROLINA
GOV. JAMES G. "JIM" MARTIN

151

NORTH DAKOTA
GOV. GEORGE A. "BUD" SINNER

155

OHIO
GOV. RICHARD F. CELESTE

159

OKLAHOMA
GOV. HENRY BELLMON

163

OREGON
GOV. NEIL GOLDSCHMIDT

167

PENNSYLVANIA
GOV. ROBERT P. CASEY

171

RHODE ISLAND
GOV. EDWARD D. DiPRETE

175

SOUTH CAROLINA
GOV. CARROLL A. CAMPBELL JR.

179

SOUTH DAKOTA
GOV. GEORGE S. MICKELSON

183

TENNESSEE
GOV. NED McWHERTER

187

THE GOVERNORS' STORY

BUS STOP: The Minnesota state Capitol was one of 50 visited by BusCapade.

The first phone call went to the Missouri governor's office. "We'll be traveling to all 50 states on a 40-foot blue-and-white USA TODAY bus. Over the course of the six-month trip, we plan to interview several thousand people, including every governor. Could you arrange for an interview with Gov. Ashcroft the week of March 16th?"

The polite response: "We'll get back to you."

Our early inquiries left a number of press secretaries puzzled. They had not yet heard of "BusCapade" and there weren't any standard procedures for dealing with anything quite like this. What should they do first? Check on the interview date or issue a parking permit?

The caller from USA TODAY had mentioned a musical horn on the bus that plays state songs, the theme from *Rocky* and *On the Road*

Again. Was this just an interview or would the governor be expected to help blow up balloons?

In time, press secretaries across the USA came to recognize our BusCapade interviews for what they were: largely traditional, back-to-basics journalism that just happened to roll into town on a largely untraditional, promotion-powered bus.

Over the course of our journey, we did indeed interview all 50 governors, becoming the first news team to tap the opinions of all the states' leaders over a six-month period. We also followed up with the nation's newest governors after the November 1987 elections.

We asked them about the people, places, politics and policies of their states. About education and the economy. Race relations and public relations. Traditions and tourism. And much more.

The governors' own words run throughout this book. Plain talk about issues of basic importance. Not just to the residents of their respective states, but to all of us across the USA.

This is the story of the USA's governors in a decade of change:

▶ Why they're more like corporate CEOs than old-style politicians.

▶ How their power has grown.

▶ What national issues they're tackling together.

▶ And who they are — their styles and their strengths, along with some personal perceptions from the news team.

The USA's top 50. These are the state leaders of today. And many of them may be among the nation's leaders of tomorrow.

PART 1

COMMON CHALLENGES

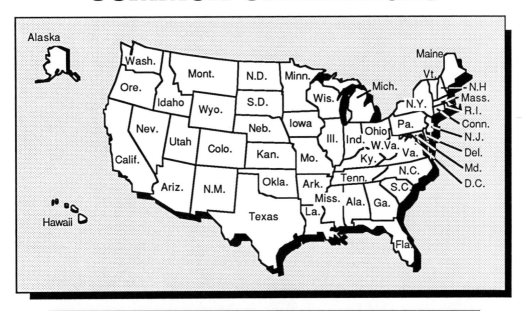

Today's governors — a new breed — face common challenges with impact beyond state borders. They are problem-solvers, with styles as diverse as the 50 states.

YESTERDAY AND TODAY

Governor.

The title evokes a distinct old-fashioned image: A hand-shaking, back-slapping, baby-kissing wheeler-dealer puffing on a big cigar. Largely male. Largely white. Largely large.

And today, that governor is largely gone.

We met only a few old-style governors on our 50-state tour of the USA. Compared with their sleeker, more competitive, modern counterparts, they seemed like political dinosaurs.

By and large, the governors of the past have been replaced by a generation whose priorities and passions, stands and styles are distinctly different.

The Louisiana governor's office is a striking example:

▶ In 1961, Gov. Jimmie Davis, songwriter and Hollywood

SUNSHINE AND SONGS: Gov.-songwriter Jimmie Davis astride Sunshine.

cowboy, rode his beloved palomino Sunshine — named for his hit song, *You Are My Sunshine* — up the capitol steps and into his office. Why? "Sunshine had never been in the governor's office before," Davis said. Meanwhile, racial tension was at a full gallop in Louisiana.

▶ In 1987, Gov. Edwin Edwards, 60, sat in the dining room of the governor's mansion and told the BusCapade news team, "The only way I could lose the next election is if I was caught in bed with a dead woman or a live boy." After a dismal primary showing, he withdrew from the race — and left behind a multi-million dollar deficit and a legacy of ingloriousness and indictments, albeit no convictions.

▶ In 1988, Gov. Buddy Roemer, 44, Harvard educated, took the oath of office, replacing Edwards. He said he wanted "a new Louisiana. . . . I'd like to reshape our image as a place where investors, businessmen and women invest and create jobs."

Another important change: The governor's office is no longer an exclusive club for white males. Among the current members:

▶ Nebraska Gov. Kay A. Orr, 49, the first female Republican governor in the USA.

▶ Hawaii Gov. John D. Waihee III, 42, a native Hawaiian.

▶ Florida Gov. Bob Martinez, 53, a Hispanic.

▶ Vermont Gov. Madeleine M. Kunin, 54, a Swiss emigre.

Today's governors range in age from 39 to 71. Of those reporting a religious preference, 29 are Protestants, 12 are Catholics, two are Jewish and one is Greek Orthodox. Forty-four are married, two have never been married, three are divorced and one is widowed. Forty have college degrees.

Despite the diversity, they have much in common:

▶ Power: The shift from the Potomac to the state houses started with President Richard Nixon's general revenue sharing. His plan was a backlash to President Lyndon Johnson's Great Society. Johnson's plan sent a lot of money to the states, but kept much of the control in Washington. Nixon's plan also sent a lot of money to the states — but the states also had some flexibility in spending it. Nixon felt the government closest to the problem would have the best solution.

That pattern continued through the 1970s, and President Ronald Reagan's fiscal policies and political philosophy have proved to be a catalyst in the 1980s. He has continued moving responsibility for domestic programs to the states — often while tightening federal funds for the programs.

"Basically since Mr. Reagan has been president, whether the Democrats or even the Republicans agree with everything he's done, he's made (all governors) more powerful," says Arkansas Gov. Bill Clinton, a Democrat.

Because of the ongoing shift in power, the Council of State Governments predicted in 1985 that the 1980s and 1990s "could be a historic 'window of opportunity' for the states. Never before have they been looked to by both their federal and local partners as leaders in dealing with domestic needs and problems."

There also are institutional reasons for governors' power, according to University of Virginia professor Larry Sabato. The governorship is "much more powerful than most of the mayorships and certainly more powerful than the presidency in some ways. For example, 43 of the governors have the item veto, something that most presidents would give at least three fingers for," says Sabato, author of *Goodbye to Good-time Charlie, The American Governorship Transformed.*

▶ A dynamic office: "People used to run (for governor) on bringing the state together, or giving people good government or basically doing the right thing," Gov. Clinton says. "Now people tend to run on 'moving forward' — better schools, more jobs, cleaner environment — all that sort of thing. I think the nature of the job is much more dynamic. It's a much more activist job than it was 10 or 15 years ago."

▶ Responsibility: Based on general revenues, all 50 states, if they were corporations, would qualify for the Fortune 500 list. California, the state with the largest budget, would rank No. 7, just behind IBM. Vermont, fiscally the smallest state, would rank No. 383.

▶ Style: "Now we have this new breed of highly educated managers. A lot of them are learning on the job. They are learning to become managers. They are learning to become CEOs," says Regina K. Brough, executive director of the Governors Center at Duke University in Durham, N.C. "We are seeing them pay a lot more attention to questions of management principles and strategies and tactics and really grabbing hold."

▶ Common goals: True, governors do compete with each other, especially for new industry. But they also have come to realize that they must cooperate. Why? Because they share some of the same problems and goals. For this reason, the National Governors' Association has become a forum for seriously sharing solutions and problems. Governors have seen, for example, that the best way to reduce welfare costs is to address teen pregnancy, drugs, adult illiteracy and other social problems that remove people from the workforce. One way they have mounted their attack is through NGA task forces that map out detailed battle plans.

Gov. Kunin sizes up today's governorship this way: "Even in the '60s, at least in Vermont, the federal government was a great resource of funds, and if you wanted to start a new program you could find a federal grant to do it. Today . . . we have to figure out how to do some of the things the federal government used to do. And I think we also have to be more creative, more innovative. Today, the process is reversed, where the states are genuinely much more the laboratories of change."

When Kunin talks about her management style, she cites Tom Peters, author of the bestseller *In Search of Excellence*. His book, which became something of a bible for corporations across the USA, gave Kunin the idea of having state managers write "mission statements" describing what they planned to do in their departments. Mission statements are now an ongoing process in Vermont state government.

Ultimately, of course, good governors turn the office, the responsibility, the power and the style into tangible results. That's the acid test. And many governors are passing, says Robert D. Behn, director of the Governors Center at Duke University — especially when it comes to three crucial issues:

"Things that have reflected the most gubernatorial initiatives of recent years have been education, economic development and, most recently, welfare."

These are top priorities for governors across the USA. They illustrate well how key state leaders are influencing the national agenda.

FROM THE STATEHOUSE TO THE WHITE HOUSE

A *conversation with former President Jimmy Carter, whose hands-on management style as governor of Georgia 1971-75 led to election to the White House.*

Is being a governor good training for the presidency?

"In my judgment, it is excellent training. In the first place, a governor has to deal with budgets, with executive responsibilities, even with managing the military in some substantial degree as commander in chief of the National Guard.

"The governors have to deal with legislatures, different from the Congress in many respects, but similar also in a number of ways. The governor has to be at the receiving end and administering end of almost all of the federal domestic programs in transportation, welfare or education, health care and so forth.

"The governors are the ones who are responsible for the actual administration of federal programs, so it gives the state executives an excellent opportunity as well as a major responsibility to assess the strengths and weaknesses of these programs that the Congress has evolved.

"Another aspect of the governorship that was very significant when I was in office was a broad range of relationships with foreign countries. I traveled extensively when I was governor, primarily to promote the investment of foreigners in my state of Georgia and also to sell and to market Georgia products. I went to nations in Latin America, to Japan, to Europe, to the Mideast. This was a major responsibility of Southeastern governors when I was in office during the early '70s, and increasingly it is becoming a commitment of governors on a nationwide basis."

How has the office of the governor changed over the years?

"Governorships had a tremendous boost in responsibilities when Nixon was president, and when revenue sharing was implemented by the Congress, giving major grants to states in lieu of the highly fragmented, smaller program grants that had been the case in the past.

"When I was in office, the major programs that related to domestic affairs and community development — welfare, education, transportation and so forth — were evolved with the closest concentration between me and my staff on the one hand and governors and local officials on the other hand.

"You have to remember that the states are the original repository of authority and power under the U.S. Constitution. The federal government only has those responsibilities that have been specifically designated to the federal government. This originated in Colonial times with the Constitutional Convention and later the drafting and ratification of the U.S. Constitution, 200 years ago, and it's very significant that the states retain a tremendous authority and responsibility not often recognized in this country.

"Some states have very powerful governors. Georgia is one of them. Other states have relatively weak governorships. For instance, I had line-item veto over appropriations bills; the Legislature was only in session for about 48 days a year. It was almost impossible for the Legislature to override one of my vetoes."

How do you think the public perceives governors?

"Beginning back in the mid '70s, there was an adverse reaction among the general populace to the policies of the federal government. This gave a negative image to even highly qualified people who ran (for office) from the U.S. Senate position, or the U.S. House of Representatives. I think that the governor escapes a stigma of longtime Washington service, whether that stigma is justified or not."

Certainly, that worked to your advantage in 1976.

"Yes."

When you came to the White House, did you apply any lessons you learned while running the state of Georgia?

"Well, I was a very tight fiscal conservative. I had a background as commander in chief of the National Guard, plus 11 years of active service in the U.S. Navy, most of it in submarines. I was aware of the need to include state and local officials in decisions that directly affected their roles or responsibilities. The job training programs and allocation of transportation funds, and community development programs. ... These were basically evolved by governors and mayors working with my staff and with me. So, I reached out to governors and mayors in a very constructive way."

For the past 12 years, the White House has been occupied by former governors. Is this a trend?

"It might be a trend; whether it's going to continue, no one can predict. But, as you know, with the Vietnam War, with Watergate, with CIA revelations, with the Iran-contra affair, the people of the nation have a tendency to want someone to serve who hasn't been in Washington for a long time. And I think that it's a political fact, whether it's justified or not."

WORKING FOR EXPANSION

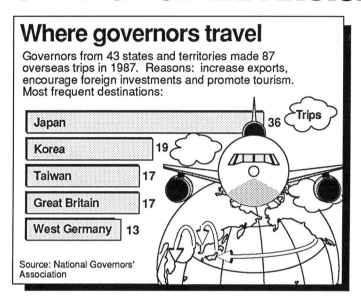

Where governors travel

Governors from 43 states and territories made 87 overseas trips in 1987. Reasons: increase exports, encourage foreign investments and promote tourism. Most frequent destinations:

	Trips
Japan	36
Korea	19
Taiwan	17
Great Britain	17
West Germany	13

Source: National Governors' Association

The modern governor is managing the economy. It's no longer enough to sit back and wait for the business cycle to do its magic. It's no longer enough to simply show up and cut the ribbon at the next factory opening.

Today's governor must be prepared to compete with other governors. They have to talk the language of corporate chieftains. They have to do their homework. They have to have a plan. Today's governor is personally involved with:

▶ Luring foreign and domestic industry.
▶ Finding markets for state goods.
▶ Helping businesses expand.

"As any governor will tell you, compared to his or her predecessor over the last 10 years, governors today are out there on the front line soliciting industry," says University of Virginia government professor Larry Sabato. His book *Goodbye to Good-time Charlie* studies how governors have changed in the past 30 years.

"I don't think there's a serious governor in the country who hasn't been abroad for a trade mission recently, who hasn't set up an international trade office in one of the major foreign capitals, and who doesn't roam the country, if necessary, competing with other states for major industry plants and new high-tech developments. It's a major part of their job today."

The facts support Sabato: All 50 states have economic development agencies. In late 1987, 38 of the states had 107 foreign trade offices — and more states and more offices are being added yearly. Four states are either planning or opening nine offices in 1988.

New Jersey Gov. Thomas H. Kean's experience supports Sabato, too. Kean went to China and Japan in September 1987 and unexpectedly bumped into five other governors.

"I guess if I want to talk to governors, I'll have to go to China," Kean quipped.

"This is a brand-new phenomenon in American life," he said. "Governors 10 years ago didn't think they were the ones who had to go and attract business from other countries."

While on the trip, Kean went to Tokyo to open a New Jersey trade office, and he found that he had company. Thirty-one other states already had offices there.

The USA's ambassador to Japan, Mike Mansfield, told us that 46 governors have visited him in Tokyo in the past 11 years.

Around the world.

Across the USA.

In every state.

Governors are thinking diversity, expansion, development. And they're doing something about it.

Some examples:

▶ In April 1987, US West Inc. announced it was looking for a place to spend up to $55 million on a telecommunications research center. Employment: 1,500. One of the 14 states in its territory would get the prize. The states were sent an extensive questionnaire that dealt with 70 criteria, and the site selection committee talked with all 14 governors.

Two governors — Evan Mecham of Arizona and Terry E. Branstad of Iowa — personally returned the questionnaire to US West's headquarters in Denver and made presentations. Other governors returned their questionnaires in one western theme or another. One used saddlebags; another selected a cowboy dressed in chaps. Colorado got the prize, mainly because

of research going on at its universities.

The center is scheduled to open in 1991.

▶ Virginia Gov. Gerald L. Baliles took three trips abroad in 1987. His itinerary included England, Sweden, Denmark, Japan, Hong Kong, Korea and Taiwan. What prompted his travel? It was partly a 1986 study showing that only 6 percent of Virginia's small businesses exported products and that 77 percent of small-business owners weren't interested in exporting. "We ignore the changes in this world at our peril," Baliles told the National Governors' Association meeting in July 1987.

▶ Maryland Gov. William Donald Schaefer made two overseas trade missions in 1987. His trade policy council also held an international trade conference for Maryland business owners. The conference title: "How To Succeed In World Trade."

▶ Nebraska Gov. Kay Orr pushed through two pieces of controversial legislation in 1987 designed to attract new businesses and to make it easier for existing businesses to expand by offering tax credits for investments, sales tax refunds and personal property tax exemptions.

In one sense, governors have long been involved in economic development. It is the way they are involved that has changed. In the 19th century, states routinely made land available for canals and railroads and helped with the financing for those ventures.

Meanwhile, the federal government regulated interstate commerce and offered protection to domestic industry in the form of tariffs. Otherwise, it was a state show.

At least that's the way it was until the Great Depression. That's when a lot of people — especially those in power — decided that too much diversification leads to chaos. They concluded that regulation and planning on the federal level was the answer. And so, for the better part of the next 50 years, Washington was the center of much of the nation's financing, promotion and planning.

Then came the recession of 1981-82. Plants closed. Welfare lines grew longer. And even when the economy picked up, many of the lost jobs were obviously lost forever — lost in large part to foreign competition.

The states — and that meant the governors — had to do something, so many of them generated better business climates, primarily by cutting taxes, analyzing their economies, deciding what was right for their states and then putting together strategies that would attract the industry the state needed.

The decline of the textile industry in the '60s already had forced Southern governors to be more aggressive in attracting foreign industry. By the end of the 1981-82 recession, governors in the rest of the USA were following their lead. Washington's role diminished.

Kean says that's precisely what happened in New Jersey.

"When I came into office, we had a recession in New Jersey — and the worst since Depression times. We had a $600 million deficit; we had an unemployment rate which was going to 10 percent.

"A state like New Jersey had been sitting back, I guess, and losing jobs and now we were in a recession and with a large unemployment rate."

Kean said he realized that Southern governors had been actively courting foreign business for years, so he talked with them for advice.

Luring new industry is the highest profile, if not the most glamorous, means of expanding a state's economy — especially when it comes to landing the big ones. The rewards are great and, usually, so are the risks. Consider:

▶ In 1985, Gov. James R. Thompson got the Mitsubishi-Chrysler Diamond Star plant for Illinois. The reward: 2,900 jobs. The risk: $88 million in incentives.

▶ In 1985, then-Gov. Martha Layne Collins got Toyota to build a plant in Kentucky. The reward: 3,000 jobs. The risk: $125 million in incentives.

▶ In 1984, Gov. James J. Blanchard got Maz-

da for Michigan. The reward: 3,500 jobs. The risk: $120 million in incentives.

▶ In 1985, then-Gov. Lamar Alexander got General Motors' Saturn plant for Tennessee. The original reward: 6,000 jobs. The adjusted reward: 3,000 jobs. The risk: $70 million in incentives.

The risks are real. The Volkswagen plant in New Stanton, Pa., proves it.

When Pennsylvania got that prize in 1976, it was the envy of many governors. VW's investment in the plant would be $250 million. There would be 4,500 jobs at the plant, as many as 20,000 related jobs. 220,000 cars per year. The $71 million and five-year local tax abatement that Pennsylvania offered looked like a bargain. Volkswagen was selling Rabbits faster than they could hop off the delivery trucks. The German company was strong. What could possibly go wrong?

What could go wrong was that VW was destined to run into more formidable U.S. competition — and into the Japanese. The result: VW will close the New Stanton plant before the end of 1988. It has been running at less than half capacity for five years. 2,100 hourly workers and 400 salaried workers will lose their jobs.

That is not to say that attracting foreign business is a crap shoot. It is not. It is a business. And as is true with all businesses, says Ralph Gerson, former director of the Michigan Department of Commerce, it boils down to a risk/reward calculation.

Gerson, a key player in Blanchard's negotiations to get Mazda, takes the business analogy even further. He says Michigan is an enterprise with 9 million shareholders, and that Blanchard and his staff felt that the $120 million they put on the line for Mazda was a good investment for those shareholders. But even Blanchard says it will be years before Michigan really knows how much Mazda will pay off.

❝ *When I came into office, we had a recession in New Jersey — and the worst since Depression times. We had a $600 million deficit; we had an unemployment rate which was going to 10 percent.* ❞

N.J. Gov. Thomas Kean

For the first 26 workers at the Diamond Star plant in Illinois, and for Larry Ellison, who works in trim and final assembly at Mazda in Michigan, the payoff is here. Their governor struck a deal, and they got a job.

Eight of the first 26 people hired by Diamond Star were unemployed — some of them victims of the soft farm economy. Ellison didn't have full-time employment when he went to work at Mazda.

When asked if Michigan paid too much for Mazda, Ellison put it this way:

"I'm not a politician. I don't know. I'm grateful for the job I got and I don't know how much it cost the state. . . . I'm glad to have a job after 14 months of picking up a job here and a job there to try to support my family. I appreciate the job. I appreciate what it took to eventually employ 3,500 people."

Jobs.

That's what terms like economic diversity, economic expansion and economic development boil down to.

Jobs.

A staple on the modern governor's priority list.

MAKING THE GRADE

Highest-paid teachers

Classroom teachers in the USA's public schools earned an average of $28,031 annually in the 1987-88 school year. Where they make the most*:

Alaska	$40,424
District of Columbia	$36,465
New York	$33,600
Connecticut	$33,515
California	$33,092

Source: National Education Association

*Average is for classroom teachers with 15 years of experience

Nowhere is the impact of the modern governor felt more strongly than in the USA's school systems.

The basic curriculum for the '80s and beyond:

Reading, writing, arithmetic — and reform.

Stung by the criticism leveled by the National Commission on Excellence in Education in its 1983 study "A Nation At Risk," the governors have aggressively tackled the task of improving the nation's schools.

The commission's report was a scathing indictment. Among the findings:

▶ A "rising tide of mediocrity" was afflicting the USA's educational systems.

▶ The scores of high school students taking standardized tests had been declining since 1963.

▶ In comparison with other industrialized nations, the USA's students had inferior skills.

The report also placed primary responsibility for governing and financing the nation's schools with state and local governments.

The governors accepted the challenge. Some more quickly than others. But by 1985, the reform movement had become a veritable steamroller and governors decided to pool their resources at a meeting of the National Governors' Association.

The association formed seven task forces, each assigned to investigate one field of education reform. The mission: Ask tough questions about improving our schools and develop a plan of action that can be applied in any state.

Why did the governors get serious about education reform? The basics:

▶ Politics: "A Nation At Risk" increased the political stakes. Voters were demanding a quality education for their children and the report helped crystallize reform efforts. "There's no question that the report kind of broke like a firestorm across the country," said Arkansas Gov. Bill Clinton.

▶ Money: Education is the single largest expense for every state.

▶ Jobs: Better education means better jobs. And better trained citizens mean a greater likelihood of attracting new industry to a state — and competing effectively in a global economy.

The governors' task forces weren't looking for any quick fixes. In fact, they named their resulting study "The Governors' 1991 Report on Education," assuming that the states would need the five years beginning in 1986 to achieve progress on all fronts.

Education Secretary William J. Bennett described the governors' report as possibly "the single most important event in American education in the last five years."

From the governors' task forces:

▶ Recommendation: Pay teachers reasonable salaries and offer them a "real voice in decisions." At the same time, require that teachers "acknowledge their basic responsibility for performance."

Simply put, low wages have driven many excellent teaching candidates away from the profession and states have to raise the ante to attract good people. At the same time, taxpayers have a right to know that improved wages will translate into positive professional performance.

▶ Recommendation: Help 4- and 5-year-old children from low-income families prepare for school so they're more likely to succeed in grades 1-12 and beyond.

These children — along with those from single-parent homes or non-English-speaking families — are described as being educationally "at risk." It's been estimated that almost one-third of the nation's schoolchildren fall into this category.

▶ Recommendation: Parents should be given some control over which public schools their children attend.

"America is a land of choices," former Colorado Gov. Richard Lamm wrote in his task force report on parental involvement and choice. "In virtually every area of our economic and private lives, we have a smorgasbord of choice. It is thus ironic that in this land of choice there is so little choice in the public school system."

Proponents of choice programs contend that if parents are permitted to "shop around" for their children's education, schools will have to offer a competitive education or risk losing students.

▶ Recommendation: Require that colleges assess what their students are learning.

The concern is whether colleges are living up to their responsibilities to students by providing an education that adequately prepares them for employment. College students have a right to this kind of consumer protection, advocates of reform say.

The governors' task force reports and the earlier "A Nation At Risk" are yielding results all across the USA:

▶ In Indiana, Gov. Robert D. Orr led the fight for the A-Plus education program approved in 1987 by the state Legislature. The program, developed by Orr and state school superintendent H. Dean Evans, provides for annual statewide achievement tests for students in seven grades, cash rewards for schools with improved performance, a longer school year, a new accreditation system and teacher and principal evaluations.

To promote the A-Plus program, Orr says he'll talk to 10,000 Indiana high school teachers by 1989, sharing his views on education and asking for their ideas.

▶ In Wisconsin, Gov. Tommy G. Thompson launched a program that provides free college tuition to qualified students attending one of five Milwaukee inner-city high schools. Another program forgives state education loans for students who go back to teach in the inner city after graduating from college.

▶ In Colorado, the Higher Education Accountability Law passed in 1985 requires that colleges be held accountable for improvements in students' skills and knowledge between enrollment and graduation. Effective in 1990, the state can withhold up to 2 percent of a college's funding if accountability standards aren't in place.

▶ In Minnesota, thousands of 11th- and 12th-grade students can take classes at area colleges and have course credits applied to their high school records. In this experiment with school choice, the college generally receives the state aid that would have gone to the high school.

▶ Under the leadership of Gov. Thomas H. Kean, New Jersey increased the minimum pay for teachers to $18,500 a year and established a high school proficiency test that must be passed before a student can graduate.

▶ In Iowa, Gov. Terry E. Branstad signed into law a bill that gave beginning teachers a minimum salary of $18,000 and provided for increased salaries for more experienced teachers.

Said Branstad: "Our concern is that some of the best graduates of our colleges and universities are being offered beginning teachers' salaries in other states far above what we can offer,

states that don't have even near the education system we do."

▶ In Connecticut, the 1986 Education Enhancement Act provided for the payment of more than $300 million over a three-year period to increase teachers' salaries.

▶ In Louisiana, new Gov. Buddy Roemer was elected on a platform that included merit pay for teachers. Roemer's long-term goal: to pay Louisiana teachers the national average salary, currently about $28,000. Louisiana's teachers now earn an average of about $20,000 a year.

▶ Neighboring Mississippi, with its landmark Education Reform Act of 1982, once was among the leaders in tackling school problems. That act provided for $219 million to open kindergartens, establish merit pay for teachers and begin competency tests for teachers and students.

But funding has not kept up with the state's ambitions and Mississippi's students now rank last in the nation on ACT test scores. Their teachers rank last in pay.

In campaigning for the governorship, Ray Mabus promised that education would be his first priority. "I'm willing to fight over everything else. But I think teachers are first." Elected in 1987, Mabus now faces the challenge of rallying Mississippi to school reform.

His argument for pay hikes for teachers: "We are entrusting them with the most valuable thing we have, and that's the children. That's our future. We as a society, and not just in Mississippi, but across the country, tend to view the value of jobs by the amount of money that's being paid. Teachers aren't ever going to get paid like lawyers, doctors and some other segments of society. But we can raise that value."

Of course, legislative support is essential to any governor's reform efforts.

West Virginia Gov. Arch A. Moore Jr. de-

❛ We as a society, and not just in Mississippi, but across the country, tend to view the value of jobs by the amount of money that's being paid. Teachers aren't ever going to get paid like lawyers, doctors and some other segments of society. But we can raise that value.❜

Miss. Gov. Ray Mabus

clared 1987 "The Year of Education" in his state, but saw his list of educational initiatives — including pay hikes for the state's teachers — flounder in the Legislature.

"We asked the Legislature for the implementation of this package and we immediately got into this political firestorm," said Moore.

The result, said Moore: "Of those 15 or 16 initiatives, only one passed. And while it was a good, solid piece of legislation, it did not materially affect the problem that we had — losing our professional educators on the elementary, secondary and higher education levels to other states.

"The Year of Education became 'The Year of Disappointment,' " Moore said.

But Moore, like others who have not achieved the gains in education they feel their states need, says he will keep trying. The governors' plans are ambitious, but progress is being made.

One particularly encouraging sign: A 1988 study sponsored by the American Council on Education and UCLA's Higher Education Research Institute found that the number of college students interested in a teaching career has increased by two-thirds since 1982.

Someone is getting the message.

REVAMPING THE SYSTEM

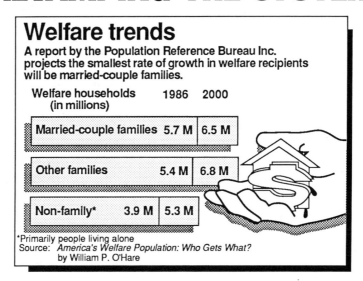

Welfare trends

A report by the Population Reference Bureau Inc. projects the smallest rate of growth in welfare recipients will be married-couple families.

Welfare households (in millions)	1986	2000
Married-couple families	5.7 M	6.5 M
Other families	5.4 M	6.8 M
Non-family*	3.9 M	5.3 M

*Primarily people living alone
Source: *America's Welfare Population: Who Gets What?* by William P. O'Hare

In Massachusetts, it's called ET — Employment and Training (ET) CHOICES program.

In Michigan, it's MOST — Michigan Opportunity and Skills Training Program.

In California, GAIN — Greater Avenues for Independence (GAIN) program.

In Delaware, First Step.

Across the USA, they're labeling it welfare reform.

Welfare was at the top of the agenda when the USA's governors gathered in July 1987 in Traverse City, Mich., for the National Governors' Association convention.

The theme of the meeting: "Making America Work."

The assumption about a welfare system based on cash handouts: It gives people a choice between "security without pride or pride without security." And that, all governors seem to agree, is no choice at all.

The answer: Programs that support people while they are learning to support themselves.

The view that something needs to be done cuts across state lines. Includes liberals and conservatives. Democrats and Republicans. It is a consensus that Sen. Daniel Patrick Moynihan, D-N.Y., has likened to a "rare alignment of the sun, the moon and the earth that causes all manner of natural wonders."

The problem is the 50-year-old Aid to Families with Dependent Children — typically called AFDC. AFDC is what most people are talking about when they talk about welfare. It is the main program that provides cash to people who are not disabled.

AFDC is not cheap. In 1986:

▶ $2 billion went to administrative costs.

▶ $15.8 billion went to benefits.

Who receives AFDC benefits?

▶ 3.7 million families or 10.9 million people.

▶ About half the people lining up at AFDC offices are young, single mothers. Many of them have never been married to the fathers of their children. Forty percent were abandoned by their husbands.

The states are responsible for running the welfare programs, although it must be within federal guidelines. The federal government picks up a little more than 50 percent of the tab. In 1986, the states spent $73 billion on welfare — including AFDC, Medicaid and other programs — and the federal government kicked in $42 billion of that amount.

It's an established system. The money gets to the hands of the needy. So what's the problem?

The problem, say many governors, is that it is not working. Cash-handout recipients receive little — if any — incentive to become self-sufficient. Even if they're offered a job, it usually pays little more than welfare and often doesn't include health insurance — a benefit all welfare recipients have.

Beyond that, the sons and daughters of cash-handout recipients are often doomed to a life of welfare. The statistics prove it. A 1987 NGA publication, "Bringing Down The Barriers," reports that for every 100 children born in the late '80s:

▶ 13 will be born to teen-age mothers.

▶ 15 will have parents who have no job.

▶ 15 will have parents who earn a below-poverty wage.

▶ 25 will end up on welfare for a portion of their childhood.

Debates about welfare are many, but they all come down to the same question:

How does the government get the most for its money?

The answer that Massachusetts Gov. Michael S. Dukakis came up with is probably now the most widely known. Most people know the Massachusetts program as simply ET.

ET has become the prototype for work-training programs across the country. It is the prototype of what most governors are talking about when they talk about welfare reform.

No doubt, Dukakis' presidential campaign has raised ET's visibility. He touts it as a national welfare model. But it also is known because it is one of the first successful work-training programs, and it has a number of "cousins," as Dukakis puts it, in other states.

The idea behind ET is not new.

The idea behind ET is not complicated.

ET calls for cutting the welfare rolls by putting people to work.

The federal government also has tried the same concept. One recent example: the Comprehensive Employment and Training Act — CETA.

What is ET's secret? It seems to be follow-through:

▶ First, ET clients choose and design employment plans. Then they receive the necessary training and counseling to reach their goals.

▶ Second, day care is offered for up to 12 months after an ET "graduate" leaves welfare for a real job. That's crucial. Many of the clients are single mothers.

▶ Third, graduates whose new jobs do not provide health insurance at first can participate in the Health Choices program. It provides up to 12 months of health benefits.

When ET was unveiled in 1983, Dukakis set a goal of placing 50,000 graduates in jobs by the fifth anniversary. That goal was achieved by June 22, 1988.

Detractors say there's more to ET's success

than meets the eye. They say people have found jobs because of a booming Massachusetts economy — not because of Dukakis and his prized work-training program.

A study by the Massachusetts Taxpayers Foundation, a respected, non-governmental group, disagrees. It says ET "has contributed significantly to the drop in the welfare caseload in Massachusetts."

The study also points out that in fiscal year 1988, it costs $5,305 to move an ET client off the welfare roll, but it costs $9,080 for one year of typical welfare assistance payments.

About 40 states have work-training programs. Some are experiments in a few counties. Others are statewide. Some examples:

▶ Michigan Gov. James J. Blanchard introduced MOST — Michigan Opportunity Skill Training — in 1984. In any given month, 91,396 people are in the program. To date, 24,601 have been placed in full-time jobs. Number of people on public assistance: 304,728.

▶ California Gov. George Deukmejian introduced GAIN — Greater Avenues for Independence — in 1985. As of June 1987, 13 of 58 counties were participating. 27,880 people were in the program, and 3,788 people had found full- or part-time work by that time. Number of people on welfare in those counties: 103,139. GAIN is expected to be in all 58 counties by fiscal year 1988-89.

▶ Vermont Gov. Madeleine M. Kunin introduced Reach Up in 1986. It is the only welfare program in the USA that allows welfare mothers to attend college. About 2,400 people have taken part in Reach Up and 1,062 now have jobs. 7,629 families are on welfare in Vermont.

▶ New Jersey Gov. Thomas H. Kean launched REACH — Realizing Economic Achievement — in 1987. Seven thousand people are in the program. Number of people on welfare: 328,000.

> **❝** *We have to reach out and make changes and try to prevent continuation of welfare from generation to generation. That's what the governors are trying to do.* **❞**
>
> **Del. Gov. Michael N. Castle**

Governors also have supported other innovative ways of aiding welfare recipients:

▶ Minnesota Gov. Rudy Perpich is introducing a program that is designed to convert 300 welfare recipients into small-business owners.

▶ Missouri Gov. John Ashcroft's Parents As Teachers program, which centers on in-home visits by parent educators, appears to be effective in increasing scores on intelligence tests. That, down the road, could reduce the number of high school dropouts.

▶ Arkansas Gov. Bill Clinton initiated the Good Beginnings program, which provides low-income women and their babies with comprehensive health care.

▶ Ohio Gov. Richard F. Celeste streamlined state services for children under age 4 by pooling interdepartmental resources and cutting duplications. The outcome: The number of services has increased from 25 to 185.

▶ Delaware Gov. Michael N. Castle's administration strictly enforces child support payments. In 1986, the state helped collect $14 million in child support. Castle was chairman of the National Governors' Association Task Force on Welfare Prevention.

Clearly, governors across the USA are channeling enormous amounts of energy toward helping the poor to help themselves. Gov. Castle makes the effort sound like more of a long-term mission than just a routine responsibility when he says: "We have to reach out and make changes and try to prevent continuation of welfare from generation to generation. That's what the governors are trying to do."

PART 2

THE 50 GOVERNORS

The USA's top 50. A fascinating mix. No two with the same background or philosophy. No two with the same style. They range from:

▶ The New England reserve of Vermont Gov. Madeleine Kunin to the evangelical zeal of Louisiana Gov. Buddy Roemer.

▶ The Western hospitality of Wyoming Gov. Mike Sullivan to the studious approach of Virginia Gov. Gerald Baliles.

▶ The frontier spirit of Alaska Gov. Steve Cowper to the methodical marketing of Michigan Gov. James Blanchard.

Still, there is much they share. They are all modern managers coming up with modern solutions to persistent problems:

▶ How to improve schools.

▶ How to get people off welfare.

▶ How to attract industry.

▶ How to maintain — or change — a state's image.

What are these key leaders like?

▶ Most are personable, not pompous.

▶ Many are part chairman, part cheerleader.

▶ Their jobs are demanding, but so are they.

▶ Ambition abounds. All have big plans for their states; many have big plans for themselves.

Week after week, in state capitol after state capitol, we found people behind the governor's desk who are recognizing society's rapid changes, facing tough challenges, making hard choices.

We found 50 of the most powerful people in the USA, many only beginning to tap their potential.

We found 50 key leaders on the forefront of the USA's future.

The governors

State	Governor	Age[1]	Party	Took office
Alabama	Guy Hunt	55	Republican	1987
Alaska	Steve Cowper	49	Democrat	1986
Arizona	Rose Mofford	66	Democrat	1988
Arkansas	Bill Clinton	41	Democrat	1979[2]
California	George Deukmejian	60	Republican	1983
Colorado	Roy R. Romer	59	Democrat	1987
Connecticut	William A. O'Neill	57	Democrat	1981
Delaware	Michael N. Castle	48	Republican	1985
Florida	Bob Martinez	53	Republican	1987
Georgia	Joe Frank Harris	52	Democrat	1983
Hawaii	John D. Waihee III	42	Democrat	1986
Idaho	Cecil D. Andrus	56	Democrat	1971[2]
Illinois	James R. Thompson	52	Republican	1977
Indiana	Robert D. Orr	70	Republican	1981
Iowa	Terry E. Branstad	41	Republican	1983
Kansas	Mike Hayden	44	Republican	1987
Kentucky	Wallace G. Wilkinson	46	Democrat	1987
Louisiana	Charles "Buddy" Roemer III	44	Democrat	1988
Maine	John R. McKernan Jr.	40	Republican	1987
Maryland	William Donald Schaefer	66	Democrat	1987
Massachusetts	Michael S. Dukakis	54	Democrat	1975[2]
Michigan	James J. Blanchard	45	Democrat	1983
Minnesota	Rudy Perpich	60	Democrat	1983[2]
Mississippi	Ray Mabus	39	Democrat	1988
Missouri	John Ashcroft	46	Republican	1985
Montana	Ted Schwinden	62	Democrat	1981
Nebraska	Kay A. Orr	49	Republican	1987
Nevada	Richard H. Bryan	50	Democrat	1983
New Hampshire	John H. Sununu	48	Republican	1983
New Jersey	Thomas H. Kean	53	Republican	1982
New Mexico	Garrey Carruthers	48	Republican	1987
New York	Mario Cuomo	56	Democrat	1983
North Carolina	James G. "Jim" Martin	52	Republican	1985
North Dakota	George A. "Bud" Sinner	60	Democrat	1985
Ohio	Richard F. Celeste	50	Democrat	1983
Oklahoma	Henry Bellmon	66	Republican	1963[2]
Oregon	Neil Goldschmidt	48	Democrat	1987
Pennsylvania	Robert P. Casey	56	Democrat	1987
Rhode Island	Edward D. DiPrete	53	Republican	1985
South Carolina	Carroll A. Campbell Jr.	47	Republican	1987
South Dakota	George S. Mickelson	47	Republican	1987
Tennessee	Ned McWherter	57	Democrat	1987
Texas	William "Bill" Clements Jr.	71	Republican	1979[2]
Utah	Norman H. Bangerter	55	Republican	1985
Vermont	Madeleine M. Kunin	54	Democrat	1985
Virginia	Gerald L. "Jerry" Baliles	47	Democrat	1986
Washington	Booth Gardner	51	Democrat	1985
West Virginia	Arch A. Moore Jr.	65	Republican	1969[2]
Wisconsin	Tommy G. Thompson	46	Republican	1987
Wyoming	Michael J. "Mike" Sullivan	48	Democrat	1987

[1] Ages are as of June 30, 1988. [2] Clinton has been governor 1979-80, 1983-present; Andrus, 1971-77, 1987-present; Dukakis, 1975-78, 1983-present; Perpich, 1976-78, 1983-present; Bellmon, 1963-67, 1987-present; Clements, 1979-82, 1987-present; Moore, 1969-76, 1985-present.

GOV. GUY HUNT

IMPRESSIONS

G uy Hunt knows all about being an underdog.

Few gave this preacher and cattleman — without a college education — much chance of winning when he entered the governor's race in 1986.

After all, his only experience as an elected official came as a county probate judge, and he had been trounced when he ran for governor in 1978.

But win he did, becoming Alabama's first Republican governor in more than a century.

A man who can beat the odds may be just what Alabama needs. The state has had an image problem and has lagged behind much of the nation in income, education and social services.

Hunt was candid when we met with him:

"I think the image of Alabama as a whole was a state of rednecks, a state of people who were behind the times and would not make the adjustments necessary for business to grow and prosper. Now we're really one of the two hot spots of the South as far as economic development is concerned."

Hunt freely acknowledged Alabama's rocky racial history and said he is genuinely committed to civil rights. But he dismissed as trivial any concerns about the Confederate flag flying above the Statehouse.

"If I start removing the rebel flag, a lot of people will never listen to me again," he said. "So, we've got to look at meaningful things and not things that are symbols."

Five months after our interview, black leaders reminded Hunt just how meaningful the Confederate flag was to them. One black state legislator threatened to personally tear down the flag and was arrested when he tried.

Overall, Hunt does appear to be making some real progress in a state with tremendous potential.

He has a tough battle ahead, but his style may finally unify what was once divided.

In Hunt's words: "If this state is ever going to move forward and move out of the bottom five, we're going to do it together."

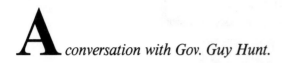

A *conversation with Gov. Guy Hunt.*

What gives Alabama a competitive edge in trying to attract business?

"A lot of the companies that have plants in Alabama talk about the high quality of the labor. Also, we've turned from a farm economy (to) where you have a lot of people in their 40s and 50s who are trying to get off the farm into something else. Plus we have the kind of training program that is said to be one of the best in the country, where we cooperate with the company to train employees."

Your state tends to show up toward the bottom of lists ranking education spending, income and social services. What's being done to elevate the state in these areas?

"We're pretty high as far as teachers' salaries. Until this past year, we were second to Virginia in the Southeast. One of our goals is to bring teacher salaries up to or above the national level during my term in office. We have some of the best schools in the country. We're trying to bring about welfare reform and jobs for people on welfare. We also have a tax reform commission."

Is it true that you want to establish a more down-home atmosphere in the governor's mansion?

"During the campaign, I told people, 'This is your governor's mansion. And when I'm elected, we want you to come for breakfast.' So I began that. I had not considered weddings until we had two or three there. There are days when we have hundreds of people through the mansion. We've tried to make people feel it is theirs. Maybe we've succeeded."

Is George Wallace a tough act to follow? Do you find yourself being compared to him?

"Not really. I think that if I had followed him in 1970, yes, there would have been that comparison. I think his health, his inability to be mobile and to be on top of things, and having to delegate more than the ordinary governor would in the last few years makes it not so much so. In fact, we had him over for dinner the other evening in the mansion, and, together with some other former governors, he told the press that he thought I'd make the best governor we'd ever had, and he said, 'I don't think I was bad.' "

You are a minister?

"Accredited Baptist minister."

Are you still practicing?

"Yes, I pastor two churches. I have two associate pastors at each place so that it does not make it difficult for me to be off if I need to be off."

What did you learn in the election when you ran for governor and lost?

"That first election more or less fine-tunes you. It teaches you how to meet the press, and how to talk, and how to watch your words, and I think that helped me in '86."

You're from Holly Pond, population 543. Now you're governor of Alabama. Is there something about small communities that prepares you to be a leader?

"I think your big difference is the down-to-earth ability of people that you gain on the farm. Really, you have more time to reflect. I think that's a real important thing. You have more time to be out in the wide-open spaces, and do a lot of thinking. I think that you're more insulated from TV there. That doesn't mean that kids on the farm don't watch TV, but you have more opportunity to be out walking in the woods and fields and pastures."

HUNT PROFILE

PARTY: Republican.

IN HIS WORDS: Being a preacher "makes you more accessible to the people. . . . It helps you be more of a realist, not exalt yourself. You talk to people eyeball to eyeball and friend to friend."

BORN: June 17, 1933, in Holly Pond, Ala., to Otto and Orene Hunt, farmers.

FAMILY: Married Helen Chambers in 1951. Mrs. Hunt, 53, is a homemaker. The Hunts have four children, Pam, 33; Sherrie, 31; Keith, 29; and Lynn, 25.

EDUCATION: No college degree. Turned down journalism scholarship to University of Alabama.

TIMELINE

1954: Joined Army.

1958: Became Primitive Baptist preacher, pastor of Mt. Vernon Primitive Baptist Church; chosen pastor, Gum Pond Primitive Baptist Church, in 1964.

1959: Began distributing Amway products; still owns distributorship and runs 140-acre cattle ranch in Holly Pond he inherited from family.

1962: Lost bid for state Senate.

1964: Elected county probate judge; re-elected in 1970.

1976: Chaired state campaigns for Ronald Reagan; chaired GOP state delegation and again in 1980.

1978: Lost gubernatorial election.

1981: Named state executive director, U.S.D.A. Agricultural Stabilization and Conservation Service.

1986: Elected governor with 56 percent of vote; surprising win is believed to be a result of voter backlash after bitter Democratic nomination fight.

NOTEWORTHY

Alabama's first Republican governor in 112 years. . . . Named one of the USA's "governors to watch" by *U.S News & World Report* for "impressive economic reform."

PERSONAL

Likes to play tennis, go bicycling. . . . Favorite food is fruit salad — has his own special recipe using apples, peaches from his orchard. . . . Loves country music, especially Roy Acuff. . . . Drives home on weekends to preach at Mt. Vernon Primitive Baptist and Gum Pond Primitive Baptist churches — a 300-mile round trip.

THE FUTURE

"We love the humble life and quiet life on the farm. But whatever entails as far as the future is concerned, we believe that Alabama is worth that sacrifice."

1991: Term expires in January; eligible for re-election.

PRIORITIES

▶ Education: Proposed teacher competency testing and reforms for funding distribution.

▶ Economic development: Revamped civil liability laws; reorganized Alabama Development Office and Alabama Department of Economic and Community Affairs.

▶ Environment: Proposed ban on new hazardous waste dumping sites and reduction of existing dump sites.

GOV. STEVE COWPER

IMPRESSIONS

He's been nicknamed "The High Plains Drifter," but no one would mistake him for Clint Eastwood.

At 5 feet 11 inches tall, with suits off the rack, Steve Cowper is rugged only by gubernatorial standards.

Still, in both style and substance, Cowper seems to embrace the frontier legacy of Alaska. He describes himself as "one of those rebels" who came to the state in search of opportunity. He found it.

Cowper, a native of Petersburg, Va., was practicing law in Norfolk, Va., in 1968 when he got the itch to move to Alaska.

"I just thought this is the kind of place I'd like to be," he said.

"I didn't know anybody here. I just sort of appeared at Alaska's doorstep."

After a stint as an assistant district attorney in Fairbanks, Cowper went to Vietnam in 1970 and worked as a free-lance correspondent.

Apparently destined never to hold a run-of-the-mill job, Cowper went on to become a partner in an air-taxi service, and a political columnist for a newspaper.

In the "Lower 48," those wouldn't be the career moves you would make on the way to the governor's mansion. But Cowper — and Alaskans, for that matter — aren't interested in playing it safe.

In 1974, Cowper was elected to the Alaska House, where he served for two terms. By 1982, Cowper wanted to be governor, but fell short in the primary by 259 votes.

By 1985, Cowper had built enough political momentum to defeat incumbent Gov. William Sheffield in the primary before beating Arliss Sturgulewski with 52 percent of the vote in the general election.

We found few governors who were as straightforward about the state of their states. No pretensions. Doesn't duck the problems. Just the style of a guy who might be sitting on the bar stool next to you.

We routinely invited the governors to drop by the USA TODAY offices the next time they were in Washington, D.C. Steve Cowper did.

Clint Eastwood? Not really. But maybe Alan Ladd.

A *conversation with Gov. Steve Cowper.*

How did you campaign for governor in a state this size?

"Actually, television is the key to this thing just like it is every place else."

You have a remarkable range of people in this state. How do they get along?

"Well, our racial difficulties, such as they are, probably relate more to the urban culture's inability to understand the indigenous people."

Are there efforts to protect the Eskimo culture?

"Yes. That is another beneficial result of the oil money. There was enough to get people together from the villages to try to rekindle the old way of life."

What do you think people in the "Lower 48" think Alaska is all about?

"Too many believe that Alaska is snow and ice everywhere, and people's heads poking up at intervals. In fact, the weather in most of the coastal areas is pretty moderate for northern climes."

Is Alaska still a frontier state?

"Yes. I hope it always is."

Is that what attracts people like you?

"Yes. There's a kind of call to the individual that goes on around here, which is an interesting myth. But it won't work in the kind of world that we're faced with now."

The oil pipeline construction boom is over. Where do you think Alaska is headed now?

"What I'd like to see happen here is the rapid development of a technologically proficient society."

Are you trying to turn the cold into an asset?

"Well, over the years we have accumulated more experience and have done more stuff in Arctic construction techniques. We're going to put a research foundation together. It would relate directly to cold-weather techniques and materials research."

What other attributes can Alaska capitalize on?

"All phases of energy. My belief is that the key to success here lies in knowledge and information."

Isn't the state also ideally located for trade?

"We are much closer to the Asian markets than any other place in this country, certainly by air and ship. And we can capitalize on Alaska's being a crossroads between Europe and Asia. If we become experts in the international marketplace, I think we're going to be major players."

How did Alaskans become so dependent on the oil economy?

"People were sitting around all winter, waiting for the sun to come out again so they could go to work. We went from that immediately into the oil pipeline construction — when everybody began to have permanent jobs and made some pretty serious money. Then oil prices went up beyond anybody's wildest imaginations. That, in turn, triggered a construction boom, which went on and sort of overreached itself. Now we're having withdrawal pains."

Did Alaska squander its money when times were more flush?

"I think some money was wasted. You have to bear in mind that there were infrastructure needs that simply didn't exist in any other state. We still don't have a decent road system. And we use money in ways other states probably haven't thought about. We spent $200 million, for instance, on a communications system."

Do Alaskans follow sports down below?

"Oh, yeah. Like everybody else. We've got a satellite hookup — everybody's become Seattle Seahawk freaks."

COWPER PROFILE

PARTY: Democrat.

IN HIS WORDS: "I'm a person who likes to cause change to happen."

BORN: Aug. 21, 1938, in Petersburg, Va., to homemaker Stephanie Cowper and Marion R. Cowper, a contractor.

FAMILY: Married third wife, Michael Margaret Stewart, in 1985. Mrs. Cowper, 35, is a lawyer. The Cowpers have a 1-year-old son, Wade. Gov. Cowper has two daughters from his first marriage, Katherine, 26, and Grace, 23.

EDUCATION: Bachelor of arts in history and law degree from the University of North Carolina-Chapel Hill.

TIMELINE

1968: Moved to Fairbanks, Alaska, from North Carolina; became assistant district attorney.

1971: Practiced law, Cowper and Madsen firm.

1974: Elected to two-year term in Alaska House; re-elected in 1976; managed Alaska Permanent Fund, state savings account that collects part of oil revenues.

1982: Lost Democratic gubernatorial nomination by 259 votes.

1986: Elected governor, taking 52 percent of the vote against Arliss Sturgulewski. Cowper had defeated incumbent Gov. William Sheffield in the Democratic primary.

1990: Term expires in December; eligible for re-election.

PRIORITIES

▶ Economic development: Hiked exports to Pacific Rim; proposed establishing endowed science foundation; lobbying to bring 1994 Winter Olympics to Anchorage.

▶ Fiscal conservatism: Balanced 1987 budget; cut spending 10 percent.

▶ Health and human services: Appointed task force to create support system for children; proposed $17.5 million budget.

▶ Education: Proposed endowment to provide special education.

▶ Environment: Promotes development of "promising" oil reserve in northeast Alaska.

NOTEWORTHY
First Alaska governor to unseat an incumbent governor.

PERSONAL
Drives a pickup. . . . Strums the banjo. . . . Refuses to use his No. 1 license plate. . . . Plays rugby for the Fairbanks Sundawgs.

THE FUTURE
Plans to remain in public service in Alaska: "I keep up with Washington . . . but I don't want to go there."

GOV. ROSE MOFFORD

IMPRESSIONS

Gov. Rose Mofford didn't set out to be governor. But as Arizona's secretary of state and, hence, next in line of succession, the office was always just a heartbeat — or, as it turned out, a conviction — away.

"Auntie Rose," who has worked in state government for 47 years and known 12 of Arizona's 17 governors, has a tough mission. Her predecessor, Evan Mecham, the man who launched his administration in 1987 by rescinding a state holiday honoring the Rev. Martin Luther King Jr., was forced out of office April 4, 1988. The Arizona Senate convicted him of obstruction of justice and misuse of funds.

Now it's up to Mofford to restore respectability to the Arizona governor's office.

Mofford says she's up to the job, partly because she's learned something from each governor she's known. Some of the lessons:

▶ Gov. Sidney P. Osborn (1941-48) taught her the importance of political organization.

▶ Gov. J. Howard Pyle (1951-55) showed her the importance of communication.

▶ Gov. Raul H. Castro (1975-77) demonstrated the importance of determination.

▶ Gov. Bruce Babbitt (1978-87) inspired her with his scholarship.

She even says that Mecham taught her something:

"I learned from him that the demands of the job are greater than anyone would ever imagine."

A few weeks after taking office, Mofford had her own problems — allegations of concealing real estate holdings and gifts and misuse of funds. Her answer: "I never misspent a penny" and failing to report some transactions was "an honest mistake."

The controversy and the challenges of being governor are not entirely new to Mofford. After all, here is a woman who was fired in 1953 as executive secretary to the Arizona tax commissioner because, as her boss put it, "It was better to have a man in that particular job."

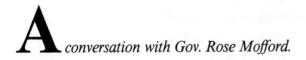

A *conversation with Gov. Rose Mofford.*

What has been the impact of Evan Mecham's administration?

"The recall, the impeachment, and the indictment — we had never had anything like that in Arizona, nor do I know of anyone in the United States that's had it. So it has been quite difficult. I just have to say that one never likes to see such problems confront a state, and as the new governor, I hope that any negative publicity will turn around into positive action."

What are your priorities?

"We have just emerged from one of the most traumatic years in our state's history. My first priority is healing Arizona's political wounds from the prior administration. I've taken this up under such adverse conditions. When this session ends, I will spend the summer developing my legislative initiatives for 1989. Number one has always been education with me."

Did you ever think you would be governor?

"No, no, I really didn't. I've liked what I did, and I had great plans for the secretary of state."

Have you ever sought advice from former governors?

"Yes, I called them in, the ones that could attend. I certainly called them for their advice and they've been most helpful and I can still call on them."

What sets Arizona apart from other states?

"Where else in the United States can one drive 100 miles south from a major population center and be in a beautiful Sonoran Desert or 100 miles north to snow ski? Arizona probably has one of the richest blends of cultures with Anglos, Hispanics, blacks, Asians and Native Americans. My one-liner would be, what sets Arizona apart — its natural resources, a picture postcard on every street corner."

What has *Arizona Highways* magazine meant to the state?

"*Arizona Highways* is our window to the world. It has many subscribers out-of-state and has been a great asset to our tourism industry, and I know that first hand because I saw it go from black and white to color. Of course, we have no advertising, but the demands for that magazine are unbelievable. You find them in doctors' offices, you find them as you travel abroad. We use them a lot for our own advertising, giving the bound volumes to visiting dignitaries."

MOFFORD PROFILE

PARTY: Democrat.

IN HER WORDS: Because her parents were immigrants, "We didn't just have to vote. We had to be the first to vote."

BORN: Rose Perica, June 10, 1922, in Globe, Ariz., to John Perica, copper miner, and Frances Perica, homemaker.

FAMILY: Divorced.

EDUCATION: Studied business and public administration at Phoenix College, Industrial College of the Armed Forces.

TIMELINE

1941: Secretary in Arizona treasurer's office.

1943: Secretary for Tax Commission; business manager for *Arizona Highways* magazine.

1953: Named assistant secretary of state.

1975: Named assistant director of administration, state Department of Revenue.

1977: Appointed secretary of state; elected to four-year term in 1978; re-elected in 1982, 1986.

1982: Elected president, National Association of Secretaries of State.

1988: Succeeded Gov. Evan Mecham after his conviction on impeachment charges.

1991: Term expires in January; eligible for election.

PRIORITIES

▶ Education: Proposed plan to recruit and retain disadvantaged students in higher education.

▶ Tax reform: Proposed plan to reform tax system and eliminate loopholes to balance budget.

▶ Human services: Proposed hiring a director of human services to coordinate drug abuse programs.

NOTEWORTHY

In 1988, became state's first female governor. . . . In 47 years as state employee, has served 12 of Arizona's 17 governors.

PERSONAL

Once rejected an offer to play professional women's basketball. . . . Inducted twice into Arizona Softball Hall of Fame. . . . As secretary of state, she did her own typing and answered her own phones. . . . Fluent in American Sign Language. . . . Favorite spectator sport is basketball. . . . Collects kachina dolls, antique rifles, handguns and Southwestern turquoise and copper artifacts.

THE FUTURE

"I enjoy the challenge of being governor of Arizona. It is the highlight of my 47 years in state government. At this point I do intend to seek another term."

GOV. BILL CLINTON

IMPRESSIONS

We visited Bill Clinton just a few weeks after he decided not to pursue the presidency in 1988. Most Democrat-watchers were surprised. We told him we were, too. He still seemed a little surprised about his decision himself.

Clinton told us he made his decision after a long talk with his wife, Hillary.

We "just concluded that the only chance I had to win was for us both to go full time, flat out immediately," he said. "Since we only have one child, and she's only 7, that would be very destructive for her, or at least potentially very bad for her."

Still, an almost astonishing move from a man who has the kind of ambition that it seems will inevitably spill over Arkansas' borders.

After all, this is the same Bill Clinton who at age 10 sat "glued to the tube" watching the 1956 Republican and Democratic political conventions.

This is the same Bill Clinton who decided at 16 he wanted to go into politics. And who just 16 years later was elected to his first term as governor.

A man in a hurry. Until now.

From time to time, we interviewed governors who were rumored to have one eye on the White House. During these sessions, one unspoken question lingered: "Is this man (or woman) really presidential material?"

In the end, only the USA's voters can answer that question. But Clinton is among a growing number of governors who appear to have many of the tools.

He's bright. Aggressive. Personable. He's been a leader in education reform, both statewide and nationwide.

And he plays a mean saxophone, as his fellow governors learned when he took the stage with Motown legend Junior Walker at a National Governors' Association meeting in Traverse City, Mich., in 1987.

'88 was not to be Bill Clinton's year in the spotlight.

But don't bet that he's not already getting in tune for '92 or '96.

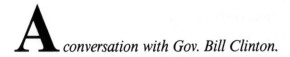

A *conversation with Gov. Bill Clinton.*

You initiated the country's first competency test for current teachers. How did you sell that?

"I sold it by going on statewide television and talking to people about it. And then by having meetings around the state and trying to encourage the people of the state to call the legislators. I basically had to say that, unless we were going to have the accountability measures, I wouldn't support my own tax increase."

What was the result?

"Thousands and thousands of teachers went out and improved their basic skills. Those who didn't pass can't have their certificates renewed. I think we did the right thing. But it was the toughest fight I think I've ever been in."

Now that broad education reforms are in effect, are you seeing the results in the students?

"For the last five years, we've seen an increase in our test scores and a reduction in the regional — and apparently racial — differences between those test scores, as well as a continued decline in the drop-out rate."

Is there a special challenge for Southern states in education reform?

"Yes, and I think that's one reason Southern states moved more quickly and more broadly. We were the poorest region of the country conditionally and the least well-educated. So, for our states, it was literally a matter of survival."

How do the people in Arkansas perceive their state?

"I believe there is a concern that maybe we are known for two things that are no longer fully representative of what we are. The first is the barefoot hillbilly image. And the second is the racial crisis, which culminated in the Little Rock Central High School conflict in 1957."

How should the USA view Arkansas?

"The truth is that two major elements of our culture are the hill-country heritage and the heritage of the delta, the farmers. But it's also true that we have a highly diversified economy and a highly diversified culture today."

How is the business climate?

"We've got some of the most impressive companies in the country headquartered in Arkansas. We have a significant number of people in very sophisticated operations. So Arkansas is a very different state than it's perceived to be."

How are you trying to change the state's image?

"A few years ago, I supported an $800,000 campaign in *The Wall Street Journal* after a $60,000 research survey among major business executives. We asked them things like, what's the biggest problem with Arkansas in terms of its business climate? And they said, 'Well, it's not centrally located.'"

And that's not quite true.

"In fact, western Arkansas is 200 miles from the geographic center of the United States. And we have all kinds of transportation networks, an enormous number of business investments and a lot of distribution centers."

What is the most overlooked tourist attraction in Arkansas?

"The Cossatot River, which the state has recently taken steps to purchase and preserve."

What is the status of race relations in Arkansas?

"Good. Certainly Arkansas, like the rest of the states, isn't totally free of racial problems and there is still much to do. But we have made great progress: Black men and women hold responsible positions on my staff, direct several major departments and agencies in my administration and hold positions of responsibility in local governments and private business."

CLINTON PROFILE

PARTY: Democrat.

IN HIS WORDS: "I decided to be in politics when I was 16. . . . I still remember people who spoke at the Republican and Democratic conventions when I was 10. I'd just sit there for hours glued to the tube."

BORN: William Jefferson Boythe IV, Aug. 19, 1946, in Hope, Ark., to William Jefferson Boythe III, salesman, who died before his son was born, and Virginia Kelley, nurse/anesthesiologist. At 15, Clinton took the name of his stepfather, car dealer Roger Clinton.

FAMILY: Married Hillary Rodham in 1975. Mrs. Rodham Clinton, 40, is a lawyer. Her insistence on keeping her own name caused such a flap that she goes by Hillary Rodham Clinton. The Clintons have one child, Chelsea, 8.

EDUCATION: Bachelor of science, Georgetown University; Rhodes Scholar, Oxford University; law degree, Yale University.

TIMELINE

1972: At 26, coordinated George McGovern's presidential campaign in Texas.

1976: Elected to two-year term as state attorney general.

1978: Elected to two-year term as governor with 63.4 percent of vote; lost gubernatorial re-election bid in 1980 — voters were turned off by "hotshot" image and car-tax increase.

1982: Re-elected to two-year term with 55 percent of vote after shortening his hair and promising not to "lead without listening;" re-elected with 63 percent of vote in 1984.

1986: Re-elected to four-year term with 64 percent of vote; elected chairman of National Governors' Association; spearheaded welfare reform initiative.

1991: Term expires in January; eligible for re-election, says he is unlikely to run again.

NOTEWORTHY

USA's youngest governor in 40 years when he was elected at age 32 in 1978. . . . Named one of the USA's five most effective governors by other governors in 1986 *Newsweek* poll. . . . First Arkansas governor ever elected to four-year term. "This is the most job security I've had since I went to work in a grocery store at 13."

PERSONAL

Childhood desire was to be another Elvis Presley. . . . Was Sen. J. William Fulbright's protege. . . . Plays the saxophone. . . . Portraits of Lincoln and Churchill hang in his office. . . . Loves to read "cheap" thrillers by Robert Ludlum and Robert Parker.

THE FUTURE

"For what it's worth, I'd like to be president."

PRIORITIES

▶ Education: Started USA's first mandatory teacher testing.

▶ Job development: Helped in-state employers create jobs.

▶ Welfare: Reforms included contract requiring welfare recipients to upgrade job skills and state-funded child care and medical insurance assistance.

GOV. GEORGE DEUKMEJIAN

IMPRESSIONS

For George Deukmejian, running the state of California is a fairly formal affair.

While many other governors could be described as self-effacing and informal, Deukmejian's style is serious, somber.

The press has said he has no charisma. His response: "I'm not necessarily an elected official who is entertaining."

That style was reflected in his office staff. Coolly efficient, they agreed to set up an interview, but they made it very clear that their boss was a busy man who had extremely important appointments both before and after our meeting.

The interview was one of the most solemn of BusCapade. Even questions about personal likes and dislikes elicited staid responses. The leader of a celebrity-laden state, we asked him whether any particular movie star was a personal favorite.

His straightforward reply: "I enjoy meeting people, including celebrities. I wouldn't say that I'm awestruck."

We asked him about his personal reaction to earthquakes. Fear? Concern?

"Not any kind of fear or anxiety. You just feel the roll or the tremor. I would generally do what I have been advised to do. You don't want to be standing next to a bunch of bookshelves or other movable objects close by."

Not flamboyant. Not warm. But most Californians will tell you he's been very effective.

He just edged Democrat Tom Bradley, mayor of Los Angeles, for the governorship in 1982. Four years later, he routed him.

He also has aggressively pursued foreign industry and trade opportunities, traveling to Japan, Great Britain, Belgium and France in 1987. The state now has trade and investment offices in Tokyo and London, and has plans to open one in Mexico City.

In a state that takes pride in being on top of every new style, there's some irony in Deukmejian's leadership.

No flash. Just substance.

A *conversation with Gov. George Deukmejian.*

Opinions vary on the best way to run state governments. Some people have suggested that state governments are most efficient when run as a corporation — with the governor acting as chief executive officer. Would you describe your management style as similar to that of a chief executive officer?

"Yes. However, a CEO does not have to seek approval from a legislative body, nor does he have to operate in the glare of press examination. A governor has to be a leader and a manager, setting the priorities of the state. There is a similarity with a CEO in that governors must ensure that state government does not operate in the red."

Every state has hidden treasures. What is the most overlooked tourist attraction in your state?

"The most overlooked aspect of California, as a tourist location, is that there are many Californias. California possesses everything from a scenic 1,000-mile coastline to the majestic Sierra Nevada Mountains. Mount Whitney is the tallest peak in the U.S. outside of Alaska, and Death Valley is the lowest point in North America. From the fertile vineyards of the Napa Valley to the sheer granite walls of Yosemite Valley, California has it all."

You came here from New York. Were opportunities greater for you here?

"Much greater. I grew up in the Albany area. They had the same political machine there for 50 years. After I had passed the California bar and had been here a few years, I went into private practice in Long Beach. Four years later, I was elected to the state Assembly. That could never have happened in New York."

California's lifestyle is world famous. How do you characterize it?

"I don't think you can generalize, because there is so much diversity. Whether you like to play golf, tennis, ski or swim, you can find it here. We've got areas where you can have snow, or you can be out in the desert area. We've got 1,000 miles of coastline, we've got areas that are rural, and we've got major urban centers."

What do you think California will look like 20 years from now?

"We'll continue to see an extension of the kind of diversity that we have in the population and economy."

Sometimes people outside the state characterize you as boring and bland, but you were re-elected by a landslide. What do Californians know that others don't?

"I followed Jerry Brown, and he followed Ronald Reagan. There's a lot of comparisons. The press sometimes likes to be entertained, and I'm not necessarily entertaining."

Are Californians realistic about earthquakes?

"There's not much you can do to prevent them. But there's a great deal that can be done to try to cut down on injuries, deaths and destruction. The planning and training is good, but it could be increased."

California's population continues to grow dramatically. What brings people to California?

"Opportunity. They see in California that you're accepted for who you are and what you are, that you don't necessarily have to have had a lot of long-established contacts. They also look at California as being a creative place where a lot of new ideas are started."

DEUKMEJIAN PROFILE

PARTY: Republican.

IN HIS WORDS: "Without funds and without knowing the culture or language, they (his immigrant parents) came in search of something more precious — freedom. They came, not seeking the best that the new nation had to offer, but willing to accept even the worst."

BORN: June 6, 1928, in Menands, N.Y., to Courken George Deukmejian, carpet merchant, and Alice Deukmejian, homemaker.

FAMILY: Married Gloria Saatjian in 1957. Mrs. Deukmejian, 55, is a homemaker. The Deukmejians have three children, Leslie, 24; George Jr., 21; and Andrea, 19.

EDUCATION: Bachelor of arts in sociology, Siena College; law degree, St. John's University, New York.

TIMELINE

1952: Began practicing law; joined Army in 1953; served with Judge Advocate Corps in Paris; returned to law practice in 1958.

1962: Elected to two-year term in state House; re-elected to two-year term in 1964.

1966: Elected to four-year term in state Senate; re-elected twice.

1978: Elected to four-year term as state attorney general.

1982: Elected to four-year term as governor, helped by GOP use of absentee ballots; Deukmejian actually lost among voters who went to the polls; re-elected with 61 percent of vote in 1986.

1991: Term expires in January; eligible for re-election.

PRIORITIES

▶ Fiscal conservatism: Developed plan that paid off $1.5 billion deficit.

NOTEWORTHY
USA's first governor of Armenian descent. . . Elected governor in 1982 by the smallest margin in California history — 0.69 percent. . . . Re-elected governor in 1986 with the largest victory in state history — more than 2 million votes.

PERSONAL
Nicknamed "Duke" in college, now called "Iron Duke" for his stubborn streak. . . . Favorite spectator sport is football. . . . Likes to golf. . . . Loves ice cream, especially jamoca almond fudge.

THE FUTURE
"I may consider a third term, I may consider some other political office or I might just decide to go back into the private sector. I just haven't made up my mind."

▶ Economic development: Initiated successful efforts to recruit business for state.

▶ Welfare reform: Established workfare program.

▶ Education reform: Signed 1983 bill requiring longer school hours, more teacher accountability.

GOV. ROY R. ROMER

IMPRESSIONS

Gov. Roy R. Romer's ranching background shows up in the way he goes about being governor.

He works hard at being down-to-earth, at being natural. Romer gives the impression that he's nothing more, nothing less than just a man on the job.

It's reflected in the way Romer's suit fits him. There's nothing formal about it. The day the BusCateers met with him, his coat was hanging open and his tie was dangling. You got the feeling that in his mind he wasn't wearing a suit at all. He had on his work clothes. And if he took off his coat, you were certain his sleeves would be rolled up a second later.

It's reflected in where he sits in his office. He prefers working at a large rectangular table at one end of the room. That's where he works when he's alone in the office. That's where he meets with people.

"Why?" we asked him.

"I think this illustrates it," Romer said, looking at us seated around the table. "We're all on common footing. We're able to talk. You see my phone here, my file there. I usually have a cookie here.

"I don't like that desk. It's an imposing barrier. It makes me feel separated from people."

Romer says Lincoln never forgot the people, never forgot where he came from and he wants to do it the same way. The homespun way.

To a point anyway. Lincoln certainly never rocked to the sounds of the "Boss." But Romer does. He's a Bruce Springsteen fan, if not a mesmerized devotee. One month after we met Romer, he flipped on a Springsteen tape in his convertible and drove 100 miles to the wrong hotel to give a speech.

"Driving myself is the only way I can get away and think," he told the crowd, once he got to the right place — 75 minutes late.

A conversation with Gov. Roy R. Romer.

What don't you like about your job?

"I worry about the trappings of public office. When you go to a convention, you find these phalanxes of security, aides and officials. It drives me wild. I think people who are elected to office — Lincoln was my model — have got to maintain that sense of where they came from. You do not allow the hurrah of the crowd to sort you out, separate you from people, either symbolically or internally."

How do you do that?

"Let me tell you what I did Sunday. I had some time, and I've got a convertible, so I put the top down. I began to drive around this town (Denver). I stopped in front of a center for the homeless. I thought I'd like to come back and spend a day there, or a night there, to get a feel for how they see the world. You've got to do that to govern well."

Denver is the only major city planning a new airport. What impact will that have?

"It's a tremendously important thing. If I were in Japan and I had one minute to give a pitch for Colorado, I'd say, 'Look, the major hub airports of the United States are as follows: four on the East Coast, two on the West Coast and three in the middle of the country. Denver is in the center.' Then I'd say, 'Why deal from the edge when you can deal from the center?'"

Is that a real advantage for the state?

"New technology will bring transpolar flight into some locations; then they'll spin them out. Think about where that might be in the United States. Denver is likely to be one of those."

In addition to location, what brings so many people to Colorado?

"Our unique geography and beauty. It is a state that has been blessed with the plains, the mountains, the Western Slope. Another characteristic that is unique is the variety of economic life. We have some agriculture, some minerals, some tourism, some small low-tech manufacturing, some high-tech."

Do these factors make Coloradoans different?

"There is a style about Colorado that is in part because of its beauty and its recreation. But if you come to Colorado, what do people do? They think about skiing, climbing mountains. It's outdoor; it's aggressive; it's not yuppie."

What effect does the economic variety have on the state?

"I view Colorado to be the Athens of the West potentially. It's a crossroads, not just of finance, commerce, industry, but a place where new ideas are applied in new ways. And that's what I think is exciting about the place."

Clean air is becoming a concern not only in Denver, but all the way down the Front Range. What can you do about it?

"One, we need to have better freeways. Secondly, we need rapid transit. Third, we need to do a more stringent job of emission control. Fourth, we need to consider converting coal-burning power plants to gas. Next, diesel. I think we have not yet come to terms with the restrictions on wood burning. That's a very substantial portion of pollutants. Next, conversion of some larger diesel engines to alternate fuels. Last, research. We have not yet done adequate research on what you do in high altitude with auto engines."

ROMER PROFILE

PARTY: Democrat.

IN HIS WORDS: "I'm always learning . . . and when I end this office I'll still be learning."

BORN: Oct. 31, 1928, in Garden City, Kan., to Irvine "I.R." and Margaret "Bessie" Romer, who ran a farm, general store and post office.

FAMILY: Married Beatrice "Bea" Miller in 1952. Mrs. Romer, 58, is a child-care professional. The Romers have seven children, Mark, 34; Paul, 32; Mary, 30; Chris, 28; Tim, 26; Tom, 19; and Elizabeth, 16.

EDUCATION: Bachelor of science in agricultural economics, Colorado State University; law degree, University of Colorado.

TIMELINE

1942: Worked on family farms and ranches for 10 years, beginning at age 14.

1952: Joined Air Force.

1956: Began practicing law in Colorado.

1958: Elected to two-year term in Colorado House of Representatives.

1960: Re-elected to state House.

1962: Elected to four-year term in state Senate.

1966: Liberal stance cost him race for U.S. Senate seat; became self-made millionaire with farm equipment stores in three states and real estate, ski resort and flying school.

1975: Appointed Colorado agricultural commissioner.

1976: Appointed chief of staff for Gov. Richard Lamm.

1977: Appointed state treasurer; elected to four-year term as state treasurer in 1978; re-elected in 1982.

1982: Appointed chief of staff for Lamm.

1986: Elected to four-year term as governor

NOTEWORTHY

Colorado's first new governor since 1972. . . . A self-made millionaire.

PERSONAL

Kept records of all his earnings, purchases as a child, still keeps these journals in his office. . . . Learned to drive tractor at age 8. . . . Piloted his single-engine Cessna 610 during campaigns; now flies for pleasure. . . . Took his staff on Outward Bound weekend to learn teamwork. . . . Abraham Lincoln, Harry S. Truman are role models. . . . Loves to swim in mountain streams and ski.

THE FUTURE

Says he hasn't been governor long enough to know if he will run again. When he leaves office he plans to buy a farm.

with 58 percent of the vote, unopposed in the Democratic primary.

1991: Term expires in January; eligible for re-election.

PRIORITIES

▶ Economic development: Created offices to assist small businesses; set up trade offices in Tokyo, Taiwan.

▶ Education: Called for merit pay, higher teacher standards, increased funding for education.

▶ Environment: Mandated fuels that burn cleaner; pushed for development of mass transit, better air quality.

▶ Infrastructure: Supported construction of new Denver airport; proposed funding to improve highways.

GOV. WILLIAM A. O'NEILL

There wasn't much tension in Gov. O'Neill's office as we sat down to interview him.

While some governors braced themselves for questions, O'Neill had the calm confidence of a man who knows things are going pretty well and is more than happy to talk about them.

When he was sworn in as governor for his first full term on Jan. 5, 1983, O'Neill promised "dependable leadership." The people of Connecticut apparently felt he lived up to his commitment, re-electing him four years later by a wide margin.

The key to O'Neill's popularity has been his state's booming economy. At the time of our visit, Connecticut had the highest per person annual income at $19,208. It also led the nation in lowest unemployment rate, at 6.3 percent. O'Neill called his state "the wealthiest."

Despite that economic success, O'Neill insisted state government had not become complacent. "We've got people in Connecticut who are starving for help," he told us. "There's McDonald's and such places around the Connecticut Turnpike that can't find anybody to work."

Many describe O'Neill as steady and low-key. He might well be all those things. But in our interview he exhibited a playful side.

When one reporter asked about Connecticut's image as a haven for Ivy Leaguers and prep school students, O'Neill laughed and pointed out the reporter was wearing distinctly preppy shoes.

When another reporter asked O'Neill for his reactions to the then-breaking story about then-presidential candidate Gary Hart's weekend with Donna Rice, O'Neill gave us a blank look and said he hadn't heard about it.

Our interview with O'Neill was notable for one other reason. It was the only interview in which the lieutenant governor was given a co-starring role. Lt. Gov. Joseph Fauliso joined us during the interview and O'Neill happily turned questions over to him.

It was the kind of generous gesture that suggests O'Neill doesn't need to have the spotlight on him all the time. When the state economy is going great guns, there's plenty of glory to go around.

A

conversation with Gov. William A. O'Neill.

How would you describe your management style?

"I believe the best way to run a state is to find the best staff available for the important cabinet posts and entrust and empower them to do the best job they can. I meet with my commissioners regularly, but I believe the operation of their departments on a day-to-day basis is left to their discretion. I chose this style because it would be impossible to run 23 departments and 45,000 employees effectively without the delegation of authority. I also am fortunate to have a group of commissioners who deserve and enjoy my trust."

Some people picture Connecticut as a tax haven for the rich, or a suburb living in the shadows of New York City. Is that accurate?

"Connecticut is not in anyone's shadows. It's a leader in the nation as far as per capita income. As far as being a tax haven for the rich, the state is doing so well that when you do live here you've got a good chance to make a very good living in all walks of life."

In your State of the State address, you talked about spreading some of the wealth around. How do you intend to do that?

"By employing people. The only way I know to eliminate poverty is through jobs. Now, it's an educational process. The people have to be trained, and all those types of things are taking place in our core cities."

Why is the job picture so uneven?

"We have a low unemployment rate, and yet there are thousands of people in the core cities who don't have jobs. We're doing everything we can to reach them through vocational and technical training."

There still are homeless and hungry people here. Does the state's reputation for wealth and growth overshadow those needs?

"Not at all. We're spending more now for housing, for example, and we'll be spending more for shelters than ever before in the history of our state."

What do you see as the state's most pressing social problem?

"Our housing stock is being replenished, but it is very expensive housing. It's almost impossible to find a home in this area for less than a couple of hundred thousand dollars. In Fairfield, you're talking $300,000 for a home."

Are you talking about palaces?

"No, we're just talking about homes. What I'm trying to do is to get people to build moderate- and low-income housing. What we have to try to do is induce them into building different types of housing. We've got $100 million of bond money for housing sitting there from last year, so in this particular year we could go forward with a couple of hundred million dollars of housing."

Some think New Englanders are cold and aloof. Is that true?

"It's a feeling of being where it all began. I like to say that we're all Connecticut Yankees, frugal and hardworking."

Why doesn't Connecticut have very many sports teams?

"There, I'm afraid, we probably do live in the shadows of New York and Boston. When you've got the best basketball team in the world in Boston, and a pretty good baseball team there, too, it's hard to build another one 100 miles away."

When you want to get away for a weekend, where do you go?

"There's a spot about 23 miles from Hartford in the town of East Hampton, and in that town is a lake, and on that lake is a little house. That's our real house."

O'NEILL PROFILE

PARTY: Democrat.

IN HIS WORDS: "The most important thing as far as leaving a legacy is that I was a square shooter. That's what I'd like to be remembered for, and that's it."

BORN: Aug. 11, 1930, in Hartford, Conn., the only child of Frances and Joseph O'Neill, who ran a tavern in East Hampton, Conn.

FAMILY: Married Natalie "Nikki" Scott Damon in 1962. Mrs. O'Neill, 52, is a former high school business teacher.

EDUCATION: Attended New Britain Teachers' College, University of Hartford.

TIMELINE

1949: Worked as draftsman; joined Air Force in 1950.

1955: Sold life insurance; took over family tavern, O'Neill's, in 1957; still owns tavern.

1960: Lost bid for state legislature; lost second bid for legislature in 1962.

1966: Elected to two-year term in state House of Representatives; re-elected four times; appointed chair of state Democratic Party in 1975.

1978: Elected to four-year term as lieutenant governor.

1980: Assumed governorship when Gov. Ella Grasso resigned five weeks before her death from cancer.

1981: Underwent open-heart surgery.

1982: Won four-year term as governor with 53 percent of vote; re-elected to four-year term with 58 percent of vote in 1986.

1991: Term expires in January; eligible for re-election.

PRIORITIES

▶ Education: Signed 1986 Education Enhancement Act ensuring minimum teacher pay, stricter standards.

NOTEWORTHY
By 1991, he will have served 10 years in office, longer than any Connecticut governor since 1809.

PERSONAL
Harry S. Truman is his hero. . . . Hobby is visiting scenic spots in Connecticut in his 1961 black Thunderbird. . . . Likes big-band music. . . . Favorite spectator sport is basketball.

THE FUTURE
"I am not interested in running for president because I already have the best job in the world."

▶ Economic development: Established revolving loan program to attract new business.

▶ Fiscal stability: "We've got money in the bank, bills paid, paying off state debt, rainy-day funds tucked away."

▶ Infrastructure: Established a 10-year program to rebuild roads, bridges.

GOV. MICHAEL N. CASTLE

IMPRESSIONS

Gov. Michael N. Castle is preppy. If he wasn't born wearing a button-down-collar shirt, he most assuredly donned one shortly thereafter. You half expect to look down and see him wearing deck shoes without socks right there in the governor's office.

He's also boyish. He grins a lot. And he slips in a little subtle humor when you're least expecting it — like when he was telling the BusCateers that he has considered teaching when he finishes his second term and that "maybe that's why we're raising teachers' salaries so rapidly in Delaware." Not a suggestion of jesting.

And he's a bachelor. But says he's not single. He's married to being governor. He obviously loves it. "The best government job in this country is to be governor of a state. And I happen to think that a state like Delaware, which is relatively easy to manage because there are so many assets going into the situation, is even much more fun to govern." Then he added, "I'm in a situation in which I have a job in which the Constitution indicates that no matter what happens, I must leave it after two terms."

Will he teach when his term ends in 1989? Maybe. But don't be surprised if you see Michael Castle in a Capitol cloakroom before you see him in the classroom. He's governor of a small state, but he's got big ideas. National ideas — like welfare. And he's comfortable pitching them on Capitol Hill. He told us about it:

"I'm very involved in welfare reform. I've been working with the White House . . . and (U.S.) Sen. (Daniel) Moynihan and a little bit with the House of Representatives trying to work something out."

Sure, he mentioned teaching. He mentioned practicing law, too. But he also said this:

"I would, probably sometime in the second term, look at the possibility of what might be available in Washington. I've never thought about working in a Washington administration, but I suppose that is a possibility as well."

Remember, Washington is just 92 miles down the road from Dover.

A conversation with Gov. Michael N. Castle.

Are governors performing like CEOs today?

"I think that's absolutely correct. I think that 15 or 20 years ago you had a number of governors who were really non-activist. I think you now have governors who are vitally involved in education. They're involved in international trade. They're dealing with social programs."

How have you applied this style?

"First, we have attempted to plan for the future so the policy and legislation were not adopted randomly. Secondly, we have attempted to use public/private sector persuasion to accomplish the end desired."

Which state has the best economic expansion program? Why?

"Delaware. Starting with the Financial Center Development Act in 1981, Delaware has passed a series of banking legislation which has led to 10,000 new jobs on an employment base of some 275,000."

Some critics of employment and training programs have said that the best way to get people off welfare is to improve a state's overall economy. How do you respond to that criticism?

"First, I don't consider that criticism. It is clear to me that a strong state economy is going to provide job opportunities, particularly at the more marginal employment levels. Our success rate in Delaware is probably the highest in the country, with 50 percent of our graduates from the First Step program (welfare and education training and employment) either working in part-time or full-time jobs."

What is the status of race relations in your state?

"Good to excellent. We had the most inte-grated school districts in America and have shown a vast improvement in test scores from minority students, as well as stable race relations in recent years."

It's difficult to come here without seeing du Pont family influence. How are they regarded here?

"Fifteen years ago, when I started in the Legislature, there was a feeling that the du Pont family was controlling things, including the newspapers. There was a feeling they were controlling the economy of the state, and what the company didn't control, the family did control. The feeling now is that there is less control."

Are you concerned about Delaware becoming too well-known?

"We do have some concerns about growth. Ecologically it's a very difficult balance. Recently, I've proposed quality-of-life plans, where the counties would have to adopt land-use planning, and they can't vary it except with a super majority. If the growth gets ahead of your highways, sewers and water, you're going to have a problem."

How many times has Delaware reduced its personal income tax?

"Four straight times. In 1979, we were the highest in the country, about 20 percent."

Have the reductions reduced services?

"They haven't. We had the highest increase in teacher salaries in the country last year. Also, by reducing income taxes, we have increased economic development activity, which has brought in more people, more jobs. They, in turn, pay in additional revenue, and that has produced the opportunity to reduce taxes again."

You've passed an evaluation system for teachers. How large a priority is education reform?

"It is a high priority, and we really don't have an evaluation program firmly in place the way we want it. We've also tried to put in a career ladder for teachers."

CASTLE PROFILE

PARTY: Republican.

IN HIS WORDS: When his father remarried at 84, bachelor Gov. Castle quipped, "For all you doubting Thomases, what the heck. There's still hope for me. I've got another 40 years or so."

BORN: July 2, 1939, in Wilmington, Del., to du Pont Co. patent lawyer James R. Castle Jr. and Louisa Castle.

FAMILY: Single.

EDUCATION: Bachelor of arts in economics, Hamilton College, N.Y.; law degree, Georgetown University.

TIMELINE

1965: Appointed deputy attorney general.

1966: Elected to serve two-year term in state House.

1968: Elected to four-year term in state Senate; drafted legislation to reform criminal laws, voting laws, education; re-elected in 1972.

1980: Elected to four-year term as lieutenant governor; groomed for governorship by incumbent Gov. Pete du Pont, who was barred by state constitution from seeking a third term.

1984: Elected governor with 55 percent of vote.

1989: Term expires in January; eligible for re-election.

PRIORITIES

▶ Economic development: Proposed mandatory land-use planning; implemented State Improvement Fund in 1985.

▶ Fiscal conservatism: Cut income tax for three consecutive years beginning in 1986.

▶ Education: Proposed teacher evaluation program and pilot program allowing teachers to run their own classrooms; proposed

NOTEWORTHY
Delaware's first Catholic governor.

PERSONAL
Drove 1972 Oldsmobile convertible during campaign, uses Lincoln Town Car for state business. . . . At first, recruited staff members to stay for dinner at the governor's mansion so he wouldn't have to eat alone. . . . Loves to watch basketball on TV.

THE FUTURE
Running for re-election in 1988.

teacher pay hike and new salary structures.

▶ Criminal justice: Appointed new commissioner of corrections and new judges.

▶ Welfare reform: Began pilot program providing medical benefits for welfare recipients who begin working; implemented First Step job training for welfare recipients; established program to provide educational, social and medical support for young children.

GOV. BOB MARTINEZ

IMPRESSIONS

When we arrived to visit with Gov. Bob Martinez, it was a hot, humid, hectic day at the Florida Capitol. The new, controversial tax on services had the governor's office sweating.

Susan Traylor, Martinez's press secretary, was literally holding off the local press just outside Martinez's office.

When the service tax — aimed at such services as advertising, legal services and even pet grooming — did come up, it was clear that Martinez's support was beginning to melt. The nation's only Hispanic governor was facing the ultimate political question: What do you do when public opinion is rolling against you — in a flood tide?

"It was the advertisers, through their associates, who continued the battle. Otherwise, it would have been over with," Martinez lamented.

Despite all the difficulties, Martinez was composed. Gubernatorial. But he was coming just a few syllables short of admitting he was a little sick of the tax himself.

That's just what he did a few weeks later. He asked the legislature to repeal the tax. It was a decision that earned him the title, "Gov. Gumby" — the green cartoon figure who can bend in all directions. By the end of the year, the tax was gone.

For Bob Martinez:

▶ Score one for political courage. He knew he would run into opposition when he pushed the service tax through the legislature. But he did it.

▶ Subtract one for guessing wrong. The tax wasn't an idea that would survive in the end. So he reversed it.

▶ Add one for a sense of humor. He handled our lighter questions with a chuckle. We asked him how he would handle the college football rivalry between Florida and Florida State. "I'll do probably what all courageous governors do, which is sit on both sides. One half on one side, one half on the other."

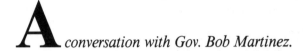

A *conversation with Gov. Bob Martinez.*

You're a first-term Republican governor, but, until four years ago, you were a prominent Democrat. In Florida politics, what's the biggest difference between the two parties?

"I don't believe we think of different issues. It's always the approach to an issue where we begin to differ. I basically believe more in home rule. I came out of local government, and I always felt that the property tax was neither a sufficient nor equitable source of revenue for local government. But the Democrats, historically, have felt that the sales tax was a state revenue and not to be used by the local government."

On social policy, how do you differ from the Democrats?

"The state government shouldn't be setting up health clinics in schools, which is counter to the Democratic philosophy. We all recognize that every youngster needs an education, but the approach may end up being somewhat different. It's a lot easier in the long run to prevent a problem than to go back to correct it. We're the second highest dropout state in the nation, so it's obvious that, upfront, something's wrong."

How would you fix these problems?

"A lot of it is dealing with how you prioritize the overall budget expenditures. We ought to concentrate on public education, public health, public works, public safety. But when you look at what we have done over decades, we're into everything. We've got a lot of programs, but very few get served, because we just don't have the resources to do it all."

How would you describe the difference in attitude between a native of Florida and a newcomer?

"I find that the native Floridian may be more aggressive in terms of economic development than those who have moved here. The newcomers are getting away from congestion and have fears that they have moved to a state that may end up being a New York City or a Chicago. The natives are looking at an expanded economy where they can make a profit."

Do you ever take your family to Disney World?

"I'm about ready to start again with grandchildren. Our children got old enough and started going on their own. You cannot find a better postmark for a state than Disney. What Disney does is attract people to Florida, and once here, they may go ahead and make other inquiries about Florida."

MARTINEZ PROFILE

PARTY: Republican.

IN HIS WORDS: As USA's first Hispanic governor, "I did not come here to be different, I came here to make a difference."

BORN: Dec. 25, 1934, in Tampa, Fla., to Serafin and Ida Martinez. His father was a waiter; his mother, a seamstress.

FAMILY: Married Mary Jane Marino in 1954. Mrs. Martinez, 53, is a former high school head librarian who resigned after her husband was elected governor. They met in high school homeroom. The Martinezes have two children, Sharon, 30, and Alan, 26.

EDUCATION: Bachelor of science in social science, University of Tampa; master of arts in labor and industrial relations, University of Illinois.

TIMELINE

1957: Taught civics in Hillsborough County schools; became labor relations consultant for Hillsborough County Classroom Teachers Association in 1963; became executive director of Hillsborough County Classroom Teachers Association in 1966.

1975: Took over family restaurant, The Cafe Sevilla in Tampa; appointed to board of Southwest Florida Water Management District.

1979: Elected to four-year term as mayor of Tampa; re-elected mayor in 1983.

1983: Switched to Republican party.

1986: Elected to four-year term as governor with 54.6 percent of the vote; appointed co-chair of Vice President George Bush's presidential campaign.

1991: Term expires in January; eligible for re-election.

PRIORITIES

▶ Education: Initiated Project Independence to train and employ welfare recipients;

NOTEWORTHY
USA's only Hispanic governor ... Florida's first Hispanic governor ... Florida's first Republican governor in 20 years.

PERSONAL
Owns basset hound, Mascotte, named after the ship that brought his grandmother to the USA. ... Avoids movies, except an occasional Western. ... Jogs two miles three or four times a week at 5:30 a.m. ... Favorite recreation is shooting baskets in back yard of the governor's mansion, working out in mansion's weight room.

THE FUTURE
"I had my chance to run for governor because I've tended to business. ... And I have no aspirations other than to be a good Floridian and a good governor for Florida."

raised teacher salaries.

▶ Economic development: Proposed project to develop USA's first commercial spaceport.

▶ Criminal justice: Proposed stiffer sentencing for career criminals and more prisons; proposed funding for alternative types of sentencing — such as electronic monitoring — to relieve overcrowding.

▶ Environment: Won agreement with federal government to ban offshore drilling in Florida Keys; established land protection program.

▶ Fiscal conservatism: Slashed $201 million in government spending.

GOV. JOE FRANK HARRIS

Gov. Joe Frank Harris embodies some of the best attributes of the Old South. He's gracious. He's polished. He's a tall, silver-haired, antebellum gentleman.

Gov. Harris also stands for the New South. The progressive South. The South of growth. The South of enlightenment — especially racial enlightenment.

Racial tension in Forsyth County, Ga., in early 1987 put Harris to the test. His challenge: help some of the ugly attitudes of the Old South come to grips with — and change with — the New South.

Harris didn't hesitate to discuss the issue. We asked if people's attitudes could change. Harris told us, "People's attitudes are already changing and have been changing for many years in the South. I think we've made probably more progress than any of the other states in the South in having a compatible relationship between the races, and the growth and momentum that we're having I think attest to that fact."

No matter how sophisticated a Southern politician might be, there's always a little country in him. It was the same with Gov. Harris, who became just "good old Joe Frank" when he learned that two BusCateers were Georgians. He was more than willing to take a few minutes and mug it up in front of the camera with his regional kindred — BusCapade driver Joel Driver of Fort Valley and reporter Paula Burton of Atlanta.

We came away with the feeling that Joe Frank Harris is basically a manager — a manager who is likely to leave office at the end of his second term in 1990 with a Georgia that hangs on to the best of the past while plotting a course for a bright future.

No revolutions.

No surprises.

Just good old front-porch common sense.

A *conversation with Gov. Joe Frank Harris.*

What is the status of race relations in your state?

"Positive and always geared toward improvement. Georgians traditionally exhibit a willingness to resolve differences through cooperation and communication."

During the recent racial incidents in Forsyth County, you said there's absolutely no place for bigotry in our society. Is Forsyth County an isolated case, or are there other Forsyth counties around the state?

"There are other Forsyth counties to some extent, not only in Georgia but all around the USA. This is not just a Georgia problem. It's a problem that exists wherever people are. It's being handled in a proper way, and it's being dealt with very effectively."

Did the Forsyth County incidents give Georgia an image problem?

"To some degree, but if it has, it's someone looking for an excuse. If you look at the track record, over the last 20 years, we've had more than 2 million new people arrive in our state. We've had over 526,000 new jobs in the last four and a half years, and we're having the kind of momentum that other states are very envious of."

How have you seen Georgia change in the past 20 years?

"When I became a member of the General Assembly 23 years ago, our budget was less than $500 million. Today our budget is over $10 billion per year. State government is a big business. If we were lined up on the Fortune 500 list of corporations, we'd probably be No. 72 or 73."

Is it true that there are two Georgias, one made up of the thriving Atlanta area and the other of depressed rural areas?

"That's been an emotional issue. Georgia is a very diverse state. But when you look at the total, there's not any separation through any part of Georgia. If there are any barriers, or any so-called two-Georgia thinking, it's disappearing."

Gradually, Atlanta has become the model for the New South. Why do you think that's happened?

"The reason Atlanta and Georgia have moved forward has been through the cooperation of people working together. Diversity would be the key, and then leadership and people working together."

At the turn of the century, what will Georgia be like?

"Projections are that we'll still be one of the fastest-growing states in the year 2000."

How is that growth being controlled?

"We have a growth strategy commission that's working right now — a diverse group of 41 people across the state. We're very conscious that unless we have orderly growth, we are not going to be able to serve some of the high-growth areas."

How do you personally feel about the future of the state?

"I like to feel Georgia's in a position almost like a locomotive going down a track. We're fueled up and moving."

We often hear that Atlanta's airport is overcrowded and another major airport is needed in the area. Do you agree?

"That's true if we continue our growth pattern and the number of flights continues. There are already several sites reserved for that second airport."

What do you want Georgia's image to be?

"As the place where the action is, where anything is possible and anything can happen if you're willing to work hard."

HARRIS PROFILE

PARTY: Democrat.

IN HIS WORDS: "I never envisioned myself as being governor."

BORN: Feb. 16, 1936, in Bartow County, Ga., to Franklin Harris, concrete dealer, and Frances Harris, homemaker.

FAMILY: Married Elizabeth Carlock in 1961. Mrs. Harris, 48, is a homemaker, former teacher. The Harrises have one son, Joe, 24.

EDUCATION: Bachelor of business administration, University of Georgia.

TIMELINE

1958: Served in Army; helped manage family business, Harris Concrete Products, with brother, Frank, and father, Franklin.

1964: Elected to two-year term in Georgia House of Representatives; re-elected eight times, serving for 18 years; chaired Appropriations Committee for eight years.

1979: Became president of family development firm, Harris Georgia Corp.

1982: Elected to four-year term as governor with 63 percent of vote; re-elected with 71 percent of vote in 1986; named chairman of Southern Governors Association in 1987.

1991: Term expires in January; not eligible for third consecutive term.

PRIORITIES

▶ Education: Enacted comprehensive Quality Basic Education Act in 1985 without raising taxes.

▶ Economic development: Created Economic Development Council and Growth Strategies Commission to develop plan for economic development and environmental protection.

▶ Affirmative action: Created Human Relations Commission in December 1987 to mediate civil rights issues. Discrimination pro-

NOTEWORTHY
The second Georgia governor to win a second consecutive term.

PERSONAL
Admires Abraham Lincoln. "He was a self-made person." ... Keeps vase of wife's roses in his office when they are in bloom. ... Loves chocolate-covered cherries. ... Favorite color is blue. ... Pet peeve is people showing up late.

THE FUTURE
Ineligible for third term in 1990. Harris says, "I don't have any political plans whatsoever. ... I think there will be a place for me somewhere, probably in the business world."

tests in Forsyth County drew national attention earlier that year.

▶ Health care: Increased access to Medicaid for pregnant women and needy families.

GOV. JOHN D. WAIHEE III

IMPRESSIONS

The word interview does not describe the BusCapade session with Gov. John D. Waihee III. It is too formal. And Waihee — although descended from royalty — is just too informal for an interview. What we had was a chat with Waihee.

Waihee likes to talk — but slowly, deliberately. He's true to his name, which translates loosely to "calm waters." It's no surprise that he studied Zen Buddhism and Werner Erhard's mellowing "est" training. It's also no surprise that Waihee is notorious for being late because he doesn't like to rush conversations.

With us, he wasn't late. And he also didn't rush the conversation.

Waihee cautiously considered each topic, ranging from the growing importance of the Pacific Rim to proper business attire in Hawaii. Waihee's thoughts on business dress told a lot about him.

"The problem is that we don't have a Hawaiian business attire," Waihee explained. "The aloha shirt is too informal for many occasions. On the other hand, the coat and tie may be too formal or too hot. I want to try to get together a sort of contest among the Hawaiians to come up with a business dress — something that is more than an aloha shirt, but not a coat and tie."

The BusCateers realized that what he had in mind was something that was right for Hawaii, but also right for John D. Waihee III. Something that's proper, but not pompous.

A *conversation with Gov. John D. Waihee III.*

The 1985 United Airlines strike posed some real dangers to your economy. Is Hawaii too dependent on tourism?

"The strike posed a number of dangers that impacted on tourism. But it poses a danger in and of itself, whether or not we have a tourism-inclined economy. And that's because 99.99 percent of our transportation for people is by air. And under the best of circumstances, we should not be so dependent on one carrier."

What can you do about it?

"One, diversify the markets from which people come to Hawaii. One of the reasons we didn't suffer as badly as we might have during the United Airlines strike was that we made up the difference with tourists from Japan, who were not bound to travel on United. The other safeguard is to diversify the number of carriers, types of carriers."

Hawaii traditionally has seen a lot of opposition to business and growth. Do you still encounter opposition to development?

"Yes. Actually, Hawaii went through a couple of swings. From when we became a state, up to the early '70s, were the formative years of the travel industry. The concern was to be sure that while the mainstream was pushing growth, there would be laws that protect the land. Then, about the time of the oil crisis in 1974, people started to think that maybe we ought to slow down a bit and that we ought to look at the supply of resources a little bit more closely. Now we're probably closer to where we were in 1962 when people wanted growth. But, whatever cycle we're in, people in Hawaii generally have a very high appreciation for their environment."

What are your top five priorities as governor?

"Education, relief of traffic congestion, construction of affordable housing, diversification and strengthening of the economy, public-private initiatives in human resources to respond to changing demographics and economic structure."

Has the Reagan administration made governors more powerful, less powerful, or the same?

"More powerful, by abdicating the long-established federal leadership role and increasing the responsibilities of statehouses."

Is this a one-party state, politically?

"Depends on your definition. This state has an awful lot of Democrats. I happen to think that this state is actually not a one-party state because the Democratic Party has so many different factions."

Do you see Hawaii taking on a greater role in national affairs?

"The Pacific, despite its importance to our country economically, has for the large part been ignored benignly by the United States. I think we can become an effective voice for the aspirations of the region. And that's why I really believe that the state has a national role to play."

You went to school in Michigan. Based on living there, what differences stand out to you between mainlanders and islanders?

"When I was in Michigan, I knew a lot of people from the country, and they were wonderful people. But there was one essential difference, and that is the idea of vastness. There's no sense of limitation. On an island, there's the isolation, and there's water on all sides of you all the time. So you get a sense that this is it. Therefore, it's a little bit more precious."

What image would you like people on the mainland to have of the state of Hawaii?

"I like the image of Hawaii being a very exciting place, that there are a lot of things happening here, that America's future lies in the Pacific Asian Rim, and that Hawaii is the farthest outpost of the country."

WAIHEE PROFILE

PARTY: Democrat.

IN HIS WORDS: As a child, "I really had a hard time accepting authority — not in a belligerent way, but intellectually. If someone said this was the way it should be, I would challenge him."

BORN: May 19, 1946, in Honokaa, Hawaii, to rancher John Waihee and schoolteacher Mary Waihee.

FAMILY: Married Lynne Kobashigawa in 1969. Mrs. Waihee, 41, is a former high school English teacher. They met in high school, attended college together. The Waihees have two children, John, 17, and Jennifer, 16.

EDUCATION: Bachelor of arts in history, business, Andrews University; law degree, University of Hawaii.

TIMELINE

1968: Coordinated community education for Twin Cities Area Human Resources Council in Michigan.

1971: Named administrator of Honolulu Model Cities program; became program manager in Honolulu Office of Human Resources in 1974.

1976: Practiced labor law with Honolulu firm Shim, Sigal, Tam and Naito; founded law firm Waihee, Manuia, Yap, Pablo and Hoe in 1979.

1980: Elected to two-year term in state House of Representatives.

1982: Elected to four-year term as lieutenant governor.

1986: Elected to four-year term as governor in upset victory with 52 percent of the vote.

1990: Term expires in December; eligible for re-election.

PRIORITIES

▶ Housing: Proposed program to build af-

NOTEWORTHY
Member of first graduating class from University of Hawaii's law school in 1976. . . . At age 39 became Hawaii's youngest lieutenant governor. . . . State's first native Hawaiian governor.

PERSONAL
Likes swimming, golf. . . . Pitches for cabinet softball team. . . . Martin Luther King Jr. and Challenger astronaut Ellison Onizuka are his heroes. . . . Has saltwater reef tank in his office; says the fish provide entertainment for him and he provides entertainment for the fish.

THE FUTURE
"I'll probably stay in public service in one way or another, but either way I'll try to get in more golf."

---

fordable housing, provide rental assistance.

▶ Economic development: Proposed establishing Office of Technology Transfer and Economic Development and innovation centers to assist high-tech businesses; proposed plans for commercial space-launch services and funding of waterfront development.

▶ Education: Proposed teacher pay hike.

▶ Welfare reform: Initiated "Project Success," voluntary workfare program; proposed job training for fathers of dependent children.

GOV. CECIL D. ANDRUS

For Cecil Andrus, deciding to run for a third term as governor was just a matter of knowing his own priorities.

After his first two terms as governor, Andrus signed on as President Jimmy Carter's secretary of the interior. He won applause from environmental groups, but four years in Washington were more than enough for him.

"My wife and I had enjoyed 37 years of marriage and I wouldn't trade a national political career for whatever years she and I have left," Andrus said. "I left Washington, D.C., with not the best taste in my mouth."

Although Andrus once lashed out at Interior successor James Watt, saying Watt had a philosophy of "If you can't dig it up or cut it down, it has no value," Andrus was more temperate in our conversation.

How did he assess the Reagan administration's management of natural resources?

"It hasn't been all that bad. The attempts at destruction have been frequent, but basically the laws are there and have been working."

The only time we saw even a flash of anger from the otherwise even-tempered Andrus came after a question about white supremacists who made Idaho their home.

"I resent that a small group of people who are a self-styled white supremacy group can take a small compound in our state and get the publicity nationwide that they have. I hate to see us transmit to the world that there's any place that has a group like that," Andrus said.

We left Andrus' office with an Idaho road map in hand.

He had heard about the speeding ticket BusCapade received in Wisconsin and told us that he didn't want to see that happen to us in the state of Idaho.

Hence, the inscription: "Good for one ticket." — Gov. Cecil Andrus.

A conversation with Gov. Cecil D. Andrus.

What made you decide to run for governor again?

"John Evans, my predecessor, was not going to run. The list of Democrats who could be elected was very short. I refused to accept the doldrums that the economy was in. I said we had to make an investment in the state. I lived here because this was home and where I chose to live, but I had a little more exposure to the outside world maybe than some of the others, and I decided I would do it. Now I'm at a point in my life where I can make a difference. Now we'll see."

What has changed in Idaho since you first served as governor in 1971?

"Our population has gone up from 670,000 to well over a million. And we had somewhat of an exodus during the depression that parts of America have been struggling through. That has stabilized and bottomed out."

How has Idaho responded to the changes?

"Idaho is more aware of the competitive nature of the world and what we have to do to perpetuate ourselves. Our basic economy now has gone through some very devastating times and we are now out there competing with the rest of them. We're the 13th largest in size geographically within the 50 states. We've got 82,000 square miles and roughly 53 million acres."

Has the job of secretary of interior changed much since you served in that position in the Carter administration?

"The role has not changed from 1849, when it was created: Your responsibility is the stewardship of all the public-owned land in America, with the exceptions of the military reserva-tions and the U.S. Forest Service, which they put into the Department of Agriculture. You have about one-third of the USA's total land area. That four years I spent was very intense, but we were in the right place at the right time to do a lot of things for America."

What did you accomplish in those four years?

"On the development side, for the first time in about 10 years, we brought back a coal-leasing program where we sold coal from the public lands. We put forth an outer continental shelf offshore and onshore oil-leasing program that had been missing for a lot of years. On the protectionist, conservationist side, we resolved the Alaska lands issue that had been bubbling there since 1972. And we resolved a lot of the national resources issues."

In your State of the State address, you said Idaho is perceived to be a haven for white supremacists. How have you tried to remedy that?

"The attorney general — a Republican — and I drew up a bill that we thought was very tight and would give us the right of confiscation of their property — like you do with a drug dealer. The one way to really drive them out was, if they violated the law, then it gave you the right to confiscate their property."

But that bill wasn't passed.

"It failed because of lobbying efforts of the National Rifle Association and others. We did pass some legislation. But it wasn't as strong."

Idaho has a striking shape. Does that shape make sense to you?

"No. It shouldn't. The surveyors were supposed to go north and cut off that piece of Montana. We would have been rectangular. But the story goes that they were very drunk for several days on end and got on the wrong ridge line. It would have increased us by about 40 percent."

How do you relax?

"Fishing, hunting, hiking. You take me out into the mountains with a rifle, shotgun, or fishing pole and I do well — much better than I do in the office."

ANDRUS PROFILE

PARTY: Democrat.

IN HIS WORDS: "Governor sounds like a fancy title. But take the gold braid off his golf cap and what you have left is a problem solver. That's what I am — a problem solver."

BORN: Born Aug. 25, 1931, in Hood River, Ore., to Hal Andrus, sawmill operator, and Dorothy Andrus, homemaker.

FAMILY: Married Carol M. May in 1949. Mrs. Andrus, 55, is a homemaker. They were high school sweethearts. The Andruses have three daughters, Tana, 36; Tracy, 32; and Kelly, 27.

EDUCATION: Studied engineering at Oregon State University from 1947-49.

TIMELINE

1945: Worked as lumberjack in sawmill where his father was part owner.

1951: Joined Navy.

1960: Elected to two-year term in state Senate in 1960; re-elected in 1962, 1964 and 1968.

1963: Worked for Paul Revere Life Insurance.

1966: Lost 1966 race for governor. He was defeated in primary, but went on to general election because primary winner was killed in plane crash. Andrus was then defeated again.

1970: Elected to four-year term as governor with 52.2 percent of vote; re-elected governor with 70.9 percent of vote in 1974.

1976: Named chair of Western Governors' Conference.

1977: Resigned governorship to accept appointment as secretary of the interior by President Carter.

1981: Returned to Idaho in 1981 to open Resource Management Consulting firm.

NOTEWORTHY

Became Idaho's youngest state senator at age 29. . . . In 1970, elected Idaho's first Democratic governor in 24 years. . . . Won second term in 1974 with largest margin in Idaho history. . . . First Idahoan to serve in presidential Cabinet.

PERSONAL

Addicted to golf, he calls himself a "total duffer." . . . Has read "most of the books about Harry S. Truman," now reads western novels, biographies, 20th century world history. . . . "Slam-hanger" bridge player. . . . Enjoys country and western and big-band music.

THE FUTURE

"I'm not sure (the presidency) is worth the pain and suffering. Besides, being governor of Idaho is a better job than being president of the United States." Hasn't ruled out a re-election bid.

1986: Re-elected to four-year term as governor with 50 percent of the vote.

1991: Term expires in January; eligible for re-election.

PRIORITIES

▶ Education: Established network of child-development centers; began job training for work force in year 2000; established task force to coordinate policies and programs for children.

▶ Environment: Co-authored bill pending in Congress to designate 1.4 million acres as wilderness.

▶ Economic development: Increased funding for Department of Commerce; proposed plan to coordinate and increase economic development; proposed tax reform.

GOV. JAMES R. THOMPSON

IMPRESSIONS

S ome governors try to make history. Gov. Jim Thompson collects it.

We met Thompson in his Chicago office because he had to be out of the state capital of Springfield on business. But this was no spare office away from home. His Chicago office contains a remarkable array of art and antiques. Thompson proudly gave us a tour before the interview.

Perhaps the most memorable item in the room was the desk that once belonged to Abraham Lincoln. Two busts of Lincoln also adorned the room.

Thompson told us how dangerous it can be to treat Lincoln's memory with anything but the utmost reverence. A recently published photograph of Thompson propping his feet up on the Lincoln desk prompted an angry reaction.

"Did I get mail!" Thompson said. "Even though Lincoln probably had his feet on top of that desk more often than I have, nobody thought I had a right to do that."

Like Lincoln, Thompson has his own problems with North and South — Northern and Southern Illinois. He acknowledged that Illinois has a history of regional pride and that the city of Chicago and Downstate Illinois don't always work together or have the same ends. But he contends that's improving.

"People will always put their regions first," Thompson told us. "But I think there's a greater understanding that a dollar earned in Chicago pays taxes to Springfield and vice versa."

Yet if Illinois sometimes has internal divisions, there's a statewide pride that revels in competing against other states, particularly in the area of sports. And Thompson is head cheerleader.

"We're a great sports state," he said. "Yeah, we'd like to be winners all the time, but we can't. That doesn't mean we don't compete fiercely or enjoy the competition."

He's a big man, 6 feet 6 inches tall, with a proportionate sense of self.

He signed his high school yearbook "Jim Thompson, Pres. of U.S., 1984-1992." Although that prophecy hasn't fit the timetable, it can't be ruled out for the future.

A *conversation with Gov. James R. Thompson.*

You have two busts of Abraham Lincoln in your office. Why?

"There is still a great feeling of affection for him. I know the Republican Party of Illinois still adores Abe, because we carry Lincoln Day banquets beyond all reasonable bounds. Foreign visitors are particularly intrigued with Lincoln. So I work hard at keeping Lincoln alive, and I think most people in Illinois do."

Is your state's fiscal record one that can be exported to other states?

"It's exportable to the nation if we finish the second half of the job. Keeping taxes low is great — unless your tax system doesn't produce enough revenue to give you a first-class state. And as I try to tell audiences around the state — who are against the philosophy of tax and spend, tax and spend — there are worse things than tax and spend. Borrow and spend is worse. And the failure to spend for things that are needed, whether it's education or transportation, is worse."

You've been pretty successful in luring the Japanese here to do business. How about selling them products from Illinois?

"There has been an increase, particularly in small businesses, in export activity from Illinois to Japan, but I would have to say that the great bulk of the work that we have done as a state government has been to bring manufacturing facilities here. I think I'm right when I say that we're the third largest state in terms of Japanese investment, after New York and California."

Chicago and Illinois have had their share of political corruption. What brings this element out?

"Corruption has been with us probably since we were founded. My recollection is that the first public building built in Chicago was a jail. So that tells you something! But the first serious efforts by prosecutors, particularly federal prosecutors, to root out corruption in local government began when I was U.S. attorney, from 1971 to 1975. I think the Graylord probe, the judicial corruption probe, has been very healthy for Illinois."

Illinois spends more money than any other state on tourism. Does it pay off?

"It has paid off for us — to the point where there is no serious disagreement about continuing the expenditure at that level. All told, our expenditures on tourism promotion will run about $15.5 million next year."

What is Illinois selling to tourists?

"We're a different kind of state, and I think we finally started to promote the difference. Nobody flies into Chicago or anyplace else in Illinois to lie on the beach for two weeks. On the other hand, more people fly into Chicago to attend conventions and trade shows and meetings than to any other city in North America."

And you're promoting other parts of the state as well as Chicago?

"That's where we've really stepped up our efforts. The notion two or three years ago that the state would be putting up dollars to promote events in Rockford, or Peoria, or in southern Illinois would have been regarded as fanciful. But we've done that, and we've succeeded."

Does the rest of the state sometimes feel like a suburb of Chicago?

"There's always this Downstate-Chicago feeling: Chicago gets it all, and Chicago is just a different kind of place than downstate. We've got the cultural attractions, but, at the same time, we've worked very hard to improve the underlying tourism infrastructure. So, we understand the dollars that are involved in business tours and the different attractions in the state of Illinois, and we intend to be very vigorous in that."

THOMPSON PROFILE

PARTY: Republican.

IN HIS WORDS: "I want to be able to point to concrete achievements. I don't just mean concrete, but achievements in social services, in conservation, in transportation, that people will remember this administration for through the years."

BORN: May 8, 1936, in Chicago, to Dr. J. Robert and Agnes Thompson, homemaker.

FAMILY: Married Jayne Ann Carr in 1976. Mrs. Thompson, 42, is a former lawyer. They met at Northwestern University. The Thompsons have one child, Samantha Jayne, 9, the first child born to an incumbent Illinois governor in 72 years.

EDUCATION: Law degree, Northwestern University.

TIMELINE

1959: Became Cook County prosecutor.

1964: Taught law as associate professor at Northwestern University law school.

1969: Appointed chief of Department of Law Enforcement and Public Protection; became first assistant U.S. Attorney in 1970; became U.S. Attorney in 1971; resigned to run for governor in 1975.

1976: Elected to special two-year gubernatorial term mandated by new state constitution, with 64.7 percent of vote.

1978: Re-elected to four-year term with 59 percent of vote; re-elected in 1982 with 49.4 percent of vote; re-elected in 1986 with 52.7 percent of vote.

1981: Named chairman of Midwestern Governors' Conference.

1982: Elected chairman of Republican Governors' Association.

1983: Named chair of National Governors' Association.

1991: Term expires in January; eligible for re-election.

NOTEWORTHY

Elected governor in 1976 with largest margin in Illinois history — 64.7 percent of vote. . . . In 1985, became longest-serving Illinois governor.

PERSONAL

Signed high school yearbook, "Jim Thompson, Pres. of U.S., 1984-1992." . . . Co-authored three texts on criminal law. . . . Once rode a horse inside the state Capitol. . . . Nicknamed "Big Jim," Thompson is 6 feet 6 inches tall. . . . Collects antiques, from Teddy Roosevelt's pince-nez to doorstops.

THE FUTURE

"If I could be president, I'd like to be president. But the act of running for it is another thing. . . . I'm immodest enough to think that I could be a good one."

PRIORITIES

▶ Tax reform: Eliminated food and drug sales taxes and state inheritance tax; proposed uniform state sales tax.

▶ Criminal justice: Signed Class X anti-crime law requiring mandatory minimum sentence for violent crimes and some drug offenses; instituted computerized system to respond to child abuse cases; expanded prison facilities.

▶ Health care: Established in-home care program for elderly.

▶ Education: Initiated Illinois Better Schools program to make schools more accountable.

▶ Economic development: Expanded tourism budget; spent more than $80 million upgrading and renovating state parks; established Build Illinois program to rebuild infrastructure.

GOV. ROBERT D. ORR

IMPRESSIONS

Robert Orr is not at all complacent. You might have expected that from a man who had been a state senator, a lieutenant governor under Gov. Otis Bowen during his two terms, and governor of the state of Indiana for his own two terms. Ineligible to run for re-election, Orr could be excused if he sat back during the BusCapade interview and bragged of his accomplishments in office.

To the contrary, Orr was most excited about what he had not yet accomplished — education reform.

In his Indianapolis office, Orr was busy leading the fight for the state A-Plus Education program, which was approved in 1987 by the state Legislature. With the assistance of state school superintendent H. Dean Evans, Orr mapped out a plan for annual achievement tests for students, as well as greater overall accountability for education quality.

To promote that program, Orr promised to take his message to teachers throughout the state.

"It's landmark legislation in that we are changing the ways schools will function," Orr told us. "We have switched from one-third of the amount of money for schools coming from the state and two-thirds coming from the local property taxes to exactly the opposite."

Although Orr had a full head of steam built up to discuss education, he was a gracious enough host to field some questions from his visitors about Indiana's brand of basketball.

"As far as basketball is concerned, Indiana likes to think that while basketball was invented in Springfield, Mass., they learned how to play the game in Indiana," Orr told us.

Orr exhibited the same mild contempt for the nation's capital that we saw throughout the heartland.

"I think Washington is distracted with itself," Orr said in response to a question about foreign policy. "Everything within the Beltway is different than what it is in the rest of the country."

Orr told us he would "like to be remembered as having spent a sufficient amount of my time thinking about the future."

Orr's strong commitment to Indiana's school children makes that prospect very likely.

conversation with Gov. Robert D. Orr.

Indiana is now the largest steel-producing state. In light of the low cost of steel that is subsidized by foreign manufacturers, what does this mean for the economy of Indiana?

"We've got to do more and more of the kinds of things that were done last week with the joint venture between Nippon Steel and Inland Steel. And there are other ways by which ingenuity can cause us to be more productive and, therefore, low enough in cost to be able to meet that competition."

Doesn't the new plant resulting from that venture displace about 300 people from another plant?

"What they hope to do is to (slowly displace) . . . over a span of time by attrition."

Has Indiana changed much from the way it was in the '50s, the period in which the movie *Hoosiers* takes place?

"Farming is not as dominant as it was then. This state, while it has always been a major industrial state, has become that much more of one. As far as basketball is concerned, Indiana likes to think that while basketball was invented in Springfield, Mass., they learned how to play the game in Indiana. There is nothing quite to compare with the Indiana high school basketball tournament, which is only one of three states where they don't have any divisions. You play in a single tournament whether you're a school of 140 or 3,000."

How has education changed in Indiana?

"School is quite different from 25 years ago. We had a different culture about education than we do now. Discipline was much more conventional. The relationship with the family had a lot more to do with it. There weren't very many single-parent families in 1954. But I think we're on the verge of turning education into something a whole lot more important than it's ever been."

Your plan to improve schools is having a rocky time in the Legislature right now.

"It's landmark legislation in that we are changing the way schools will function. We have switched from one-third of the amount of money for schools coming from the state and two-thirds coming from the local property taxes to exactly the opposite. This (legislation) sees to the evaluation of individual schools, to the measurement of the performance of students in a very careful way with, among other things, testing. It provides a mechanism by which — instead of accrediting schools on the basis of their assets, size of the auditorium, the number of books in the library, and so forth — they are rated on results."

How would you like to be remembered?

"I'd like to be remembered as having spent a sufficient amount of my time thinking about the future. I have greatly enjoyed the experience of taking a look at China. It is bound to make a huge difference in the future of this world as it finally gets its act together. I'd like to see the country a part of that act. And I might even want to try to do some things that might facilitate it."

ORR PROFILE

PARTY: Republican.

IN HIS WORDS: "Indiana is coping with the disruptive forces of almost constant change. My first duty ... is to lead Indiana's efforts to keep pace, to see change as the best door to opportunity."

BORN: Nov. 17, 1917, in Ann Arbor, Mich., to Samuel Orr, who owned Orr Iron Co., and Louise Orr, homemaker.

FAMILY: Married Joanne "Josie" Wallace in 1944. Mrs. Orr, 67, is a homemaker. She is also a licensed pilot, former Air Force WASP bomber pilot and former nurse's aide. The Orrs have three children, Robert Jr., 41, and twins Susan and Marjorie, 39.

EDUCATION: Bachelor of arts in business, Yale University; attended Harvard University business school, 1940-42.

TIMELINE

1942: Served in Army.

1946: Named officer, director at Orr Iron Co.; became part owner, Sign Crafters Inc., in 1947; consultant, board of directors for Hahn Inc., from 1957-69.

1962: Named chairman of board, Indian Industries Inc., recreational products.

1968: Elected to four-year term in state Senate.

1972: Elected to four-year term as lieutenant governor; re-elected in 1976.

1980: Elected to four-year term as governor with 58 percent of vote; re-elected to four-year term in 1984 with 52 percent of vote.

1986: Elected president of Council of State Governments.

1989: Term expires in January; not eligible for third consecutive term.

NOTEWORTHY

In 1980, elected governor with a record vote margin for Indiana — 58 percent. ... In 1984, campaigned with what aides called USA's first MTV-style political ad.

PERSONAL

Enjoys skiing. ... Favorite books include: *The Reckoning* by David Halberstam, *War and Peace* by Tolstoy. ... Plays golf, tennis. ... Heroes are Charles Lindbergh and Dwight D. Eisenhower.

THE FUTURE

Not eligible for re-election in 1988. Plans "to do something interesting that will draw on the great experience I've gained in the last seven years."

PRIORITIES

▶ Education: Established "Prime Time" program to reduce class size, proposed "Principals Leadership Academy" to develop student competency standards, initiated "A-Plus Program" to measure results and reward performance.

▶ Economic development: Created Indiana Corporation for Science and Technology to support innovation, strengthen economy; established Corporation for Indiana's International Future to develop international strategy.

▶ Licensing reform: Pushed through License Branch Reform Act to redistribute proceeds from license plate sales for cars.

GOV. TERRY E. BRANSTAD

IMPRESSIONS

Interviewing Gov. Terry Branstad was easy. All we had to do was walk into his office, turn on our tape recorders and he erupted in enthusiasm. He was genuinely excited about Iowa.

No matter how soft the farm economy was. No matter how bad things were. Gov. Branstad was convinced that the worst was over. He was determined, not despondent about his state. And he was clearly having fun talking about it. So much so, that it was all we could do to squeeze in a question during the first 15 or 20 minutes of the session.

Branstad sat in a large chair behind a large desk and held forth. Early in the interview, he read us the "Ambassador's Creed," a motto his office had come up with for Iowans living across the USA:

"Iowa is the America that you grew up believing in. It is faith, hope and caring about each other. It is freedom, but through hard work and integrity. It is the belief that the future will be better than today if we make it that way. Iowa is a place where the dream still works, and it is our challenge as ambassadors to tell the world about it."

We left there realizing it also was his motto.

Branstad's plan for Iowa is not much different from what other farm-state governors have in mind for their states: Create a broad economic base to protect the state against swings in agribusiness.

No one can be sure what the weather will do to the crops, but Branstad seems determined to hoe to the end of the row.

A conversation with Gov. Terry E. Branstad.

Would you describe your management style as similar to that of a chief executive officer?

"Yes, while recognizing that government's bottom line is services, not profits. In 1985, I proposed and implemented a reorganization of state government that cut the number of departments from 68 to 24, cut 10 percent of the state payroll and created a Department of Management. Because of this, I can now conduct monthly progress review meetings with each agency and manage for efficiency, effectiveness and accountability."

You want more diversification in the economy. How are you going about getting that?

"The first thing I did was recommend a major new initiative for excellence in education. I signed that bill recently."

How does it work?

"It was a program to raise beginning teachers' salaries to $18,000 and to provide some general increases to reward our good teachers and encourage them to stay in the classroom."

That $18,000 floor compares with —

"It's about $14,500 for the average beginning teacher salary. We are well below the national average. Iowa students have traditionally scored very high. We scored No. 1 in the country last year in both the American College Test scores and SAT. But some of the best graduates of our colleges and universities are being offered beginning teachers' salaries by other states far above what we can offer."

What is the mood of Iowans?

"People are recognizing that the worst is indeed behind us, and there are some real opportunities. I also think we've got to change the way we're going to do things."

And how would you do that?

"We should build on education. I mentioned that. I've also embarked on a very ambitious transportation program and asked for a major revision of our tax structure. Unfortunately, we were not successful in getting the tax reform approved this year. Iowa does have a reputation as being a high-tax state. We're trying to change that."

What do Iowans think of President Reagan?

"I think Ronald Reagan has been a strong national leader. I think he's restored faith and confidence in America. I don't think he's been very well liked in the state of Iowa. In fact, I think if you look at the national polls, he has the lowest approval rating in this state."

Why is that?

"Some of the statements that have been made on agricultural policy. I respect him, but I've been disappointed with the way they handled the farm credit problem and the agriculture issue generally."

Many people think of *The Music Man* when they think of Iowa. That image of River City — small town, people caring about each other — does that kind of town still exist in Iowa?

"Absolutely. People really care about each other, and they care about their community."

Aren't many Iowans concerned that these small towns will become a thing of the past?

"That's why it's so essential that we aggressively work on rural development, and diversification, and providing job opportunities. The ones that are aggressive, that work out, really go after economic opportunities."

Are farms in Iowa doing better now?

"I remember Oct 1, 1985. Because of farm foreclosures we were asking for help. Now, land prices have bottomed out. Livestock prices have improved significantly. So the farm situation is improving modestly."

BRANSTAD PROFILE

PARTY: Republican.

IN HIS WORDS: "I've learned to manage stress. I've got to learn to accept the fact there's going to be unfair criticism and there's going to be things you get blamed for that you have no control over. You can't let it bother you."

BORN: Nov. 17, 1946, in Leland, Iowa, to Rita and Edward Branstad, farmers.

FAMILY: Married Christine Johnson in 1972. Mrs. Branstad, 36, is a homemaker. The Branstads have three children, Eric, 12; Allison, 11; and Marcus, 4 — first baby born to an incumbent Iowa governor in 137 years.

EDUCATION: Bachelor of arts in political science, University of Iowa; law degree, Drake University law school.

TIMELINE

1969: Drafted by Army.

1972: Elected to two-year term in state House of Representatives; re-elected in 1974, 1976.

1974: Practiced law as senior partner in firm Branstad & Schwarm.

1978: Elected to four-year term as lieutenant governor.

1979: Bought farm in Lake Mills, Iowa; still owns, runs it.

1982: Elected to four-year term as governor with 52.8 percent of vote; re-elected governor with 52 percent of vote in 1986.

1984: Chaired President Reagan's Iowa campaign.

1991: Term expires in January; eligible for re-election.

PRIORITIES

▶ Economic development: Lowered business taxes in 1985; cut income taxes in 1987; initiated statewide commercial transportation network in 1988.

NOTEWORTHY

In 1983 became youngest governor in Iowa's history, saying, "Some people say that life begins at 40, so I'm excited about the opportunity. Plus, the alternative isn't very good."

PERSONAL

Has collected more than 200 political campaign buttons since 1972. . . . Camps out with daughter Allison and her Indian Princess troop. . . . Enjoys state, county fairs. . . . Loves to read about Harry S. Truman.

THE FUTURE

"I have no interest in Washington, D.C., and I've been there enough to know how much better I like living in Iowa. My goal is to stay here and see the state through to a strong, diversified economy."

▶ Education: Excellence in Education program raised teacher salaries, provided performance-based pay.

▶ Welfare reform: Established "Project Promise" to provide training and increase child care and medical benefits for welfare recipients returning to work.

▶ Budget control: Implemented reorganization; cut 10 percent of state payroll; created Department of Management.

GOV. MIKE HAYDEN

IMPRESSIONS

Mike Hayden has that Midwestern, solid-rock, farm-boy way about him. No flash. No fake.

He knows his responsibilities; he'll take care of them. He always has. He always will. He told us that his values come from growing up in a rural community:

"You develop very strong traditional values, family values. That is, your family is very close-knit, and you learn to depend on other people, and they learn to depend on you. You build on that dependency."

He values having played a part in the Vietnam War. He felt his country needed him, and he went. Platoon leader. Company commander. Soldiers Medal, two Bronze Stars, the Army Commendation Medal.

Regarding the controversy surrounding Vietnam, Hayden says:

"There is a tremendous awakening in this country of the sacrifice that was made over there — the ultimate sacrifice that was made by some 58,000. I felt like (the appreciation) would come some day.

"It wasn't so hard for me, because like I said, from a small town, I was never that rejected. But there was a tremendous number of people I was over there with, who have never been properly recognized for their commitment, and today people are starting to realize that we really owe those folks."

Hayden says he plans to stay in public service. He thinks that's where he's needed.

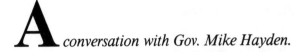

A*conversation with Gov. Mike Hayden.*

Would you describe your management style as similar to that of a chief executive officer?

"No. Since government is not operated on a for-profit basis, it seldom can be run with a corporate management style. My preference is to recruit a strong cabinet and delegate management authority to them. In state government, the Legislature is the board of directors, and, to be successful, one has to work with them in a much different manner than a CEO working with a board of stockholders in the corporate environment."

You've been holding "Tell the Governor" sessions that allow any Kansas resident to come by and talk with you for a few minutes. How are the sessions going?

"They're going quite well, and they drive my security crazy. I have an inherent belief in the grass roots. I also believe that we suffer in government — in every capital, and they probably do worse in Washington than anywhere — we suffer from what we call 'the Topeka Bubble.'"

Which means?

"It's easy to lose touch with the common folks. It's just hard to feel the pulse. So, we established this program called 'Tell the Governor,' where people simply line up at the door for an opportunity to, in five minutes, say whatever they want to the governor. We have one scheduled next month in Kansas City, Kan. We're going to move around the state. We're going to try to do it about six times a year."

Many people think of *The Wizard of Oz* when they think of Kansas. Is that the right image?

"That's an image that a lot of outsiders have of our state. It's not an image that most Kan-

sans ever entertain in their own minds because they live here every day."

But like the movie says, "There's no place like home."

"That's exactly right. And to most of the 2.3 million people here, that's absolutely true."

How is Kansas different today from what it was 50 years ago?

"We find ourselves today not only very much involved in national affairs, but international affairs. Kansas — being the largest producer of wheat in the nation and the No. 1 state in production of red meat — finds that we've got to sell that red meat in the other 49 states and abroad. And we have to sell 70 percent of all our farm commodities overseas in order for our farmers to find prosperity."

Are you actively courting overseas markets?

"We recently received a trade delegation of the Taiwanese. They bought in excess of $30 million worth of corn. We just sent our lieutenant governor to the People's Republic of China to work out trade relations on how we might buy products and commodities from them and how they might buy from us. Our secretary of commerce next week will be in Germany, where we're going to open a new office, so that we might have direct representation with the European Economic Community."

Kansas is known for its farm tradition. What's happening to the family farm? Is it disappearing?

"There's no doubt because of technology the number of family farms will be diminished. They already have. We lose on the average between 1,000 and 2,000 farms a year in Kansas. And we've been doing that for a long, long time."

HAYDEN PROFILE

PARTY: Republican.

IN HIS WORDS: "Growing up in a small town and working on the farm taught me the value of hard work, discipline, honesty and courage."

BORN: March 16, 1944, in Atwood, Kan., to Ruth and Irvin Hayden, farmers.

FAMILY: Married Patti Rooney in 1968. Mrs. Hayden, 40, is a homemaker and graduate school student. The Haydens have two daughters, Chelsi, 12, and Anne, 7.

EDUCATION: Bachelor of science in wildlife conservation, Kansas State University; master of science, biology, Fort Hayes State University.

TIMELINE

1967: Joined Army, Vietnam War veteran.

1972: Elected to two-year term as state representative; re-elected six times.

1973: Named executive manager of Rawlins County promotional council.

1976: Worked for E.C. Mellick (insurance) Agency.

1986: Elected to four-year term as governor with 51.9 percent of vote.

1991: Term expires in January; eligible for re-election.

PRIORITIES

▶ Economy: Established Kansas Partnership Fund to develop industrial sites.

▶ Environment: Created Department of Wildlife and Parks; proposed funding for pollution cleanup project.

▶ Fiscal conservatism: Cut spending by $60 million; submitted balanced budget in 1988.

▶ Education: Proposed Margin of Excellence program to raise teacher salaries at state universities; proposed more funding for elementary, secondary schools.

NOTEWORTHY
First Kansas governor trained in conservation.

PERSONAL
Favorite politicians are U.S. Sen. Bob Dole and Alf Landon. ... Loves to hunt, fish. ... Favorite musician is Johnny Cash. ... Displays paintings, bronze sculptures of wildlife in his office. ... Pet peeve is littering.

THE FUTURE
"I've spent 15 years in public service. I very much enjoy the job as governor. I would hope to be in a position to seek a second term and continue in public service throughout my career."

GOV. WALLACE G. WILKINSON

IMPRESSIONS

Wallace Wilkinson is an unusual politician. He has a reputation for shunning publicity. Just a few years ago, he even refused to have his picture taken for a newspaper.

Maybe that's the reason we had a tough time getting a slot on Wilkinson's schedule. We first talked with his staff in December 1987, and the governor finally responded to our questions in June.

Fact is, Wilkinson did have a busy beginning to his administration. He got into office and discovered $56.7 million in red ink for the fiscal year ending June 30, 1988. What had gone wrong? A credit-card mentality, he said.

In his first State of the Commonwealth address, Wilkinson, a self-made millionaire, bluntly sized up the situation:

"We're broke. Busted. Tapped out."

But Wilkinson didn't even appear tempted to renege on his campaign promise not to raise taxes:

"We cannot tax our way out of our problems. We must work our way out of our problems with a vibrant and growing economy that provides jobs for those who want and need to work."

To put it another way, Wilkinson said Kentucky was on its knees, but "not down for the count."

Wilkinson has the background to tackle the fiscal problems. Business associates have described him as a shrewd operator who converted a small book business into a multimillion dollar enterprise. Can he work similar wonders for the state of Kentucky?

He certainly seems to have the necessary fighter instinct. As he once said, "Winning is the ultimate revenge and losing is the ultimate punishment."

A conversation with Gov. Wallace G. Wilkinson.

It has been said that you're someone who values privacy. Why enter politics?

"The governor's race was my first venture as a candidate into politics. The fact that I won the governorship, and won it in convincing fashion, indicates that the people of this state were looking for someone who would make changes. Someone who would change the way we do business and change the way we educate our children. The opportunity to pursue these goals and to contribute to my state in a unique way attracted me to politics."

Before you took office, you said, "Being governor is not really going to be much fun." Have you changed your mind?

"It is not as much fun being governor as it used to be because money is tight. That's true in every state. However, that makes the job more challenging than it's ever been, and I like that."

Some governors have told us the office is more powerful than ever before. Do you agree?

"The center of activity in government today is in the governors' offices. The job of governor is unique in American politics because the governor has so many tools with which to work and has the ability to maintain personal contact with the people. The strength of the office is in the support of Kentuckians for our programs. As governor, I have the opportunity to make changes that can have a lasting and positive impact on all Kentuckians. We are investing Kentucky's resources in jobs and better schools. As governor, I can direct our resources where they can do the most good."

Why have you been such a strong advocate of a state lottery?

"A lottery is a source of new revenue and will enable us to keep money in state that is being spent on lotteries in states that border Kentucky. The traditional political approach to raising revenue would be to raise taxes. Before we consider that, however, we owe the people our best effort to generate revenue from every available source and the lottery is a source."

What are your top priorities?

"Jobs and improving schools."

What sets Kentucky apart from other states?

"Our people and our determination to compete. The people of Kentucky are our greatest asset. Anyone who has ever been to Kentucky knows that our hospitality is legendary. Kentuckians are the friendliest, most determined, and hardest-working people in the world. In tourism, economic development, transportation and other areas, our location — within a day's drive of two-thirds of the country's population — is a unique advantage."

What's Kentucky's image?

"Kentucky is viewed, I think, primarily as an agrarian state. I'm proud of our rural heritage, and there is no question that agricultural products are a mainstay of our economy. But, Kentucky is much more. We are viewed as a great vacation spot and justifiably so. From the mountains in the East, to the rolling hills of the bluegrass — home of the world's great thoroughbreds — to the lake region of Western Kentucky, this state combines beauty and excitement in a way that is unmatched."

In your inaugural address, you said, "Kentucky's character is such that we will not accept defeat." Can you elaborate a bit on that?

"Kentuckians pioneered the West. Kentuckians brought education, art and family values to the wilderness. That pioneer spirit and determination to compete for everything that our country offers is still strong in Kentucky."

WILKINSON PROFILE

PARTY: Democrat.

IN HIS WORDS: "From my earliest recollections, I wanted to have something. I knew about haves and have-nots, and I was determined to be a have. I never had any other ambition, and I always knew I'd succeed."

BORN: Dec. 12, 1941, on 140-acre Casey County, Ky., farm, to Hershel and Cleo Wilkinson, who owned the farm and a small grocery store. His parents sold store, farm goods on a truck route.

FAMILY: Married Martha Carol Stafford in 1961. Mrs. Wilkinson, 46, manages family farm. The Wilkinsons have two children, Glenn, 18, and Andrew, 15.

EDUCATION: Studied electrical engineering at University of Kentucky; general studies at Campbellsville College.

TIMELINE

1963: Opened Kentucky Paperback Gallery at age 22 while still in college; opened used-textbook store in 1965; expanded bookstore into Wallace's College Book Co., which owns 14 book stores and wholesale textbook firm; later founded Wilkinson Enterprises, with interests in management firm, Wilkinson Flying Service, real estate development; owns or leases 2,500 acres of farmland, two banks.

1983: Named finance chairman for Louisville, Ky., Mayor Harvey Sloane's unsuccessful gubernatorial bid; chaired former Gov. John Y. Brown Jr.'s short-lived bid for U.S. Senate nomination.

1987: Elected to four-year term as governor with 64.9 percent of vote.

1991: Term expires in December; not eligible for consecutive terms.

PRIORITIES

▶ Economic development: Pushed state lottery through legislature; proposed emphasis

NOTEWORTHY

Wilkinson was elected in 1987 in Kentucky's most expensive gubernatorial campaign — he spent nearly $6 million. . . . His 1987 win by a 64.9 percent margin was the largest ever for the Kentucky governor's race.

PERSONAL

Wrote in high school yearbook that his ambition was to be a millionaire and, "Caesar was short. Napoleon was short. And I'm not real tall myself." . . . Loves opera. . . . Swims, plays tennis and skis.

THE FUTURE

Will return to private business when term expires in 1991, unless state amends constitution to allow consecutive terms.

on job training certificates for adult education and vouchers for jobless to obtain free training.

▶ Education: Developed incentive program to reward schools for improvement; established program to test new concepts in education.

GOV. CHARLES 'BUDDY' ROEMER III

IMPRESSIONS

BusCapade visited Louisiana twice. Once in April to interview Gov. Edwin "Fast Eddie" Edwards. Again in December to meet with Louisiana's new governor, Charles "Buddy" Roemer III.

What a difference eight months can make.

Edwards had been the quintessential governor of the past. A "good-time Charlie" if there ever was one. When we had lunch with him at the mansion, he said: "The only way I could lose the next election is if I was caught in bed with a dead woman or a live boy." He faltered in the primary and dropped out of the race.

Roemer appeared to us to be the quintessential governor of tomorrow. A progressive governor if there ever was one. Key quote from his interview: "I want another look for Louisiana. But we have to deserve it. And in some areas where we are behind the curve — education, campaign financing laws, economic development incentives, both for companies already here and for companies we'd like to have come — we've got to be a competitor."

When we dropped by Roemer's office, he was governor-elect. His office was small. His staff young. But there was an excitement about the place. It felt like the cavalry headquarters just before the big charge.

The commander of this group — known throughout the state as "Buddy" — was short and small compared to most of the governors we met.

"Buddy" struck us as painfully honest — honest with the zeal of a Southern Baptist minister. Ask him a question and you got the feeling he would say what had to be said, even if he would rather not be saying it.

We left feeling that this new 44-year-old governor with a Harvard education is the best hope Louisiana has had in the governor's office in a long time. A mix of good old boy and hard-nosed know-how.

A conversation with Gov. Charles "Buddy" Roemer III.

You've said a few times, "Let's tell this country to take another look at Louisiana." Clearly you recognize there's an image problem. How do you plan to change Louisiana's image?

"Two ways. The most important way is through performance. If the numbers over the next two or three or four years show that our ranking in education begins to rise, we don't have to go to number one. We can't do that in three or four years, but we can get off number 50. If our performance deserves a second look, I can agitate to make that performance be reviewed in the marketplace. That's going to be over a period of time."

And the second way you plan to change Louisiana's image?

"The second way is using the publicity of the election itself."

Are governors performing like CEOs?

"I think it's good politics for a governor to be a CEO. And I think that the governor's office is just a continuation of my education."

If you turn the state completely around, you're going to attract a great deal of national attention. Would you like to follow your hero, John F. Kennedy, to the White House?

"Oh, it's possible, sure. But I'm not agitated or ambitious to that extent. I mean, I'm 44. When I was 34, I had no idea I'd be sitting here talking to you. What I'll be doing at 54, I have no idea. I'll be involved, I'll be on the leading edge somewhere. I'll be talking about and to and for people. That's my dream. And if that's in the White House, fine. If not, that's fine too. I really see an eight-year job here, and I don't mean to take for granted a second term. But I think to do what we have to do in Louisiana is going to be very difficult, there's no guarantee that we can do it. We're going to need the best and the brightest and some luck and some help, and it's going to take a while. So, I'm in no hurry. Would I like to be president of the United States some year, some time? You betcha! Am I eaten up with it? No way."

Does your election — a person with a Harvard background — say something about broader changes in the Deep South?

"I don't know. Harvard was an important part of my life, made possible by my father and mother. My brother went to Harvard, also. He's younger than I am. It's a good question. There is a change of leadership across the South; forget Harvard or Yale ... there's a change of leadership, generationally speaking. People are beginning to step down, there are new faces. It's happening."

How would you characterize race relations in Louisiana today?

"Not where I want them to be. We have a high number of elected officials who happen to be black, and that's positive. I received the second largest black vote in this election. It was only 15 percent. I'm not happy with where the relationships are because we've talked education but haven't put our dollars in the classroom, and our minority populations have suffered accordingly. There's some anxiety, there's some fear, there's some trepidation because I'm succeeding a popular governor among the minority, very popular. We've never seen one as popular, who gave a lot of rhetoric but not much performance. I'm going to give some rhetoric, but a lot better performance. I think over time the angst will diminish."

ROEMER PROFILE

PARTY: Democrat.

IN HIS WORDS: "I'm new, fresh. I have one foot in the future rather than both feet in the past. . . . The future will beat the past; it better."

BORN: Oct. 4, 1943, in Shreveport, La., to Charles E. "Budgie" Roemer II and farm manager Adeline Roemer. Father was Louisiana commissioner of administration under former Gov. Edwin Edwards.

FAMILY: Married Patti Crocker in 1973. Mrs. Roemer, 34, is an adult-literacy volunteer. They met at the state constitutional convention. The Roemers have one child, Dakota, 6. Gov. Roemer has two children from his previous marriage, Caroline, 20, and Charles E. "Chas" IV, 18.

EDUCATION: Bachelor of science in government and economics, Harvard University; master's in business and finance, Harvard Business School.

TIMELINE

1971: Named aide to Gov. Edwards during his election campaign.

1972: Elected delegate to state constitutional convention.

1973: Chartered Red River Valley Bank; chartered the Bank of the Mid-South in 1979.

1978: Lost first bid for U.S. House seat.

1980: Elected to two-year term in U.S. House; re-elected without opposition three times.

1987: Came from last place to win four-year term as governor with 33 percent of vote; incumbent Gov. Edwards conceded election before runoff, saying, "It never occurred to me that I would run second."

1992: Term expires in March; eligible for re-election.

NOTEWORTHY

In 1987 handed former Gov. Edwards his first election defeat in 33 years. . . . First Louisiana governor to limit individual campaign contributions to $5,000 and refuse political action committee funding and cash contributions.

PERSONAL

Promised to quit poker if he became governor, hasn't played since. . . . Reads during lulls in football and baseball games and finishes nearly a dozen books a month, especially on government and foreign policy. . . . New York Yankees fan. . . . Loves Robert Frost's poetry. . . . Plays tennis, racquetball.

THE FUTURE

Elected in 1987, Gov. Roemer says, "My focus in the next four years is helping to turn this state around."

PRIORITIES

▶ Education: Recommended establishment of "super board" to oversee higher education policy and budget decisions; supports teacher evaluations, incentive pay hikes, reducing class sizes, school accountability, redirecting funding into classrooms, dropout prevention programs.

▶ Economic development: Proposed creation of department of economic development and reforms of workers' compensation, unemployment compensation and product liability laws.

▶ Environment: Proposed increased funding for and reorganization of Department of Environmental Quality; proposed expanded environmental monitoring programs.

GOV. JOHN R. McKERNAN JR.

IMPRESSIONS

The capitol in Augusta has an open, airy, informal feeling about it. It feels more like a high school building that was built in the early part of the century than a state capitol.

And John McKernan seems a lot like the kind of guy who was elected president of the senior class. Maybe it was his age. When we met him he was a young, yet serious, 39. He also displayed a sense of humor. It showed up a number of times. He was all business when we were, but when we were ready to have fun, so was he. We asked him about what people from Maine should be called:

"I think that you probably call a person from Maine a Mainer. But you'll hear various things, like Maineiac, and other aspects. I don't know what the correct, technically correct, term is, but believe me, I didn't go around during my campaign referring to everybody as Maineiacs!"

Later we asked about the red telephone in his office. We hadn't seen a "hot line" in any other governor's office and we were curious:

"Just in case anybody gets out of hand in here. It goes to the state police barracks. Nobody picks it up there, they just come running."

"Have you ever used it?" we asked.

"No, I haven't. But the woman who guards the door has the phone out there, too, and she's knocked it off a couple of times!"

Then we asked him if Stephen King, Maine resident and prolific writer of horror novels, is a blessing to the state.

"A mixed blessing," he quipped. "He was a major supporter of my opponent. But we're trying to heal that."

We wanted to know if King got his inspirations from Maine communities.

"I hope not," McKernan said. "But as long as he keeps getting those inspirations" and keeps insisting they be filmed in Maine, "God bless him."

A conversation with Gov. John R. McKernan Jr.

What do most people think of when they think of Maine?

"They think of the natural beauty, the coast, the absolutely clean air, the freshness. And they also think of rural poverty. They don't realize what there is here, and the kind of opportunities that there are, and that Portland is probably one of the best metropolitan areas in the country to either live in or work in."

What would you like Maine's image to be?

"We want to get the word out that we have an opportunity that's missing in some parts of this country. We are working to provide opportunities for people to not only invest, but also to address some of the shortcomings we have in parts of the state. We also must raise some aspirations in some of the northern and eastern parts of the state, so that we can provide the skilled work force that people are going to need to make those kinds of investments."

Maine is still very much pioneer country with a lot of open area. How does that affect people's lives?

"It changes your values. A woman from Massachusetts told me, 'The difference is that when you live here, you don't have all the other activities that lure you out on Friday, Saturday nights, even during the middle of the week. Your life has a tendency to revolve around your children and their events. And that brings a community together.' "

Tourism is the second-largest industry in the state behind paper manufacturing. How does that translate into dollars?

"Four billion dollars — but we only spend a million dollars. One of the lines in all of my speeches is that there are 47 states in the country that spend more on advertising for tourism than Maine."

Why hasn't Maine spent more to promote tourism?

"Because there has been the feeling in the past that, well, we've got enough people here in July and August anyway. The point that we're trying to make is that there are other things that we ought to be doing to help get people into the state and into areas other than along the coast between July and August."

Shortly after you were inaugurated in January, you said, "It's time our children were no longer Maine's No. 1 export." Why did you say that?

"Young people in the state, after they graduate, go to Massachusetts or Connecticut and find work. Then, years later, they come back. That was really brought home to me at my 20th high school reunion last summer, when I realized how many in my class had done the very same thing. What really struck me is there's something about the uniqueness of Maine that really runs deep in people."

You've got this marvelous perspective of having been in the state Legislature and then in Congress in the legislative branch, now in the executive branch. How do you like your job, and how do you feel about running a state versus being one of several people running a state or a country?

"First of all, it's the big difference between the executive and legislative branches. Having served in the state Legislature, that helped me going into Congress. I noticed that a lot of the newer members, both my year and even afterwards, the ones that had the most trouble adjusting were the ones who hadn't served in the legislature. But there just is no question in my mind that the real crucial decisions that are going to be made, that are going to affect the quality of people's lives, are going to be in the states."

McKERNAN PROFILE

PARTY: Republican.

IN HIS WORDS: "I spent an awful lot of time trying to decide whether to run for governor, asking 'What is it that we really can do that would make a difference?'"

BORN: May 20, 1948, in Bangor, Maine, to John R. McKernan, newspaper publisher, and Barbara McKernan, homemaker and former city councilor.

FAMILY: Divorced. One son, Peter, 16.

EDUCATION: Bachelor of arts in government, Dartmouth College; law degree, University of Maine.

TIMELINE

1972: Elected to two-year term in state House of Representatives; re-elected in 1974; drafted state's returnable bottle law.

1975: Practiced law with Stearns and Finnegan in Bangor; in 1976, joined Verrill Dana firm in Portland, and ran President Gerald Ford's campaign in Maine.

1982: Elected to two-year term in U.S. House of Representatives; re-elected in 1984.

1986: Elected to four-year term as governor with 40 percent of vote.

1991: Term expires in January; eligible for re-election.

PRIORITIES

▶ Economic development: Tripled funding for tourism promotion; commissioned study to develop blueprint for state's economic development, which led to $7 million in funding; created "job opportunity" zones; won 3-cent hike in state gas tax to fund infrastructure programs.

▶ Education: Established accountability for schools; increased funding for drug education, higher education.

▶ Welfare reform: Established a program to provide training, medical insurance, child care and transportation for welfare recipients; doubled state child-care resources.

▶ Tax reform: Proposed $19.2 million in property tax relief for homeowners and overhaul of state personal income tax.

NOTEWORTHY
In 1986, elected USA's youngest governor at age 38 and Maine's first Republican governor in two decades.

PERSONAL
Star basketball player in high school. . . . Sails with friends in summer, skis at Maine resorts in winter. . . . Likes to "eat as much lobster as I can get." . . . E.B. White is his favorite author. . . . Loves to play tennis.

THE FUTURE
Eligible for one more term in 1990 but says it's too early to make a decision.

GOV. WILLIAM DONALD SCHAEFER

William Donald Schaefer was the first governor we met who would rather be mayor.

He's held three jobs in public office — city councilman, mayor and governor. Being mayor was most appealing.

"Do you think you'll enjoy being governor as much ultimately?" we asked.

"No."

Schaefer's affection for the office of mayor stems in large part from his hands-on management style. He enjoyed walking the sidewalks of Baltimore and surveying how things were going. If he saw garbage cans kicked over or a particularly nasty pothole, he could remedy it with a phone call to a department head.

"When you're mayor, you're right with people," Schaefer said. "Walk along the street and the senior citizens know you're going to do something for them personally. Walk along the street and kids know you're going to try to do something."

His critics characterize him as blustery and bullheaded. Maybe. But he's also a bulldozer of a man, tough to stop when he sets his mind on doing something.

He was largely responsible for renovating Baltimore's downtown, developing prime tourist attractions in an area that could have been a bleak urban landscape. He did that with energy, drive and a refusal to take "no" for an answer.

We may have been most surprised by Schaefer's hostility toward the press. He's been in public office for a long time, yet critical editorials clearly rankle him.

"I'm not loved by the media because if I don't like what they're saying, I don't mind telling them. I'm not one of the darlings of the media. I have my own ideas on how things should go," Schaefer said.

We saw the same kind of sensitivity when Schaefer was reminiscing about his days as mayor and how his constituents would let him know how his administration was doing.

"They write you letters. They get on talk shows and blast you. Every once in a while someone says something kind and you almost drop dead."

A conversation with Gov. William Donald Schaefer.

How would you describe your management style?

"We depend heavily on a cabinet-style of management for the state. The cabinet meets every Thursday morning for two hours. We discuss the important issues facing the state, activities for the month ahead and other policy decisions. Some observers have described my staff as 'diffuse.' We do not aim for a chain of command. I prefer to have my top people report directly to me. I do not have a chief of staff but have divided those duties among several staff members."

Some say Maryland is this nation in miniature. What does that mean?

"We've got a big metropolitan area, an ocean, farm land, and little villages. There are places just bursting with energy. Baltimore has good museums and an aquarium, and a lot of things tourists can see. Mountains out in Western Maryland — they don't know how beautiful their area is. Ducks flying all over the place. So anything in the United States is right here."

And then there's the Chesapeake Bay. It's a recreational and economic treasure, but what about its pollution problems?

"We can save the bay. I've got to get across that every person can do something to save the bay. Now, how do I do it? I need a million people — a million people of the 5 million people in this state committed to saving the bay."

What's an example of something an individual can do to help save the bay?

"A sponge crab is a female crab that has that sponge on the bottom of its eggs. I would never keep a sponge crab under any circumstances. I would put it back so it could lay eggs. I am very meticulous in never catching or keeping a fish that isn't right. I don't catch fish just for the sake of catching them. Now that's something I'm personally doing."

Your approach is credited with revitalizing Baltimore when you were mayor. What lessons did you learn there that other large cities need to learn?

"Go to the neighborhoods and work with people in the communities. Build strong neighborhood organizations. Let people do things for people. The mayors don't spend time in the communities. They don't organize. The second thing is a very close association with the business community. The city couldn't have moved forward if we didn't have cooperation from the business community. The third thing is brain power."

While you were mayor, the Baltimore Colts left for Indianapolis. Will NFL football return to Baltimore?

"We've got a good chance. When the owner pulled the team out, all the owners were embarrassed. They felt there was some moral obligation to put a team back, but as time goes on and ownership changes, the moral obligation gives way to the bottom line."

SCHAEFER PROFILE

PARTY: Democrat.

IN HIS WORDS: "There are certain words I like to use. 'People.' 'Do it now.' 'Get it done right the first time.' Time is important, there is so much to do. . . . If we finish one thing, there's a pile of things right behind it to do. And we can't wait until next year."

BORN: Nov. 2, 1921, in Baltimore, to William Henry Schaefer, lawyer, and Tululu Irene Schaefer, homemaker.

FAMILY: Single; lived with his mother in Baltimore row house until her death in 1983.

EDUCATION: Law degree, master of arts in law, University of Baltimore.

TIMELINE

1943: Joined Army, where he administered military hospitals.

1950: Practiced real estate law with Schaefer, Waltjen and Arabian.

1955: Lost first race for House of Delegates. Elected to four-year term on Baltimore City Council; re-elected to City Council in 1959, 1963.

1971: Elected to four-year term as mayor of Baltimore; re-elected three times.

1986: Elected to four-year term as governor with 82 percent of vote.

1991: Term expires in January; eligible for re-election.

PRIORITIES

▶ Economic development: Consolidated Office of International Trade; reformed workers' compensation benefits and insurance laws; won approval for construction of two sports stadiums; created Department of Economic and Employment Development; established Economic Development Opportunities Fund to support business expansion or relocation into state.

▶ Education: Increased funding for elementary and secondary schools; consolidated state college governing boards.

▶ Transportation: Pushed through nickel-a-gallon gas tax increase to fund highway, bridge projects; initiated light-rail project in Baltimore area.

▶ Health and human services: Created Children's Trust Fund to provide grants to child-abuse prevention programs; reorganized and streamlined day-care regulations, established Direct Loan Fund for day-care facilities.

▶ Criminal justice: Signed handgun law that supporters call USA's first state law banning manufacture and sale of "Saturday night specials."

▶ Environment: Signed 1987 Bay Agreement to clean up Chesapeake Bay; created Department of the Environment.

NOTEWORTHY

Elected by biggest margin in USA's 1986 gubernatorial races and in Maryland history — 82 percent.

PERSONAL

As Baltimore's mayor, painted streets and sidewalks pink to cheer up the city. . . . Gen. George Patton is his hero. . . . Favorite vacation spot is "my trailer in Ocean City, Md." . . . Longtime companion is Hilda Mae Snoops. . . . Known to friends as "Don" and critics as "Willy Don."

THE FUTURE

No current ambitions for national office.

GOV. MICHAEL S. DUKAKIS

IMPRESSIONS

Mike Dukakis — the man who would be president.

We visited Dukakis in his Boston office in May 1987 to talk about the state of Massachusetts. But one question lingered in the background: Does this guy have the stuff to be president of the USA?

At the time, Dukakis was just another face in the political crowd. One of the so-called "seven dwarfs" — most in the USA had never heard of him. He was viewed as somewhere in the middle of the pack among Democratic contenders.

Dukakis would later have to try to overcome the label of being stiff and unglamorous. But he was undeniably personable and engaging in our meeting. Perhaps that illustrates what some have said about Dukakis — that the man who can be aloof from a speaker's podium can be a charming conversationalist in closer quarters.

Anyone running for the presidency of the USA has to be prepared for certain questions from the press. The danger in that, of course, is that many of a candidate's answers become canned, never straying far from a set response.

We heard some of that from Dukakis. When we asked him about his lack of experience in foreign policy, he responded:

"Well, I usually have two answers to that question. One is that there was a fellow shortly before Carter (Nixon) who had more experience in Washington than anybody I can think of and he had to resign in disgrace. I've always had a very strong interest in foreign policy. I don't think you have to live in Washington, D.C., necessarily, to know something about foreign policy."

Some have suggested similarities between Dukakis and President John F. Kennedy. We didn't see any, beyond the fact that both are Democrats from Massachusetts.

The people of the USA have yet to cast their final vote on whether Michael Dukakis is presidential material. But we came away from Dukakis' office that morning in May with a sense that this man had the background, the intelligence, character and style to be a top contender for the top office in the land.

A conversation with Gov. Michael S. Dukakis.

How would you describe your management style?

"I try to use a hands-on, activist style, hiring good people to whom I can delegate authority. But I also must work with my Legislature, build coalitions, work directly with citizens and community groups and communicate effectively with my constituents. In that sense, a governor's job is very different from a corporate chief executive."

Whom among the 50 governors currently in office would you describe as the best manager? Why?

"A difficult question because the states have so many different needs and problems. Among governors whose leadership styles I admire are Vermont's Madeleine Kunin, Arkansas' Bill Clinton, Michigan's Jim Blanchard, and New Jersey's Tom Kean."

Massachusetts' Employment and Training (ET) CHOICES program has received praise nationally for preparing welfare recipients for jobs. Is this a national blueprint?

"You can train people until you're blue in the face. But if there aren't any jobs out there, you can't do much. We probably this year will get out of Congress national welfare reform legislation, which is very much like ET."

How else would you help regions with severe economic problems right now?

"You can pull any region out of the economic doldrums if you work hard at it, if you put in some public resources and you bring the private sector in with you and you begin to work."

Is that how it worked in Massachusetts?

"Southeastern Massachusetts has been chronically depressed since the 1930s. The unemployment rate was 14 percent. I went down there on the 20th of January 1983 and said, 'Folks, we're going to put together a regional development effort.' Today, in South Massachusetts, we've got a labor shortage — we're trying to bring people in. We have 33 new plants either completed or under construction in Taunton. And 31 of them had some kind of help from state government."

Hasn't high-tech industry been a major factor in your economic growth?

"High-tech is very important to us, but in terms of overall employment, it's maybe 10 percent of the total economy. Tourism employs many more people than high-tech. It's the diversity that we've been able to create here that really is our great strength."

On foreign policy, how do you feel about U.S. policy in Central America?

"We have a president who in 1984 in a debate with Fritz Mondale said that the alternative to Marcos was a communist regime in the Philippines. I don't believe that. But if that's going to be our policy, then we're going to find ourselves facing one radical revolution after another, and I don't think that's what this country ought to stand for."

So you don't think we should be sending aid to the Nicaraguan contras?

"I'm against it. It's doomed to failure and has been from the beginning. Not only that, it's illegal. The Rio treaty and the charter of the Organization of American States say in explicit terms that what we are doing in Nicaragua is a violation of those treaties. I don't know when we're going to stop making these mistakes."

Do you think the press is overzealous in its coverage of presidential candidates?

"When you run for the presidency, you've got to assume that you're going to be the subject of intensive public scrutiny. That's something that goes with the territory."

DUKAKIS PROFILE

PARTY: Democrat.

IN HIS WORDS: "My mother and father summed up the American dream for me in 11 words, 'Much is given to you. And much is expected of you.'"

BORN: Nov. 3, 1933, in Brookline, Mass., to Greek immigrant parents, Dr. Panos Dukakis and Euterpe Dukakis, a teacher.

FAMILY: Married Katharine "Kitty" Dickson in 1963. Mrs. Dukakis, 51, is director of Public Space Partnerships, Harvard University, and a former dance teacher. The Dukakises have two daughters, Andrea, 22, and Kara, 19. Mrs. Dukakis has a son from a previous marriage, John, 30.

EDUCATION: Bachelor of arts in political science, Swarthmore College; law degree, Harvard University.

TIMELINE

1955: Joined Army.

1960: Practiced law with Hill & Barlow.

1962: Elected to two-year term in state House of Representatives; re-elected three times.

1967: Sponsored USA's first no-fault auto insurance bill.

1970: Lost bid for lieutenant governor; moderated TV show *The Advocates*.

1974: Elected to four-year term as governor with 55.8 percent of vote.

1978: Lost gubernatorial primary bid.

1979: Appointed director, lecturer in Intergovernmental Studies, Harvard University.

1982: Elected to four-year term as governor with 59.5 percent of vote; re-elected with 68.7 percent of vote in 1986; elected chairman of Democratic Governors' Association.

1991: Term expires in January; eligible for re-election.

NOTEWORTHY
Rated USA's most effective governor in 1986 *Newsweek* magazine poll.

PERSONAL
Dedicated fitness walker, covers three miles a day. . . . Frugal — grows own vegetables in front yard, takes subway to work. . . . Writes own speeches. . . . Favorite poet is John Greenleaf Whittier. . . . Speaks five languages in addition to English — French, Greek, Italian, Korean and Spanish.

THE FUTURE
Announced bid for presidency April 29, 1987, "We can bring the message of Massachusetts to the people of our country. It is a message of good jobs and economic opportunity and vibrant, sustained economic growth for every American."

PRIORITIES

▶ Economic development: Created 12 agencies to offer low-cost business financing; established Centers for Excellence program to encourage high-tech research.

▶ Welfare reform: Established Employment and Training program for welfare recipients.

▶ Tax reform: Initiated state tax amnesty; increased personal exemptions; cut taxes five times in five years.

▶ Education: Made proposals to guarantee college tuition and lower dropout rate.

▶ Health and human services: Initiated Governor's Alliance Against Drugs to make schools drug-free by 1990; expanded homeless shelters; instituted plan to build affordable housing and provide rental assistance.

▶ Environment: Signed bill to clean up landfills; approved bond issue to buy, reserve open space for future generations.

GOV. JAMES J. BLANCHARD

IMPRESSIONS

We observed throughout BusCapade that many of the nation's governors operate like company presidents. James Blanchard could be chairman of the board.

Blanchard was elected governor in 1982, and immediately inherited a state in trouble.

Michigan had a $1.7 billion budget deficit and an unemployment rate of more than 17 percent.

To head off the deficit, Blanchard asked for a temporary — and highly unpopular — 38 percent income tax increase.

Ask Blanchard how things have gone since then and he lights up, reveling in this "before and after" picture.

"At that point, we had 17.3 percent unemployment. Now it's probably 8.5 percent. We were bankrupt. Now we're not only solvent, but have the strongest finances at any time in modern history."

No idle boasts there. Blanchard has led a successful — and continuing — diversification of the economy. He's also developed a unique program that lets parents invest in a fund that guarantees college tuition for their children.

Like only the most polished politicians and after-dinner speakers, Blanchard speaks in quotes.

Listening to him discuss his programs is like hearing a war hero or great athlete recount past glories. He's told these success stories so many times that the rough spots are all gone.

Still, for all his boosterism, Blanchard didn't hesitate when asked for a candid appraisal of Michigan's problems:

"The kind of unemployment we have in some of our major urban areas leads to very serious social problems: crime, welfare, despair, ugly neighborhoods, racial strife. We have ideas and systems and programs to deal with them, but we're by no means on top. If we succeed, America succeeds. If we fail, America will fail. We're on the front line."

And Blanchard already knows that the key to winning on the front line is keeping an eye on the bottom line.

A conversation with Gov. James J. Blanchard.

How does Michigan's tuition-guarantee program work?

"Somebody puts down $3,500 now, or the equivalent in payroll deductions. And we guarantee, when the child reaches 18, there will be four years free of tuition at any one of our public colleges or universities. They get to pick the college at the time, assuming they can get admitted. If they decide not to go to school, the purchaser gets the money back with interest."

Do you think other states can benefit from this type of program?

"Every state's going to end up doing it. Each state's a little different, and they'll have to tailor it to their own needs. If a child is told his name is on a certificate that says if you study hard and work hard, your college is paid for, they're much more likely to work hard and study hard. I see the tuition-guarantee program as a great motivator."

Do graduates of Michigan universities stay in the state?

"Now, yes. Two years ago, no. The percentages are up from what they used to be. There are cycles. I'd like to keep them all here. As a matter of fact, I'd like to draw the brain power from other states in here. Brain power, not brawn power, is the key to the future."

Chrysler is planning to buy American Motors. What does that mean to Michigan in terms of jobs and economic growth?

"It represents another milestone in Chrysler's remarkable comeback. AMC is located here, too, but its plants are really located elsewhere. So Chrysler is very much committed to Michigan — they've invested $3 billion this last year. Chrysler's technology and brain center is in Michigan, and they're going to build a whole new manufacturing facility in Detroit."

The Chrysler-AMC pact adds another chapter to an automobile industry in transition. How is it changing within Michigan?

"There's going to continue to be reorganization and further automation. Walter Reuther negotiated an agreement in 1954 that said, basically, the United Auto Workers will accept automation requiring fewer workers per car each year in return for higher wages. That has gone on forever. We will continue to see a reshaping and an incredible surge of new technologies in the industry for reasons of survival and competition."

Why did GM pick Tennessee over Michigan as the site for its new Saturn plant?

"General Motors has invested $9.5 billion in Michigan in the last four years. They put their Saturn headquarters in Troy, Mich., and their Saturn research and engineering center. The brain center and central nervous system are here. The assembly line will be in Tennessee. In the initial talks with us, GM indicated it wanted to create a whole new culture of management and labor attitudes."

How do you feel about that?

"There's some real wisdom there, because the labor-management relations at GM are the worst of the Big Three. The size of the company just lends itself to bureaucratic problems, and it's hard for them to be flexible with the kind of size you're dealing with. It's no accident they picked the state where they don't have a single plant or facility or a UAW relationship."

What do you consider the best points about Michigan?

"Michigan is one of the most beautiful states. We have more shoreline than Florida and California. We're a center of high technology, and great public institutions, great public universities. We're a state of ideas."

BLANCHARD PROFILE

PARTY: Democrat.

IN HIS WORDS: "I'm an optimist. I believe that when we all work together there's nothing we can't accomplish."

BORN: Aug. 8, 1942, in Detroit, to James Blanchard, metallurgist, and Rosalie Blanchard, an office manager and bookkeeper. Father left home when his son James was 9.

FAMILY: Divorced; one son, Jay, 17.

EDUCATION: Bachelor of arts in history, master's in business administration, Michigan State University; law degree, University of Minnesota.

TIMELINE

1964: Named page to Democratic National Convention; met his hero, Adlai Stevenson.

1968: Named legal aide to Michigan secretary of state.

1969: Became assistant state attorney general.

1974: Elected to two-year term in U.S. House of Representatives; re-elected three times.

1982: Elected to four-year term as governor with 51.4 percent of vote.

1986: Re-elected with 68.1 percent of vote.

1991: Term expires in January; eligible for re-election.

PRIORITIES

▶ Economic development: Created 1985 Michigan Strategic Fund, a cooperative state financing program; appointed Governor's Commission on Jobs and Economic Development, a coalition of business, labor, education and government; established Michigan Modernization Service for industry; streamlined unemployment system and reformed worker's compensation system; signed legislation to establish $339 million no-interest loan program for farmers.

NOTEWORTHY
First Democratic governor to win re-election in Michigan since 1958.

PERSONAL
Wanted to be three things when he grew up: a baseball player for Detroit Tigers, a school janitor, a politician. . . . At age 10, worked at neighborhood Democratic Party headquarters after school. . . . Set campus record for tree-sitting at Michigan State University. . . . Enjoys playing golf. . . . Chronically late, says his mother: "He always wants to talk to one more person or shake one more hand."

THE FUTURE
"Once you have national ambitions, you don't have any influence. I'm not about to trade away my influence for some ego trip down hopeless lane. I'm here in Michigan."

▶ Fiscal conservatism: Paid off $1.7 billion state deficit in 1985, which changed state credit rating from worst to best in nation.

▶ Education: Established USA's first college tuition-guarantee program in 1986; helped Michigan become the first state to require AIDS education; established tuition incentive program and drug and alcohol abuse education program; increased funding 74 percent since 1983.

▶ Jobs: Established Michigan Youth Corps program in 1983, a public works and construction program.

▶ Criminal justice: Halted early release of inmates due to overcrowding; proposed mandatory sentencing for some crimes and "work and learn" camps for youths.

▶ Tax reform: Proposed 0.2 percent cut in state income tax; proposed property tax relief; reduced business tax $18.5 million.

GOV. RUDY PERPICH

IMPRESSIONS

It must be something in the water.

The land of lakes has contributed a dramatically disproportionate number of presidential candidates in the past two decades. Walter Mondale. Eugene McCarthy. Hubert Humphrey. Rudy Perpich.

Rudy Perpich?

Well, not quite or not yet. But during our visit to Perpich's office in Minneapolis in May 1987, he was clearly toying with a run at the top.

"I felt that Cuomo or Hart was just going to go all the way. Then Cuomo dropped out and then Hart. Of course, it becomes wide open. I'm just waiting to see what's going to happen between now and September," he told us.

During that time, Perpich decided not to pursue the presidency. Still, his indication of a potentially serious run for the top office in the land caught us a bit by surprise.

After all, Rudy Perpich is not a household name. There were no signs of a behind-the-scenes campaign organization. And there didn't seem to be any appreciable ground swell of support.

So we asked him, point blank: "Could you do the job?"

His response: "Yeah, I can do the job. I wouldn't have any problem."

With Gary Hart's problems in mind, he said, "I can answer any of the *Miami Herald*'s questions."

Perpich was cordial and at ease throughout the interview. A former dentist, he has clearly spent plenty of time making small talk with patients and his easygoing demeanor rarely changed during the interview, whether he was discussing the use of National Guard troops in Central America or Minnesota's frigid weather.

Perpich has spoken eloquently about how dedicated teachers helped shape his life — as a 5-year-old U.S.-born son of Croatian immigrants, he couldn't speak English when he began school.

Perpich has returned the favor by becoming a firm advocate of quality education. Minnesota has led the nation in exploring the concept of school choice, an approach designed to bring greater competition and greater quality to schools throughout a region.

A conversation with Gov. Rudy Perpich.

Is Minnesota's political tradition as liberal as its reputation?

"It's far more conservative than most people think. Nationally, they think of Minnesota as being a very liberal state. It has to do with our German and Scandinavian background. Thirty-five percent of the people are Scandinavian, and about 40 percent have German roots. So it comes from that background of caring for each other — compassion and caring for each other. That kind of builds on this. Literally, it's a very conservative state. The people are very independent here."

Do you think there has ever been one prototypical political figure in Minnesota?

"Hubert Humphrey, Eugene McCarthy, Harold Stassen, Warren Burger, Harry Blackmun — many. No. There really hasn't been. Humphrey was a leader, but it's a stretch of the imagination to say that he was a kind of a party boss. There just isn't any control to the state as such."

Why are you opposed to the use of National Guard troops in Central America?

"We have our men in Scandinavia; they've been over in the Far East, in Korea, and the rest of the world, and there wasn't any problem. Then all of a sudden, they decide they're going to send them abroad without permission of the governors. I believe the National Guard is a citizens' guard. The governor is the commanding general. There isn't any governor who's going to say 'no' if there is a real need."

Is there a need in Central America?

"For what they're doing? No, absolutely not."

For many of us, the word "cold" immediately comes to mind when Minnesota is mentioned. Does that present an image problem for the state?

"When people think of Minnesota, they think not only of cold, but clean water, clean air, clean environment, clean politics, clean government. People here do care about each other. So we have a very special quality of life in Minnesota. Without the cold weather, we'd be overrun. Literally."

Your parents were Eastern Europeans. In fact, you spoke Croatian.

"People who left Eastern Europe did so because of political, economic, religious reasons. That's why I believe they're such good citizens. I remember my father and mother would get dressed up — they were laboring people, my mother worked in a laundry, my father in the mines — to go to vote."

Why did so many Eastern Europeans wind up in the mining industry?

"They were very hard workers, and they didn't have an education. So, where did you go? You went into the mines. You went into the woods. Or you went in the packing houses or steel mills. And that's how they ended in those areas. They were also determined to get a good education for their children, and did."

How are cities like your home town of Hibbing recovering from the downturn in the iron and steel industries?

"It's stabilized. It's a very slow turnaround because we had about 14,000-plus jobs. The full-time equivalent now maybe would be about 4,000 jobs."

What are some indications?

"We don't have the people moving out like we did. That has definitely stabilized. And people on the main streets say their businesses are improving."

PERPICH PROFILE

PARTY: Democratic-Farmer-Labor.

IN HIS WORDS: "Education was my passport from poverty. When I was 5 years old — a first-generation American who couldn't speak English — dedicated teachers taught me the English language and opened a window on the world."

BORN: June 27, 1928, in Carson Lake, Minn., to Croatian immigrants. His father, Anton Perpich, was a miner, and his mother, Mary Perpich, was a laundry worker.

FAMILY: Married Delores "Lola" Simic in 1954. Mrs. Perpich, 57, is a homemaker. The Perpiches have two children, Rudy Jr., 29, and Mary Sue, 28.

EDUCATION: Associate of arts in general studies, Hibbing Junior College; doctor of dental surgery, Marquette University.

TIMELINE

1946: Joined Army.

1954: Opened private dentistry practice.

1956: Elected to Hibbing Board of Education.

1962: Elected to four-year term in state Senate; re-elected in 1966.

1970: Elected to four-year term as lieutenant governor; re-elected in 1974.

1976: Succeeded Gov. Wendell Anderson when Anderson became a U.S. senator.

1978: Lost gubernatorial election.

1979: Named vice president of World Tech Inc., subsidiary of Control Data.

1982: Elected to four-year term as governor with 59 percent of vote; re-elected in 1986 with 56 percent of vote.

1991: Term expires in January; eligible for re-election.

PRIORITIES

▶ Farm crisis: Signed omnibus Minnesota

NOTEWORTHY

State's first governor from working-class Iron Range region in northeastern Minnesota. ... Has held office longer than any other Minnesota governor — seven years — and his term doesn't expire until 1991.

PERSONAL

Son Rudy Jr. is his closest political adviser; also consults his three brothers, wife and daughter. ... Wishes he had more time to go canoeing at his lakeside home in Gilbert, Minn. ... Enjoys basketball and football. ... Drinks hot Minnesota cider instead of coffee. ... Displays valuable collection of Yugoslavian paintings in his office.

THE FUTURE

On possibility of running for an unprecedented fourth term: "I'm going to stay governor until I put Minnesota on what I consider a job-creating (course), including tax reform and education and the whole thing in human services."

farm bill, including model mediation and financing legislation.

▶ Economic development: Signed bill banning corporate raiders from selling target companies' assets for five years.

▶ Tax reform: Cut personal income tax 26 percent over three-year period from 1985 to 1987; slashed state corporate tax and inheritance tax; abolished 10 percent income tax surcharge and tax on firms with foreign subsidiaries; cut property tax and sales tax.

▶ Education: Signed open-enrollment bill, USA's first law allowing parents to choose children's school; established student-incentive program for high schools and program to pay tuition for high school students taking college classes.

GOV. RAY MABUS

IMPRESSIONS

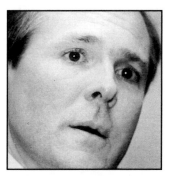

At the time we dropped in on Ray Mabus, he should have been tired, maybe a little harried, even apprehensive. It would have been understandable. His campaign was only a month behind him. He was trying to put together a staff and in six weeks he would be taking the oath of office.

Yet, we found Mabus to be calm and confident. He clearly wasn't suffering "buyer's remorse." He wanted to be governor — and he seemed to be ready, right down to his dark blue suit.

In many ways, he's the typical governor of the '80s:

▶ He's young: On Jan. 12, 1988, took office at age 39 — the youngest governor in the USA and the youngest in Mississippi since 1915.

▶ He's educated: bachelor's degree from the University of Mississippi, master's from Johns Hopkins University, law degree from Harvard.

▶ He's accomplished a lot at an early age: His work as Mississippi state auditor was the subject of a Page One article in *The Wall Street Journal*; *Esquire* magazine named him one of its "Achievers Under 40"; *U.S. News and World Report* listed Mabus among 30 rising figures in U.S. politics.

Now he's determined to make his mark on Mississippi — especially when it comes to education. Mabus says it's a given: He's going to raise teachers' salaries and pull his state out of the pits in education. And he's going to do it without raising taxes. He made that clear to us:

"We pay our teachers less than anybody in the country. Today, in our university system, for every three teachers we train, two of them don't teach in Mississippi. They either leave the profession or leave the state. We've got to do something about that. We simply can't compete as long as we don't pay people a living wage. I think that symbolically making sure that Mississippi isn't at the bottom is an important step in that direction."

Mabus has been called a "yuppie governor." But he seemed more selfless than selfish when it came to his new mission — Mississippi.

A conversation with Gov. Ray Mabus.

Two Harvard graduates, you and Gov. Charles "Buddy" Roemer of Louisiana, are running two Deep South states. Does that say more about Harvard or the New South?

"I don't know if it says a whole lot about either one. It says more about the mood of the state being willing to make some basic change, give some younger people an opportunity to manage government. I think it speaks more to frustration . . . that the 'good ole boy system' hadn't gotten us where we needed to go."

To what degree will you be a CEO of Mississippi rather than a traditional politician?

"I don't think anybody's mistaken me for a traditional politician. I think that you're going to have to be more like a CEO. You've got a lot more board members to answer to and a lot more constituents that are going to pass on your work than a normal CEO does. In Mississippi, we've got a $4 billion-a-year budget. We've got more than 20,000 state employees, more than 25,000 teachers. If it was a business, it would be a Fortune 100 company. I think we've got to take some of the lessons they've learned: goal-oriented management, priority budgeting."

What do you have planned in the way of economic expansion?

"I think the main thing we can do for economic development and economic expansion in Mississippi is education. I think if we make sure we are training, giving a good, basic, solid education from pre-school to graduate school, then we'll do fine in economic development."

What about race relations in Mississippi?

"If we allow ourselves to be divided racially, geographically, educationally or economically, we're not going anywhere. Mississippi has known the pain and the futility of a divided society. We simply can't afford that anymore. We've made great strides. The fact we have more black elected officials than any state in the union shows how far we've come."

What can be done to improve education in Mississippi?

"We've got to lower the dropout rate. We've got to make sure we have a better basic education nationwide, don't forget humanities and don't just train a nation of technocrats. Give people an education they can use interchangeably and not for a specific job that may not be there in 10 years, 15 years.

What has been the reaction to your plan to raise teachers' salaries?

"Well, I got 53 percent of the vote (in his election as governor). At least the majority, I think, want to do that. I've gotten reaction both ways. I'll tell you why I did it. . . . We as a society tend to view the value of jobs by the amount of money paid. Teachers aren't ever going to get paid like lawyers, doctors and some other segments of society. But we can raise that value. The Education Reform Act upped the requirements for teachers, and I think that's a process that needs to continue."

To what degree should state government get involved in setting AIDS policy?

"I'm willing to do anything in order to try to halt the spread. If testing will do it, let's test. What I don't want to do is drive people out of the health-care system. . . . I frankly don't think it's going to be successful if it's state by state. I think you're going to have to have a national policy on it."

What do you think of work-training welfare programs?

"I think you can learn a good bit from programs like that. I hope the federal government will give the states, or give pilot projects in the states, some opportunity to be a little bit more flexible, and do some things like the work-training program in Massachusetts."

MABUS PROFILE

PARTY: Democrat.

IN HIS WORDS: "Public service is a high calling, one of honor and one of trust. I think you have to be honest and straightforward with the people you represent and try to work toward their highest ideals and goals."

BORN: Oct. 11, 1948, in Ackerman, Miss., to Raymond Mabus Sr. and Lucille Mabus, who ran the family tree farm.

FAMILY: Married Julie Hines in 1987. Mrs. Mabus, 36, is a certified public accountant.

EDUCATION: Bachelor of arts in English, University of Mississippi; master's in government, Johns Hopkins University; law degree, Harvard University.

TIMELINE

1970: Joined Navy.

1972: Managed father's tree farm in Choctaw County, Miss.; began learning business in high school.

1980: Named aide to Mississippi Gov. William Winter.

1983: Elected to four-year term as state auditor; earned reformer reputation recovering more than $1.5 million in misspent state funds.

1987: Elected to four-year term as governor with 53.4 percent of the vote in the general election.

1992: Term expires in January; 1986 state constitutional amendment makes Mabus the first governor eligible for a second term since 1890.

PRIORITIES

▶ Education: Raised annual teacher pay an estimated $3,700.

▶ Economic development: Instituted consolidation of economic development agencies; advocates increased support for "home-grown" businesses, expanded processing

NOTEWORTHY

Set state record for campaign spending in 1987 governor's race — estimated $3 million. . . . In 1988 became USA's youngest governor at age 39 and Mississippi's youngest governor since 1915.

PERSONAL

Runs about three miles every night after work. . . . Works on speeches, does research on his personal computer at home. . . . Lives in a restored Victorian house. . . . Collects art, enjoys photo-realist and romantic period paintings.

THE FUTURE

Hasn't ruled out a bid for U.S. Senate but, "I'm interested in governing the people of Mississippi and I'm looking toward another term in the governor's office."

of raw products into finished goods; proposed executive-branch reorganization.

▶ New state constitution: Initiated referendum to rewrite state constitution.

GOV. JOHN ASHCROFT

IMPRESSIONS

In our coverage of Missouri, we described the state as "middlemost" — in geography, lifestyle and philosophy. The same adjective seems to fit Gov. John Ashcroft. He wasn't the most colorful governor we met in our travels, but neither was he colorless. Like many we met in the "Show Me State," he was warm, congenial and matter-of-fact about what he wanted to accomplish:

"If I have a dream for Missouri, it's this: Missouri would be a place where each person has the opportunity to reach his or her maximum, God-given potential. If I have a second dream for Missouri, it would be a place where each person had a dream."

If that "dream" imagery sounds a bit like one of President Reagan's addresses, it's probably not a coincidence.

Ashcroft's admiration for the president was apparent:

"From watching him, I've learned some things. I've learned to never underestimate your opponent. People in Washington underestimated him over and over again. I'm not sure that Tip O'Neill ever came to grips with the power of this president."

Ashcroft is one of the more conservative governors in the nation and one of the most visibly religious.

The son of an Assembly of God minister, Ashcroft doesn't drink, smoke or use profanity. In his free time, he's a gospel singer and songwriter. And a Bible sits prominently on his desk.

Ashcroft told us traditional values prevail throughout Missouri.

"There's a strong adherence to the work ethic in this state. There is a strong respect for family. This state has a set of family values and a respect for life that could make us probably the most pro-life state in the USA when it comes to electing public officials."

Ashcroft was one of the first governors we interviewed on BusCapade, but 49 states later we still had one strong impression: Ashcroft was one of the few governors equally qualified to lead a state or a Boy Scout troop.

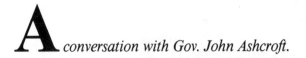

A *conversation with Gov. John Ashcroft.*

How do you describe Missourians to the rest of the nation? What makes them unique?

"I don't think in any way you could characterize Missourians as flamboyant, which is not to say that they're backward. 'Common sense' is a phrase that leaps into my mind. We have a diverse group of communities. When you get down into Springfield, my home territory, it's probably even a little bit different, with a little more emphasis on 'If it ain't broke, don't fix it.'"

What do you think the nation's perception of Missouri is?

"I don't think there is a national perception of Missouri. But Missouri is largely 'under-reputed,' if that would be an appropriate phrase for me to use. St. Louis, for instance, is thought to be a pretty old city but is under-reputed. It's not understood for its excellent neighborhoods and outstanding civic features. St. Louis is one of the great cities of the world. St. Louis is the westernmost eastern city of the USA. Kansas City, on the other hand, is the easternmost western city of the USA."

You've said Missourians tend to elect pro-life officials. Do you support the death penalty?

"Yes, I do."

Isn't that a contradiction?

"Not at all. You save lives by implementing the death penalty. First of all, it's a deterrent. A death penalty surely will deter the person who is executed from committing additional crimes. If you think it's likely to deter other people from committing crimes, you're saving lives. I'm talking about people who have committed a heinous crime of murder. To me, there is no comparison between that kind of a person and a person who is yet unborn."

Is Missouri playing a role in making U.S. industries more competitive in international markets?

"Yes, by having good workers. And by maintaining a tax structure which does not put inordinate burdens on the community that would manufacture goods. Missouri is a low-tax state. If taxes are too high, it hurts that product in the marketplace."

Missouri also has become home to several overseas plants.

"About eight different Japanese companies have come to locate plants and facilities in the state. Some German firms have done the same. It's my judgment that there will be more companies non-domestic in ownership that will want to be domestic in production. I would encourage them to select Missouri."

How did former Tennessee Gov. Lamar Alexander win over other states, including Missouri, to have the $3.5 billion General Motors Saturn plant built in Spring Hill, Tenn.?

"You'll have to ask General Motors Chairman Roger Smith what made Lamar the winner. I'm not sure Lamar was the winner. But the whole process made Missouri a winner."

How?

"Within two weeks after I became governor, we asked communities to inventory what they could do to welcome industry in the state of Missouri. We had about 30 communities that made proposals, when it became clear that the General Motors plant would be located east of here. I sent letters to 1,500 different companies after that and said, 'Look, you've heard about Saturn and what we would do for them. We'll do the same for you.' We have companies that are now doing business in the state of Missouri as a result of the Saturn effort."

ASHCROFT PROFILE

PARTY: Republican.

IN HIS WORDS: "I have a sign on my desk that I read every day. Its message is: There is no limit to the good you can do if you don't care who gets the credit."

BORN: May 9, 1942, in Chicago, to Grace Ashcroft, homemaker, and the Rev. James Robert Ashcroft, Assembly of God minister and president of Valley Forge Christian College.

FAMILY: Married Janet Roede in 1967. Mrs. Ashcroft, 43, is a lawyer. The Ashcrofts have three children, Martha, 19; Jay, 15; and Andrew, 10.

EDUCATION: Bachelor of arts in history, Yale University; law degree, University of Chicago.

TIMELINE

1967: Named associate professor of business law, Southwest Missouri State University.

1972: Lost bid for U.S. House of Representatives.

1973: Appointed to fill unexpired term as state auditor; lost 1974 election bid for state auditor.

1975: Named assistant state attorney general; elected state attorney general in 1976; reelected in 1980; mounted three unsuccessful court fights against St. Louis desegregation plan.

1984: Elected to four-year term as governor with 56.7 percent of vote.

1989: Term expires in January; eligible for re-election.

PRIORITIES

▶ Education: Pushed through Excellence in Education Act requiring new evaluation of students and teachers, providing career ladder for teachers; proposed higher education

NOTEWORTHY

Won 1980 attorney general's race with 64.5 percent vote margin — a Republican state record. . . . First Republican governor since 1928 to succeed a Republican governor in Missouri.

PERSONAL

Gospel singer, songwriter, performs for church groups with friend, former Judge Max Bacon. . . . Co-authored two legal textbooks with his wife, Janet. . . . Says white shirt is "the sign of a civilized man." . . . Enjoys "gigging " — nighttime spearfishing — and rod-and-reel fishing. . . . Plays piano to relax, basketball to exercise. . . . Hero is Abraham Lincoln.

THE FUTURE

Running for re-election in 1988. "As governor and as a father, I want to build a future of progress in Missouri."

assessment program, a plan to crack down on crime in schools and school report cards for communities.

▶ Welfare reform: Initiated pilot program to educate and train welfare recipients.

▶ Economic development: Reorganized Department of Economic Development to shift focus to job training; established "Buy Missouri" program to promote state products and the linked-deposit loan program to lower interest rates on farm loans.

GOV. TED SCHWINDEN

IMPRESSIONS

You can tell a lot about a governor's style by how easy it is to get in touch with him.

Some governors seem to have a platoon of personnel whose primary job is to protect them from unwanted intrusions.

And then there's Ted Schwinden. The governor of Montana has his home phone listed in the phone book.

"The average Montanan feels very little hesitation in picking up the phone and telling me exactly what they think or don't think about something I do," Schwinden told us. "It happens on a regular basis — here and at home. So it's personalized.

"That's just the way they do things in Montana," Schwinden said. "Politics are intensely personal in this state. It would be fairly unusual for a citizen in Miles City who I bumped into in a coffee shop, or on the street, to call me anything other than Ted."

It's probably a little easier to call your governor "Ted" when he's become as familiar a figure as Schwinden has.

A wheat farmer, Schwinden was elected to the Montana House of Representatives more than 30 years ago. He later served as president of the Montana Grain Growers Association and in 1969 was appointed commissioner of state lands. He was elected lieutenant governor in 1976, went on to become governor in 1980 and was re-elected in a landslide in 1984.

Schwinden stressed the importance of being responsive to the public.

Nowhere in the USA did we see a governor who seemed quite so receptive to contact with the press and public. We had to wonder whether any governor had the time or inclination to be quite this "hands-on."

The answer to our question came in the mail a few months later.

We had sent a follow-up questionnaire to governors as part of the research for this book.

Arriving well ahead of most questionnaires was the response from Montana — filled out by hand by Gov. Ted Schwinden.

A *conversation with Gov. Ted Schwinden.*

Montana will celebrate its 100th birthday in 1989. Is that renewing people's interest in the past?

"We've gone through a very exciting process of self-examination as a political entity. Montana's a state that is probably more known for its period of corporate domination than it is for public control, and once the people sort of seized control in the 1960s, they've been downright determined that they're going to shape their own future."

How?

"We have, I think, the only new constitution in the last 20 years. We've completely reorganized the executive branch. We've put together some of the most progressive — I hesitate to call it 'environmental,' but I guess that's the right word — legislation; our strip-mine legislation is basically the parent of the federal legislation that was passed several years later."

Street signs with names like "Last Chance Gulch" echo the Old West tradition in Montana. How much of the Old West still lingers?

"There clearly are some western influences. I moved here in 1969 from a small town in the eastern part of the state where our farm is, and I heard about a house. I took a look at it. I said, 'What do you want for it?' The guy said, '$28,500.' I said, 'That's a deal.' We shook hands. You can still do that here."

What do you see as being the most important issues in Montana in the next four or five years?

"The easy answer is jobs. We've gone through not only the same kind of economic dynamics as the rest of the country — the shift from the basics into the service industries — we saw industries fall right off the table with the collapse of oil prices a couple of years ago."

Mining was in trouble, also. How is it doing now?

"Mining has turned around dramatically. There's a tendency, because coal is so important to our state revenue, to focus on coal production, which is flat or falling. But in the area of precious metals, we're seeing probably the most aggressive development."

What about agriculture?

"In 1985, we had the worst agricultural year since the 1930s. In a state that normally produces 140 million to 180 million bushels of wheat, we didn't even make 50 million. This is a combination of drought, grasshoppers, and then, of course, we had a shrinking price."

How are Indians faring on the seven reservations here?

"It certainly varies from reservation to reservation."

What are the major problems facing the reservations?

"Depending upon the number of non-Indians who live on reservations, we have some fairly serious jurisdictional problems relating to things as simple as tobacco shops selling cigarettes without state taxes, and selling liquor. Also, there are very serious disagreements at times over reserve-water rights, sharing of revenues from coal production. And, historically, they've been among the highest areas of unemployment in the state."

What is the most important environmental issue in Montana today?

"It would depend on where you are in the state. Billings and Yellowstone County have one of the highest ambient pollution levels in the country. The biggest environmental challenge that we have is the Clark Fork River. It is going to test our ability not only to protect the stream from further damage, but to find ways to deal with over 100 years of abuse of that river."

SCHWINDEN PROFILE

PARTY: Democrat.

IN HIS WORDS: "Gubernatorial popularity is a little like teen-age romance. It can rise and fall very quickly."

BORN: Aug. 31, 1925, in Wolf Point, Mont., to Michael James Schwinden, farmer, and Mary Martha Schwinden, farmer, homemaker.

FAMILY: Married Jean Christianson in 1946. Mrs. Schwinden, 62, is a registered nurse. The Schwindens have three children, Mike, 40; Chrys, 39; and Dore, 31.

EDUCATION: Bachelor of arts and master of arts in history and political science, University of Montana; postgraduate study in history and economics, University of Minnesota.

TIMELINE

1943: Joined Army.

1958: Elected to two-year term in state House of Representatives; re-elected in 1960.

1959: Named to state Legislative Council; named commissioner of state lands in 1969; re-appointed commissioner in 1973.

1976: Elected to four-year term as lieutenant governor.

1980: Elected to four-year term as governor with 55.4 percent of vote; re-elected with 70.3 percent of vote in 1984.

1983: Named chair of Western Governors Conference.

1989: Term expires in January; rejected re-election bid.

PRIORITIES

▶ Diversify economy: Initiated "Build Montana" program, including: highway building program, incentives for business investment and establishment of Science and Technology Alliance to invest in high-tech research

NOTEWORTHY
In 1984 re-elected governor with largest margin in Montana history — 70 percent.

PERSONAL
Attended one-room school as child. . . . "Governor Ted" lists his home phone number in directory and answers phone himself. . . . Says he and his wife, Jean, "try to do the things we did before we got this job. We still shop at K mart and have lunch out on the park bench." . . . Likes to play golf, watch pro football on TV. . . . Enjoys listening to Broadway musical scores; favorites are *Cats* and *West Side Story*. . . . Favorite author is Robert Ludlum. . . . Hero is Harry S. Truman.

THE FUTURE
Ruled out 1988 re-election bid. "Eight (years) is enough."

and program to promote state products; plans to open trade office in Japan in 1988.

▶ Education: Initiated "School Night for Excellence" to survey parents as basis for reforms, including tougher requirements for high school graduation and college admission.

▶ Tax reform: Cut coal severance tax 10 percent to stimulate production; 1981 bill gives senior citizens an income tax credit for property tax paid on their home.

▶ Human services: Established Priorities for People Project to develop budget plan; created Department of Family Services.

GOV. KAY A. ORR

Kay Orr is the governor of Nebraska, not a "woman" governor. And before that, she was a candidate, not a "woman" candidate.

Here's what she told us about the historic 1986 campaign, in which her opponent was a woman:

"Both candidates made every attempt to focus on what the state needed, such as economic development. We didn't want to be identified with the 'women's issues.' ERA and abortion were both questions that could divert attention from other things we felt were more important."

In short, Orr was trying — still is trying — to diversify Nebraska's economy so that it is no longer solely dependent on agribusiness. That's what she likes talking about.

BusCapade revisited Orr by telephone a few months later. We wanted to know if two pieces of tough economic development legislation she had pushed through the Nebraska state house were producing any results. The legislation provided an incentives package designed to attract new business to the state and help existing businesses expand. She had come under attack by some people in the rural community. They said her measures weren't designed to help them. Orr was understanding but stern when she talked about the criticism:

"What they are saying is they didn't understand how a job creation act could help them in rural communities. Until each one of them can look to job creation in their very own community as a result of this economic development, it's hard for them to see how it helps them.

"They have to recognize that if the community getting the jobs is located 50 miles from them, or 500 miles, it's still good for Nebraska."

Quiet class. Patience. Persistence.

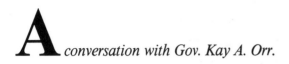

A *conversation with Gov. Kay A. Orr.*

Is the family farm surviving in this state?

"I believe it is. If you're going to look at agriculture, and the family farm, you start back 50 years ago and look at what's happened in agriculture in the Midwest. It's been rather dramatic, the amount of suffering that's gone on in agriculture, but that's something that is repeated throughout history — tough times. But there's been a decline in people on the family farms for better than 50 years. Now they're just getting more efficient."

In what ways?

"You get those Steiger tractors and those big discs, and they can run around that field one time and put down herbicides and fertilizer all at one time. They've taken down the fence rows and don't even have to mend the fence anymore. It's still family farming in Nebraska, just in a different way."

Do people across the USA have the right image of Nebraska?

"It's a unique blend of the Midwest and the West, but I would like people in the USA to get to know us better, through our people, because that's our greatest asset. We've got extraordinarily friendly people, easy to meet, courteous, thoughtful — and they're a great help in bringing in businesses, because they're a productive work force."

How seriously are you pushing your campaign proposal to have the state legislature convene every other year rather than every year?

"That's going to take some time. I'm interested in someday seeing the unicameral become a two-party unicameral and meeting only every other year."

Is every other year enough?

"Yes. We can do this business of the state in a session that meets every other year, and I certainly think we can have more discipline and accountability through a partisan legislature. But it's misunderstood by Nebraska people. They're very proud of their unicameral and the uniqueness of it."

How do you rate the job you have done so far?

"I give us strong marks for what we've actually gotten done. I give us poor marks for getting out and educating the public. We still have one of the smallest governor staffs per capita in the United States. So, it's just extraordinary to bring a small group of people in, hit the floor running, and keep going."

Why is Nebraska so renowned for having such passionate college football fans?

"It's Nebraska's way of focusing attention on our state and saying to a national audience, 'Here's Nebraska, and we have something we're very proud of in the state.' And of course, success and sports are understood by most people. Now I'd like to get them to go a step beyond that and talk about pride in Nebraska and in our people, and things that we offer, and the quality of life that we have here."

How is Nebraska unique?

"I often talk about our rich heritage, and I've always been intrigued by history. We have both the rolling hills of Iowa and the range land of the West. We've struggled to make it productive."

Nebraska has more one-room schoolhouses than any other state. What kind of education are the children receiving there?

"Nebraskans are very proud of the education that's received in those schools. They feel that they may not have all the new equipment or new curriculum, but they still send forth young people well prepared educationally. On the other side are those who favor consolidation, who feel that it's long past due. So, we will be working to find some common ground."

ORR PROFILE

PARTY: Republican.

IN HER WORDS: "Women are risk-takers. Women don't just seek safe havens. They don't accept a single role. They don't look at things as, 'It can't be done.' They just go ahead."

BORN: Kay Stark, Jan. 2, 1939, in Burlington, Iowa, to Ralph Stark, farm tools dealer, and Sadie Stark, homemaker.

FAMILY: Married William D. Orr in 1957. Mr. Orr, 53, is an insurance company executive. The Orrs have two children, John, 27, and Suzanne, 25.

EDUCATION: Studied liberal arts, University of Iowa.

TIMELINE

1964: Worked as campaign volunteer for Sen. Barry Goldwater's presidential bid.

1976: Elected delegate to GOP National Convention, platform committee member; vice chair of Reagan campaign in Nebraska; elected delegate to 1980 GOP National Convention; elected again in 1984 and served as co-chairman; platform committee member; named Platform Committee chairperson at 1988 Republican National Convention.

1978: Named volunteer co-chairman of Gov. Charles Thone's successful campaign; named Gov. Thone's chief of staff in 1979.

1981: Appointed state treasurer; elected to four-year term in 1982.

1986: Elected to four-year term as governor with 52.8 percent of vote.

1991: Term expires in January; eligible for re-election.

PRIORITIES

▶ Economic development: Four-part legislation includes tax-reduction incentives to spur business expansion or relocation to Nebraska.

NOTEWORTHY

Elected state treasurer in 1982 — first woman elected to Nebraska constitutional office. . . . In 1986 elected Nebraska's first female governor. She won the USA's first gubernatorial race that pitted female candidates against each other. . . . In 1988 named first woman to chair Republican Platform Committee.

PERSONAL

Former Sunday school teacher. . . . Favorite spectator sport is football. . . . Requires women in her office to wear skirts or dresses to "maintain a professional image." . . . Loves to ride her bicycle two or three times a week in her neighborhood. . . . Grows wildflowers at home. . . . Owns two dogs and two cats and an Arabian horse; one of the dogs is named after Tom Selleck.

THE FUTURE

Not interested in working in Washington, D.C. "That's not in my thinking at all. . . . I have much to do here in Nebraska."

▶ Tax reform: Pushed through comprehensive tax reform legislation with new structure not dependent on federal tax system.

▶ Education: Proposed $10.7 million increase in school aid and $60 million increase in research funding for University of Nebraska; won $10 million hike in college teacher pay.

GOV. RICHARD H. BRYAN

IMPRESSIONS

It's a sharp contrast between Nevada's casinos and Gov. Richard Bryan's subdued office in Carson City. Not that we expected one-armed bandits in the waiting room. But Bryan, a second-generation Nevadan, caught us a bit by surprise when he told us he never gambles.

"I can't say I haven't put a quarter or a nickel in the slot machine but I can't remember the last time when I did," he said. "I've never won a jackpot. I don't think I've played anything in the last 20 years."

You'd never mistake Richard Bryan for a pit boss. To the contrary, he's probably the ideal representative of the "other" Nevada — the fiercely independent Western state that has little in common with the glitz and glamour of Las Vegas and Reno.

Bryan grew up in Las Vegas before the big gambling boom.

"When I started school in Las Vegas, there were about 8,500 people," Bryan recalled. "Nevada had fewer than one person per square mile and every man, woman and child in our state could comfortably watch the Olympics in the Los Angeles Coliseum."

Somehow, Bryan's success story rings particularly true in Nevada, a state full of people who came seeking opportunities, a state in which family lineage seems to count for less than ambition and energy.

Bryan counts among his hobbies the study of history and that was reflected throughout the interview.

Ask about Las Vegas' styles and he'll begin his explanation with a reference to the Boulder Dam and World War II. Ask about gambling and legalized prostitution and he'll trace the history of the state from the Comstock Lode era.

Bryan deftly handled questions about less wholesome aspects of Nevada's heritage. Discussing brothels and gambling houses, his tone was that of an older brother explaining the actions of a family black sheep.

When we visited Bryan, he was toying with the idea of running for the U.S. Senate. Since then he has decided to challenge Republican U.S. Sen. Chic Hecht.

Bryan doesn't drop coins into slot machines. But from a political perspective, he's clearly not afraid to gamble.

A *conversation with Gov. Richard H. Bryan.*

Many people think of gambling and prostitution when they think of your state. What else should they have in mind?

"They should think of an extraordinary amount of diversity and scenery. Nevada now has a national park — the Great Basin National Park in the eastern part of the state. (The park opened in 1987). In the southern part of the state, you've got the first of the state parks — the Valley of Fire. There's a tremendous recreational potential above and beyond our gaming and tourism."

Do you feel the state has an image problem because of the gaming, legal prostitution and quickie divorces?

"The problem is that the image is primarily that which is perceived by people who have not been here, who do not see the diversity that I've just described; people who do not know that Nevadans are a good people who value the work ethic, that they are fiercely independent, proud of their heritage, and that it is a state in which opportunity abounds."

What kinds of opportunities?

"Someone can come to this state and, in a relatively short period of time, make his or her mark. People tend to accept you as you are, not for your family lineage or your last name."

Does the state have gambling, prostitution and speedy marriages and divorces because Nevadans have a "live and let live" attitude?

"Some of the things which you refer to were born out of economic necessity. Nevada has been heavily dependent upon a single industry. Initially, it was mining. When the Comstock mines played out, the economic dislocation was severe. In the 1930s, we embarked upon this great social experiment. As gaming in one form or another has been expanded, it suggests to us that Nevada's experiment has proved extremely successful."

Nevada ranks in the top five in categories such as school dropouts, suicide, teen pregnancies. What are you doing to attack these problems?

"This past session of the legislature enacted mandatory sex education for elementary and high schools. That certainly is a response to the concern that we have, not only as it relates to teen-age pregnancy, but the problem of AIDS as well. In the past legislative session, we expanded our mental health budget by about 49 percent, added $19 million in new funding."

Does the state have a problem attracting new business?

"Ask the person who has come to Nevada to establish a business. Those people are our most eloquent sales force because people do have misconceptions about Nevada. But once they get here, they recognize the opportunity. We have a business climate that is certainly very favorable both in terms of tax structure and in terms of attitude of the community."

You said you don't want the nation's high-level nuclear waste depository in Nevada. Do you think you'll be able to keep it out?

"Yes. I get more encouraged as we move along the line. There is a growing recognition that the Department of Energy's policy with respect to high-level nuclear waste and its disposal is bankrupt, morally as well as technically. We think that the evidence is overwhelming that the placement decision has been political. I think there is some support for going back to square one and trying to get this program back on line. There's at least some thought in Congress that we ought to take a look at some of the proposals that have come out for monitored retrieval storage, which would be an intermediate, not a long-term, solution."

BRYAN PROFILE

PARTY: Democrat.

IN HIS WORDS: "I've wanted to be governor since I was in high school. . . . This represents the ultimate for me."

BORN: July 16, 1937, in Washington, D.C., to Oscar Bryan, lawyer, and Lillie Bryan, who worked in court clerk's office.

FAMILY: Married Bonnie Fairchild in 1962. Mrs. Bryan, 49, is a homemaker. The Bryans have three children, Richard Jr., 24; Leslie, 22; and Blair, 21.

EDUCATION: Bachelor of arts in history, University of Nevada; law degree, University of California.

TIMELINE

1959: Joined Army; joined reserves in 1960.

1963: Began practicing law; named deputy district attorney in 1964.

1968: Elected to two-year term in state Assembly; re-elected in 1970; named counsel to Clark County juvenile court in 1968.

1973: Elected to two-year term in state Senate; re-elected in 1975.

1974: Lost bid for attorney general's office; elected state attorney general in 1978.

1982: Elected to four-year term as governor with 53.4 percent of vote; re-elected in 1986 with 72 percent of vote; elected president of Council of State Governments in 1987.

1991: Term expires in January; not eligible for third consecutive term.

PRIORITIES

▶ Tourism promotion: Established Tourism Commission; opened tourism office in Japan.

▶ Economic diversification: Opened trade office in Japan; reorganized Economic Development Department; created Motion Picture Division; called special legislative session to

NOTEWORTHY
In 1966, became Nevada's first public defender — and USA's youngest in that office.

PERSONAL
Enjoys reading about history, especially about the Civil War or Winston Churchill. . . . Enjoys cross-country skiing. . . . Favorite snack is Oreo cookies, keeps a jar full in his office. . . . Calls hamburgers "Epicurean delights."

THE FUTURE
Announced bid for U.S. Senate in March 1988. "It is a decision which I have not made lightly because as your governor I am fulfilling my boyhood vision of serving Nevadans as their highest state official."

clear way for Citicorp to build regional credit card center.

▶ Education: Won salary increases for teachers and tougher high school graduation requirements; increased education funding; won approval of School of Engineering at University of Nevada.

▶ Drug abuse: Created Governor's Alliance for a Drug Free Nevada.

▶ Health and human services: Implemented program to roll back patients' bill charges 25 percent; won passage of Comprehensive Child Protection Act; proposed comprehensive review of state's nursing homes and changes in nursing home care.

GOV. JOHN H. SUNUNU

IMPRESSIONS

We knew everything we thought we needed to know before we went to interview John Sununu. We had talked to people on the streets in New Hampshire. We had studied the issues. We had worked up our list of questions. There was just one lingering detail — we weren't sure about how to pronounce his name.

Various BusCateers were putting the accent in various places. In the end, however, we handled it like enterprising reporters. We simply called him "governor." (It's pronounced "soo-NOO-noo." Accent on the second syllable.)

The "governor," as we knew from our research, was an engineer. And it showed up in the way he answered questions. In the way he gauged success in office. In the way he thought about being a politician. Sununu clearly was a practical man. What works is what counts.

▶ His answers: He goes right to the heart of the question and answers with mathematical precision — plus an occasional twist of dry humor. We asked Sununu, "Is it proper for the New Hampshire primary to have the kind of impact that it has?"

"I just assumed that's the way God intended it to be," he said.

▶ His success in office: It's clearly performance — make that "empirical evidence" — that counts with Sununu. We asked him about New Hampshire's economy while he's been in office.

"We're at about 2.5 percent unemployment. We've had the lowest unemployment in the country for the last five years. Over that period, the state has gone from about 26th in per capita income to eighth in the nation."

▶ His thoughts on being a politician: "I've found this a very satisfying job. I've had more fun as a governor than anything else I've done in my life. That doesn't mean I'm going to stay with it forever. I've said I'm going to die an old engineer, not an old politician. I really do mean that."

A
conversation with Gov. John H. Sununu.

How do you like your job, and which do you prefer, the executive or the legislative branch?

"I ran for the U.S. Senate in 1980, and I lost in the primary by 2,000, 3,000 votes. In retrospect, I suspect I'm probably a heck of a lot happier as a governor, where I can get something done, than as a senator, where there's a level of frustration of trying to move 99 colleagues to deal with each and every issue."

Are there down sides to your state's 2.5 percent unemployment?

"The business community keeps telling me they can't find anybody to hire. That's the only down side. But with the pressure on the employers, they are willing to train and take the extra step to help folks."

How do you get firms to move into New Hampshire?

"I'll go and spend time with them and encourage them to come up here. In the last few years, we have worked on the theory that if we get the fundamental manufacturer up here, their suppliers and peripheral services will follow. And that seems to have worked very, very well."

Your neighboring state of Massachusetts is enjoying prosperity right now, too. Would you give Gov. Michael Dukakis credit for that?

"Most of the major changes I have seen in the attitude of businesses willing to stay in Massachusetts have been because of policies put into place by previous administrations. Their population and economic growth in terms of numbers of people working has been virtually flat in comparison to New Hampshire and a couple of other states in the Northeast."

How do you assess Massachusetts' highly praised Employment and Training program?

"There's a lot less than meets the eye. Their vaunted ET program brought the folks receiving state assistance from 88,000 to 85,000. That's about a 3 percent drop. They said it was equivalent to a 25 percent drop if it had continued to grow as it had before. That's fictional statistics. We've had a real reduction in New Hampshire of 41 percent."

Do the voters of New Hampshire take the primary seriously?

"I don't think they cast their votes lightly. My favorite story is about the old farmer in the North Country. Just before the 1980 primary, there were TV crews at his door, trying to find out whether he was going to vote for Ronald Reagan. His answer was, 'I'm not sure, I've only met him three times.' The point is that the voters do go out to see the candidates and get involved in trying to understand the differences among the candidates, and for the most part they hold off a commitment until the very end."

How is New Hampshire recovering from the loss of Christa McAuliffe, the teacher who was killed in the Challenger accident?

"The people of New Hampshire were impacted at a very personal level. We have established a Christa McAuliffe program, which is a sabbatical for teachers. The Legislature has been dealing with funding a lasting memorial to Christa in the form of a planetarium. Most of the discussion is not in a melancholy sense, but in an upbeat sense about building on what they felt was positive."

When do you expect to sign the AIDS testing bill for marriage applicants into law, and why do you feel so strongly about it?

"The real question is, why are the Centers for Disease Control and some of the medical community so strongly against it? The worst thing in the world is for a married couple to bring a child into this world with AIDS."

SUNUNU PROFILE

PARTY: Republican.

IN HIS WORDS: "If you want to be an effective leader you have to be willing to do the hard work of getting as much information as possible and then making a clear decision on the hard issues. Too many of our policy makers substitute the easier, safer course of following the crowd — that may be good politics but it isn't really good government."

BORN: July 2, 1939, in Havana, Cuba, to John Sununu, importer/exporter for the film industry, and Victoria Sununu, homemaker. They were U.S. citizens living in Cuba.

FAMILY: Married Nancy Hayes in 1958. Mrs. Sununu, 49, is a homemaker. The Sununus have eight children, Kathy, 28; Elizabeth, 27; Christina, 25; John E., 23; Michael, 20; James, 19; Christopher, 13; and Peter, 8.

EDUCATION: Bachelor of science, master of science and doctorate in mechanical engineering, Massachusetts Institute of Technology.

TIMELINE

1960: Co-founded Astro Dynamics Inc.

1965: Founded two consulting firms, JHS Engineering and Thermal Research Inc.

1966: Named associate professor of mechanical engineering, Tufts University; named associate dean, College of Engineering, Tufts University in 1968.

1972: Elected to two-year term as state representative.

1974: Lost bid for state Senate, lost again in 1976; lost race for governor's Executive Council in 1978; lost bid for Republican U.S. Senate nomination in 1980.

1982: Elected to two-year term as governor with 51.9 percent of vote; re-elected in 1984 with 66.8 percent of vote; and in 1986 with 53.7 percent of vote.

1984: Elected chairman of New England

NOTEWORTHY
First governor of New Hampshire to hold doctorate in thermal engineering.

PERSONAL
Celebrated his second and third inaugurations by inviting 3,500 people to breakfast catered by McDonald's. "I'm a great Egg McMuffin man. And if my wife isn't looking I'll sneak a Danish." ... Enjoys downhill skiing, softball, baseball and golf. ... Collects stamps and baseball cards. ... Current favorite author is Tom Clancy. ... Thomas Edison is his hero.

THE FUTURE
Rejected third re-election bid in 1988. "It has been a tough decision."

Governors' Conference Inc.; elected chairman of Republican Governors Association in 1985.

1987: Elected chairman of National Governors' Association.

1989: Term expires in January; will not seek re-election.

PRIORITIES

▶ Education: Initiated program to give computer training to teachers and establish gifted-student programs.

▶ Economic development: Signed trade pacts with Canada, Italy and Japan.

▶ Health and human services: Improved mental health services; expanded programs for developmentally disabled; increased aid to dependent children and funding for support services and cut caseloads; expanded access to child-care subsidies.

▶ Criminal justice: Built maximum-security prison system.

▶ Environment: Developed national model for acid rain reduction programs.

GOV. THOMAS H. KEAN

IMPRESSIONS

Tom Kean was elected governor in 1981 and immediately had to come to grips with an image problem. Not his. His state's.

To many in the USA, New Jersey was synonymous with pollution. Organized crime. Urban decay.

Many view New Jersey as little more than a poor cousin to New York.

"New Jersey had an image that wasn't in touch with reality. It was in part encouraged by some of her own citizens who laughed at the New Jersey jokes, who almost were apologetic about the state," Kean told us.

Kean has fought those negative images with some positive images of his own. Bright, outgoing and youthful looking, Kean has taken to the television screen to tout the merits of New Jersey as a tourist attraction. Beautiful images of the Garden State flash past the viewer while Kean buoyantly invites us to share in the state's wonders.

Ask him a tough question about pollution in New Jersey and you'll hear: "We've got a toxic-waste problem. We recognized it earlier than the rest of the country. We still have the best program in the country in that area."

Ask him about New Jersey's links to organized crime and you'll hear: "We've had some of the strongest U.S. attorneys in New Jersey and some of the best attorney generals in recent years, and I don't think anybody would make a statement anymore that New Jersey is a haven, not even a safe place, for organized crime."

He has aggressively addressed environmental issues — though not always to the satisfaction of activists in this area — and led the fight for an ambitious welfare reform program.

In the process, Kean has developed a national political presence.

By presiding over New Jersey's economic turnaround in the '80s, he has become an up-and-comer in the Republican Party. His name invariably pops up as a potential vice-presidential candidate.

Not that there's much enthusiasm for that job from Kean. "That's not the kind of job that I think I can be terribly attracted to," Kean said. "A governor likes to make decisions, you like to be your own boss."

A conversation with Gov. Thomas H. Kean.

What are your favorite features of New Jersey?

"You can drive for a couple of hours and you're in the mountains. It's a state that people think of as urbanized, and yet almost two-thirds of New Jersey is farms and woods. The northwest has its ravines and canyons. You get more ethnic groups than any other state, except one, in the country. We have a farm economy, and we're ranked in the top five in the number of farm products produced."

At one time, New Jersey was considered anti-business. Is that still true today?

"What you do to be successful is create the climate. We've cut taxes. We now have a lower tax climate than most of our neighbors. That's an asset. When I came into office, we were thought to have — and very justifiably so — a very anti-business climate. Government officials thought of business as something that they taxed and regulated. And that was about it."

Has that changed?

"We consider business an asset, something to be encouraged. I get personally involved with trying to get through to the companies that I think would be assets to come to New Jersey — but only when they're looking at other states. I've been governor now for six years. I have never yet initiated a call to a company."

What would you say needs to be done to enable a city like Hampton, a city like Asbury Park, and some of the other cities in the state to share in the economic boom? The cities seem almost immune to the economic recovery.

"Let me say first of all that the cities are not immune. That the economic recovery in the state has already helped the cities to a large degree, and if you look at statistics, you'll find for instance that black employment, black incomes, have increased four to five times as fast as for whites. Of course, they have further to go, but there is very much improvement."

Has casino gambling been good for the state?

"No question, it's created jobs. As people come to Atlantic City, they go see other parts of the state. On the other hand, gambling is not without its problems. We have fully one-half of the attorney general's office working one way or another to make sure that it stays straight. I was one of the people who led the referendum against it. But now that it's here, as governor, I want to make sure it works for everyone."

New Jersey is looking for a baseball team. Will you get one?

"Yes. This is the greatest serious sports market in the country, where we're going to build a stadium. It's going to be within 20 miles of 4 million people. And we're willing to guarantee attendance of 2 million a year."

What does Bruce Springsteen mean to New Jersey?

"He's a symbol. Wherever he goes, he talks about the state. He loves the state, obviously. He still comes back here to write songs. If we were the Japanese, we'd make him a national landmark and not allow him to leave."

KEAN PROFILE

PARTY: Republican.

IN HIS WORDS: "I like to make decisions; I like to be my own boss. I like to think I've done something almost every day that has changed people's lives."

BORN: April 21, 1935, in New York City, to U.S. Rep. Robert Winthrop Kean and Elizabeth Kean, homemaker.

FAMILY: Married Deborah Elizabeth Bye in 1967. Mrs. Kean (refuses to reveal her age) is a homemaker. The Keans have three children, twins Reed and Thomas Jr., 19, and Alexandra, 13.

EDUCATION: Bachelor of arts in history, Princeton University; master of arts in history, Columbia University.

TIMELINE

1967: Elected to two-year term in state Assembly; re-elected four times. Joined Realty Transfer Co. as chairman and president in the late '60s.

1974: Lost bid for GOP nomination for U.S. House of Representatives.

1976: Managed former President Gerald Ford's election campaign in New Jersey.

1977: Lost bid for GOP gubernatorial nomination.

1979: Appeared as commentator and reporter on *The New Jersey Nightly News*.

1981: Elected to four-year term as governor with 49.45 percent of vote; re-elected in 1985 with 69.6 percent of vote.

1990: Term expires in January; not eligible for third consecutive term.

PRIORITIES

▶ Education: Launched educational reform package raising teacher salaries, establishing system of merit rewards for teachers and recruiting professionals from other fields for teaching positions; established

NOTEWORTHY

Descended from New Jersey's first governor, William Livingston. . . . Elected governor in 1981 by tightest margin in state history — 1,797 votes. . . . Re-elected in 1985 by New Jersey's biggest landslide — 70 percent.

PERSONAL

Father and grandfather were U.S. congressmen, "I was a congressional brat." . . . Frugal — buys one can of tennis balls for whole summer. . . . Cheers for Washington Redskins, New York Giants , New York Jets and Yogi Berra. . . . Tries to read a book a week — favorite is Tolstoy's *War and Peace*. . . . Sings along with opera, Bruce Springsteen in the car.

THE FUTURE

"I have not focused on my life after my term as governor ends. I intend to remain active but I have not decided what form that activity will take."

school monitoring program that allows the state to take over districts that fall below standards.

▶ Welfare reform: Drafted program requiring welfare recipients to get training, education or work. The program includes child care, medical benefits.

▶ Economic development: Pushed through a $500 million waterfront redevelopment project in Hoboken, N.J.; established 11 urban enterprise zones.

▶ Environment: Established clean water environmental trust fund; proposed creation of Coastal Commission and increased funding for coastal protection and cleanup; signed 1986 toxic waste cleanup package.

▶ Criminal justice: Doubled prison space; cracked down on armed crimes and drug-related crimes.

GOV. GARREY CARRUTHERS

IMPRESSIONS

Some budding politicians get their feet wet by running for mayor or city council.

The more ambitious may make a bid for the state legislature.

The first time Garrey Carruthers ran for elective office, he pursued the governorship. And he won.

We met with Carruthers in his Santa Fe office just 115 days into his first term.

How does a rookie get elected governor of New Mexico? "We are in a state that wanted something different," Carruthers said.

Carruthers' background certainly is different: a professor of agricultural economics at New Mexico State University and assistant secretary of the Department of the Interior under President Reagan.

Carruthers insisted that he's not a novice at politics, however.

"Campus politics are the toughest politics in the world. I launched my career at New Mexico State by being on the faculty Senate, athletic council, and graduate council. The essence of politics, very simply, is you must like people. If you like people, you'll do well."

Carruthers was a few minutes late to our scheduled interview. He'd been delayed while touring a state prison. As he walked in, he was eager to talk about what he had just seen. After a prison riot in New Mexico in 1980 led to the deaths of 33 people, the state redesigned its prisons to tighten security. Carruthers spoke confidently about the redesigned prisons.

"They're almost riot proof," Carruthers said.

If Carruthers is taking his new job seriously, he doesn't take himself too seriously. At one point, one of our reporters joked about the difficulty most people have in spelling Albuquerque and asked — with tongue in cheek — if that was a deterrent to future development.

Carruthers didn't miss a beat. This was clearly the most ridiculous question he'd ever been asked, but he just smiled and said most people find "Aztec" more difficult to spell.

The governorship may be Garrey Carruthers' first elective office, but chances are it won't be his last.

A conversation with Gov. Garrey Carruthers.

How are you coping with New Mexico's image problem? Some people seem to think it's a foreign country.

"We're going to come out with an advertising campaign. We may start off by saying, 'Guess who just joined the 50? We're now in the United States.' We also have people who insist that we put USA on our license plates. We believe that New Mexico truly is the land of challenge. The word we like to use is a union state."

What does that mean?

"According to some sources, we have no dominant ethnic group here. The Hispanics are about 35 percent, native Americans 10 percent, blacks and other minorities, about 14 percent. You get a blanket of people in New Mexico, which leads to a unique character of the state."

What other things will you boast about?

"We have great artists, and we have some of the most diverse environment that you've ever seen. Two of the largest wilderness areas in the USA are in this state — the Pecos and the Gila wilderness. We have about everything you could ask for here, except one saving grace: We don't have all that many people. We have about 1.5 million people."

How are the Indian populations faring in New Mexico?

"Economically, not well. Some of the highest unemployment in the state is on Indian reservations, and some of the highest suicide rates are on reservations — drug and alcohol abuse. We did not help them sometimes when we introduced them to all our bad habits."

Indian groups are charging that nuclear waste and other toxic materials are polluting their lands. What is the state doing to counter this?

"I would suspect that our most significant pollution problem at the moment is the air quality. We will soon be the repository of low-level, military nuclear waste. That is going to become an industry itself. There have been debates over whether we ought to have that here."

What's the debate over?

"The most significant debate today is not the consequences of putting nuclear waste here. Everybody is fairly satisfied with the science. But there is some discussion as to whether we would have to haul nuclear waste down Main Street."

The first nuclear bomb was tested here and from that early start the Los Alamos Scientific Laboratory was developed. At what stage is the nuclear research now?

"Now the emphasis is on the safe use of nuclear energy and economic development since we have a lot of resources here: coal development, solar energy. So we've taken that collection of scientists who originally started out in the nuclear business and now expanded them into almost every conceivable scientific endeavor. This makes us very competitive for the Supercollider."

Is nuclear research important to your economy?

"It's very important to New Mexico. There's a major facility going in the White Sands project, and that will affect the economy of Las Cruces, and, to a degree, El Paso, Texas. If they expand to the larger model, then a major share of the work at White Sands will deal with the Strategic Defense Initiative."

Unlike your predecessor, you favor capital punishment. Do you think it's a deterrent?

"My predecessor chose to commute the sentences of the people on death row. I happen to be pro-capital punishment, because I do think that it's a deterrent."

CARRUTHERS PROFILE

PARTY: Republican.

IN HIS WORDS: "This was the first time I ever ran for office. It was a challenge. I get a kick out of it."

BORN: Aug. 29, 1939, in Alamosa, Colo., to William Carruthers, dairy farmer, and Frankie Jane Carruthers, nurse, farmer and homemaker.

FAMILY: Married Katherine "Kathy" Thomas in 1961. Mrs. Carruthers, 45, is a community and political activist. They met and married in college. The Carrutherses have three children, Debi Joyce, 26; Carol, 21; and Steven, 18.

EDUCATION: Bachelor of science in agriculture and master of science in agricultural economics, New Mexico State University; doctorate in economics, Iowa State University.

TIMELINE

1968: Named professor of agricultural economics and agricultural business, New Mexico State University.

1974: Named White House Fellow.

1976: Named director, New Mexico Water Resources Research Institute.

1977: Named chairman, state Republican party.

1981: Named assistant secretary, Department of the Interior.

1986: Elected to four-year term as governor with 53 percent of vote.

1990: Term expires; ineligible for second consecutive term.

PRIORITIES

▶ Streamline state government: Merged four state agencies into two new departments;

NOTEWORTHY

New Mexico's first Republican governor since 1970.

PERSONAL

Plays golf with handicap of 18. . . . Owns Cessna with some friends; has been a pilot for 12 years. . . . Jogs, lifts weights and rides a bike to stay in shape. . . . His pride and joy is his blue '68 Ford Mustang. . . . Loves country music and baseball, especially Los Angeles Dodgers. . . . Favorite artist is New Mexico sculptor Duke Sundt, who works in bronze.

THE FUTURE

Asked about his plans when he leaves office, Carruthers says, "I'm more concerned with doing a good job as governor than worrying about what I'm going to be doing in the future."

reorganized economic development and tourism departments.

▶ Economic development: Implemented interstate banking law to allow out-of-state banks to acquire New Mexico banks; established business advisory council; signed federal agreement to give state access to international databank.

▶ Education: Instituted biannual seminars to develop educational agendas; won $2 million funding for high-tech and agricultural doctoral programs.

▶ Welfare reform: Established minimum levels for child support; initiated "Project Mainstream," which funds day care for mothers trying to re-enter work force and creates tax credit for employers.

▶ Public safety: Proposed tougher penalties for drunk drivers.

GOV. MARIO CUOMO

IMPRESSIONS

Months after he ruled out a bid for the presidency, Mario Cuomo's non-candidacy was still one of the hottest political topics around.

Could this colorful and charismatic governor who cruised to victory in 1986 really be passing up a shot at the top job?

Cuomo told us he meant what he said.

"The statement was inevitable," he said. "Once I ran for governor again in '86 and won, I could not run for president."

Why not? "I called two people regarded as truth-tellers and asked, 'What do I have to do to run for the presidency?' They said 'You have to go to Iowa 50 times.' They said I could theoretically try to make a television appearance. Forget about that. Some Iowa farmer says, 'This joker wants me to vote for him, but he's too busy to talk to me. He's in New York.'"

Cuomo's denial didn't convince many. A year later, some political analysts saw Cuomo's failure to endorse a candidate in the New York presidential primary as a last-ditch effort to keep the door open for a draft Cuomo movement.

While that scenario never materialized, the conjecture was understandable. Cuomo sends out mixed signals: the rational man says he won't pursue the presidency; the ambitious man wants it more than anything else in the world.

"To be able to say I was the first Italian-American president in history — that would mean something to me," Cuomo told us. "I do regret that I don't have that opportunity."

As presidential as Cuomo may sometimes appear, he's one of the first to recognize that he has image problems.

In Cuomo's words:

"I'm always running into situations like one I had at Tulane. This anthropologist turned to me and said, 'You know, Gov. Cumo, Kemo, Cucomo, you know, you're not as ugly in person as you are on TV.'"

A *conversation with Gov. Mario Cuomo.*

How do you manage to stay popular statewide despite the conflicting interests between New York City and upstate areas?

"I don't think politics and making yourself popular is a very elusive science. You've got to give people on the issues what they understand is good and right, and you have to be with the people."

Is that why President Reagan is so popular?

"Reagan does it by magic. He stands up there — so nice, so thoroughly non-menacing that his very appearance on television is like being in your living room — and everybody feels better for seeing him."

Don't you share that magical quality?

"That's not true in my case. I have to do it differently. I have to spend time with people."

New York has been in the news lately because of political corruption. What can be done to remove the stain?

"I don't want to excuse us by spreading the blame to the rest of the country, but the truth is — Irangate, Washington, Chicago, New York City — it's universal. It's not New York. It's not Washington. There are situations all over."

What can be done about it?

"The temptation of the politician is always to hunker down as soon as that squall comes. There's a good experience here that says, if there's a scandal, take a vacation. But that would be the worst thing to do here. This one's not going to go away, this one should not go away until it's been dealt with. So what we should do is, to use one of my favorite approaches, do a jujitsu."

Can you give an example of this jujitsu?

"Take this moment of adversity and use its force to give yourself an opportunity for advance. Use this as an opportunity to do the toughest ethics law in the country."

What can the people of New York expect from you 10 years from now?

"My mother has this wonderful expression, 'Between now and then a pope will be born.' Everything happens between now and then. If 15 years ago someone had suggested that I'd be governor, I would have laughed. It would have been an absurdity."

Why?

"As a lawyer who regularly sued Wall Street firms for fun, it just didn't make any sense to think that you could actually get to be the governor of New York. Then I got devastated in two elections. Mayor Koch ate me for lunch in 1977, just awful. So, this notion that you can figure out the future, it's not like that. I love what I'm doing."

CUOMO PROFILE

PARTY: Democrat.

IN HIS WORDS: "There comes a point where the eagerness to change can become an intent to pander, an intent not to lead, but simply to win. The unfortunate fact for those of us who prefer winning is that what is right is sometimes not popular, or at least not likely to get you elected; that sometimes the price of saying what you believe is to be rejected."

BORN: June 15, 1932, in Queens, N.Y., to Andrea Cuomo and Immaculata Cuomo, who ran small neighborhood grocery store.

FAMILY: Married Matilda Raffa in 1954. Mrs. Cuomo, 56, is a homemaker and former teacher. The Cuomos have five children, Margaret, 33; Andrew, 30; Maria, 26; Madeline, 23; and Christopher, 17.

EDUCATION: Bachelor of arts in English, law degree, St. John's University.

TIMELINE

1952: Played center field with Brunswick Pirates, a Georgia farm club of Pittsburgh Pirates; career cut short by head injury.

1956: Became law clerk to Judge Adrian T. Burke, state court of appeals; practiced law as associate in Corner, Weisbrod, Froeb and Charles law firm in 1958; became partner in Corner, Finn, Cuomo and Charles law firm in 1963; named adjunct professor of law, St. John's University, in 1963.

1974: Lost bid for Democratic nomination for lieutenant governor; elected to four-year term as lieutenant governor in 1978.

1975: Appointed New York secretary of state.

1977: Lost race for New York City mayor.

1982: Elected to four-year term as governor with 50.9 percent of vote; re-elected with 64.6 percent of vote in 1986.

NOTEWORTHY
Won re-election in 1986 with 64.6 percent of vote — a record victory margin for a New York governor.

PERSONAL
Has taken two vacations since 1954 — one was his honeymoon. . . . Wrote two books, *Diaries of Mario M. Cuomo: The Campaign for Governor* and *Forest Hills Diary*. . . . Plays softball and basketball despite bad back. . . . Wakes up at 5 a.m. every day to write in diary, kept in loose-leaf notebooks. . . . Admires Joe DiMaggio, Abraham Lincoln, St. Thomas More.

THE FUTURE
Rejected 1988 bid for presidency. Anything is possible including a judgeship, and "I haven't ruled out playing center field for the Yankees."

1991: Term expires in January; eligible for re-election.

PRIORITIES

▶ Economic development: Established 10 enterprise zones in 1987.

▶ Education: Increased funding 57 percent since 1983; increased teacher pay; proposed pre-kindergarten program.

▶ Environment: Signed USA's first acid-rain control bill in 1983; won voter approval of $1.4 billion bond issue to clean up hazardous waste.

▶ Housing: Allocated $4 billion for low- and moderate-income housing and shelter for homeless.

▶ Criminal justice: Built 17,000 more cells; tougher penalties for drug dealers.

▶ Tax reform: Cut personal income tax in half; reduced corporate tax rate.

GOV. JAMES G. 'JIM' MARTIN

IMPRESSIONS

One of the things that struck us as we visited governors around the USA was the general lack of security. There was very little. In many cases, it appeared the only security most governors had was the fact that it was almost impossible to find their offices — even after we got inside the capitol.

That was not the case with James Martin. We interviewed him in a room at the Grand Traverse Resort in Traverse City, Mich., at the National Governors Convention. The night before the interview, an advance man and a plainclothes state trooper dropped by to check out the room. We were impressed by the governor's foresight.

We also were impressed by his faith. Martin is the son of a minister, and he lets religion thread its way through much of his thinking.

We asked him why he was opposed to a holiday honoring Dr. Martin Luther King. He said:

"When I was in Congress, I voted for a holiday on Sunday, which I thought would be an appropriate day. He was a minister of the gospel; so was my dad. It's just that I don't think we need more days off, and I don't think that Martin Luther King Jr. crusaded for more days off."

And when we asked him who embodies the spirit of North Carolina, he said Billy Graham.

"Billy Graham epitomizes the kind of personal commitment and expression of deeply held beliefs that would be appealing to most North Carolinians," he said.

We expected Martin to be a basketball fan. After all, he was the governor of North Carolina. We were right. And when it came to sports, it was interesting the way politics worked its way in.

Martin said that he once went to a Carolina-State game and applauded good plays on both sides. At half time he was asked: "Are you for Carolina or are you for State?"

"Yes," he answered.

A *conversation with Gov. James G. "Jim" Martin.*

A recent report rated North Carolina as a leader in attracting corporations. What is the strategy?

"One thing we haven't done yet is to offer tax incentives for specific businesses to invest as other states have. We've offered a good business climate, a modest tax rate that is a uniform burden on everybody. This means once you're established, you don't have to pay taxes while your competitor comes in tax-free."

There's a tradition of unions being unable to gain a foothold in North Carolina. Why is that?

"Most workers like the relationship that they have with their employer. There is still the possibility of organizing a plant if that relationship breaks down. We've often heard the saying that a plant that gets unionized in North Carolina is probably one that deserved it."

How do you evaluate Super Tuesday, the regional primary in the South?

"I saw that all along as the briar patch. That was an initiative of the Democratic legislatures in the South. They thought it would be a powerful way to press the Democratic Party back toward the middle by putting a major barricade in front of candidates who couldn't appeal in the South. I said it would be good for political moderation if the Democratic Party does respond in a more conservative direction to that barricade, or opportunity — however you choose to look at it."

Some people refer to "the Carolinas" instead of distinguishing between North and South. Does that bother you?

"No. We do that, too. We have a lot of good relationships with people in South Carolina. I say this not just as someone who grew up there, though I recognize that the voters of North Carolina didn't hold that against me."

North Carolina has been the king of tobacco, a title that has generated a lot of pride here.

"Still does, in a way."

But now smoking is widely believed to be a health hazard. How does that affect North Carolinians' pride in tobacco?

"It affects the market. And also, the tendency of Congress to look toward cigarettes as a revenue source. When they don't want to raise taxes on anything else, they'll raise them on cigarettes. We've seen some weakening of the market in this country in recent years."

What has hurt the most?

"The farm markets have been growing, but we've been losing our share of markets overseas. That has hurt our production quotas more than anything else. North Carolina is still No. 1 in tobacco. In a way, it's a spiritual issue. It's so much an ingrown part of society in all of our rural communities."

How are the farmers' efforts to diversify working out?

"In the first year of my administration, poultry passed tobacco as the No. 1 source of income for farmers. You'll see two distinctive features as you fly low over our state. You'll see the neat, orderly, small plots of tobacco, with four rows planted and one row open for the equipment to go through. You'll recognize it. And the other thing is, you'll see these long turkey barns and chicken barns."

North Carolina's political races attract a lot of attention. What makes them so colorful?

"The big one was between Sen. Jesse Helms and former Gov. James Hunt in 1984. You had two people who had been prominent in political life here for 12 years going head to head, and that had to be quite a donnybrook. Sen. Helms is not a retiring, shy violet. He is the focus for those who are with him and those who are against him."

MARTIN PROFILE

PARTY: Republican.

IN HIS WORDS: "There is no greater challenge today than improving quality of life for our citizens. That challenge can be met through a commitment to teamwork and a management approach that allows those around you to fulfill their potential."

BORN: Dec. 11, 1935, in Savannah, Ga., to the Rev. Arthur M. Martin, Presbyterian minister, and Mary Grubbs Martin, homemaker.

FAMILY: Married Dorothy Ann "Dottie" McAulay in 1957. Mrs. Martin, 51, is a former kindergarten teacher and real estate agent. They met at church youth conference. The Martins have three children, James G. Jr., 28; Emily, 26; and Benson, 16.

EDUCATION: Bachelor of science in chemistry, Davidson College; doctorate in chemistry, Princeton University.

TIMELINE

1960: Named assistant professor of chemistry, Davidson College.

1966: Elected to two-year term on Mecklenburg County Board of Commissioners.

1968: Founded Centralina Regional Council of Governments.

1972: Elected to two-year term as U.S. representative; re-elected five times.

1984: Elected to four-year term as governor with 54.3 percent of the vote.

1989: Term expires in January; eligible for re-election.

PRIORITIES

▶ Economic development: Established task force to help farmers restructure debt; opened information clearinghouse for small businesses; established Traditional Industries Division in commerce department; proposed five-point financing plan for new business and expansions; proposed more trade missions, trade office in Pacific Rim, reinstating merchant sales tax discount.

▶ Education: Proposed expansion of career-development-ladder program for teachers; increased funding for Basic Education Program and public schools; led fight to focus on infrastructure for aging school buildings; proposed $3.5 million for pilot pre-school program.

▶ Criminal justice: Proposed tougher DWI laws, $12.5 million to improve health care and custody for prisoners, $31.8 million for new prison construction; increased number of highway patrol troopers; expanded minimum-security prison construction.

▶ Tax reform: Pushed through largest tax-cut package in state history, repeal of inventory tax; trimmed intangibles tax by $24 million.

NOTEWORTHY

Gov. Martin is only the second Republican governor to be elected in North Carolina in this century.

PERSONAL

Composes music — one of his pieces, based on the Jude Benediction, was performed at his father's funeral. . . . Loves to play golf and watch college basketball. . . . Known as voracious reader. . . . Developed award-winning chili recipe. . . . Enjoys sailing his boat *Genesis*. . . . Likes to dance, can do a mean Carolina shag.

THE FUTURE

Running for re-election in 1988. "If I'm able to win, my energies will be directed to continuing our efforts to lift North Carolina's education, transportation and business resources, with a special effort to improve adult literacy as well as early childhood readiness."

GOV. GEORGE A. 'BUD' SINNER

IMPRESSIONS

Which way to the Capitol? After dozens of domes, we were a bit taken aback by this distinctly different building before us.

We had not expected this open, rural state to be governed from a skyscraper, but there it was, looming above the grassy green mall: a 19-story building, made of gray limestone, flanked by a striking pair of shorter structures — a staid square-shaped judicial wing to the right, and a circular legislative wing to the left.

As it turned out, this unexpected piece of architecture housed the offices of an unexpected kind of governor.

Gov. George A. "Bud" Sinner is a former sugar beet farmer, but his interests extend far beyond what's growing on North Dakota soil. He demonstrated an impressive grasp of the world economy and its impact on his state.

George Sinner's global view:

▶ "Until we do realize that there really isn't any such thing as free trade in energy sources, we're in for some terribly difficult and volatile markets and volatile supplies. Eighty percent of the world's oil is owned and marketed by governments."

▶ "All the hype about the dollar having dropped is only partly true. It's really only dropped against five currencies. And for many of the currencies against which we compete, it still hasn't changed."

While some other governors seemed determined to give us a checklist of their accomplishments in office, Sinner seemed more interested in giving us an education. We had a sense that we should be able to go to the University of North Dakota and receive three credit hours for our wide-ranging session with the governor.

When we asked about what people do in their spare time in North Dakota, he began to respond with a lighthearted remark about having 10 children, but then he stopped, suddenly conscious that what he was saying might work its way into print.

"Don't you dare!"

A *conversation with Gov. George A. "Bud" Sinner.*

How do you think most of the nation perceives North Dakota?

"The perception is that it's up there where it's cold. And probably that it's an agricultural state. The reality is that it's cold some months. It's probably not nearly as cold as other states with a much higher humidity. It also has an uncommon culture and some of the most literate people in the USA."

In what ways?

"It was the first state to have statewide public broadcasting done with an incredibly intelligent central programming plan. It was the first state to have regional mental health clinics for all of its people. To this day, it maintains more nursing home beds for the elderly than any state in the nation on a per capita basis."

Fargo has been described as the least stressful place to live in the USA. Does that apply to the rest of North Dakota, as well?

"No question about that. That's why the crime rate remains low. We're low on suicides. We're low on incidences of mental illness."

Your state's economy has been badly hurt in oil and farming, two of your biggest sectors. How are North Dakotans dealing with that?

"In the near term, it's going to be pretty tough, but there are some good things showing up. The cattle industry has come back. The rancher has done very poorly, but finally this year, they're getting good prices for their feeder cattle, if they're selling. The oil industry crisis is over, provided we stop this reliance on OPEC."

You are the spokesman for 29 oil- and gas-producing states. What's ahead for them?

"Until there's a national energy policy devel-oped that's clearly understood and much more clearly articulated than anything we have now, it's pretty uncertain. We have not developed, in the USA, any defined quantification of how much reliance we can intelligently have on foreign energy sources, particularly liquid fuels."

How is North Dakota's experiment with limited casino-style gambling going?

"It's done some good things. The modest approach that's been taken here recognizes that it's perfectly all right for people to engage in recreational gambling. But there are some real risks, and if you're going to move into the area, you might want to do it on a gradual basis and feel your way along."

If the state is going to allow casino gambling, why are blue laws banning the sale of alcohol on Sunday still in effect in some areas?

"There are different reasons for different blue laws. If you're talking about Sunday marketing or Sunday business activity, it's always been a surprise to me that when you get into the Sunday-closing issue, you'll find a wide disparity of ideological thinking that supports the retention of that quiet time for society."

Do blue laws retard economic growth in North Dakota?

"They certainly have in some ways — mostly because of the growing tourism phenomenon here."

What effect has the Reagan administration had on this state?

"Devastating, really. I don't lay it all on his doorstep. Some of the problems we have seen in agriculture and the production sector — mining, forestry, manufacturing, energy — were coming. But deficit spending and overvaluation of the dollar exacerbated the crash in ways that are almost unforgivable."

SINNER PROFILE

PARTY: Democrat.

IN HIS WORDS: "Good ideas are achieved because more than one person believed they were good ideas. And the art is to get them done, not be up there waving a banner that says, 'I did this.'"

BORN: May 29, 1928, in Fargo, N.D., to Katherine A. Sinner, homemaker, and Albert F. Sinner, farmer.

FAMILY: Married Elizabeth Jane Baute in 1951. Mrs. Sinner, 57, is a "home manager and mother." The Sinners have 10 children, Robert, 36; George B., 34; Elizabeth, 33; Martha, 32; Paula, 31; Mary Jo, 30; James, 29; Gerard, 27; Joseph, 24; and Eric, 14.

EDUCATION: Bachelor of arts in philosophy, St. John's University, where he was studying for priesthood.

TIMELINE

1951: Active duty with Air National Guard during Korean War.

1953: Co-founded family partnership, Sinner Brothers and Bresnahan, a diversified family farming operation.

1962: Elected to four-year term in state Senate.

1964: Lost bid for U.S. House of Representatives.

1967: Named to State Board of Higher Education; elected chairman in 1970.

1972: Lost bid for Democratic gubernatorial nomination.

1982: Elected to two-year term in state House of Representatives.

1984: Elected to four-year term as governor with 55.3 percent of vote.

1988: Term expires in December; eligible for re-election.

PRIORITIES

▶ Economic development: Established USA's

NOTEWORTHY

In 1986 became first North Dakota governor to chair Interstate Oil Compact Division.

PERSONAL

Refuses to use chauffeur; prefers driving his van instead of Lincoln Town Car to save money — "It's a very small state, and the budgets are tight." ... Plays classical music on "boom box" in his office. ... Tennis is his favorite sport to play in good weather. ... Favorite authors include Louis L'Amour and Andrew Greeley. ... Recently started collection of baseball caps. ... Loves to watch hockey, football and boxing. ... Heroes are Eugene McCarthy, John F. Kennedy and Thomas Jefferson. ... Fan of Broadway musicals and TV star Bob Newhart.

THE FUTURE

Announced re-election bid in 1988: "I love the work. The people here are the most intelligent, responsive and attentive in the whole world."

first farm-debt restructuring program; opened trade office in Japan in 1987; initiated four-part plan to: highlight expanding industry, develop information seminars for economic development planners, attract new business and support community economic development.

▶ Health and human services: Proclaimed 1987 as Year of the Child to emphasize children's needs; declared 1988 as Year of the Family.

GOV. RICHARD F. CELESTE

IMPRESSIONS

There was a moment in our interview with Richard Celeste when we thought a major revelation might be coming.

We had heard that he had presidential aspirations and one BusCateer asked him whether he planned to run in 1988.

"He wants an honest answer, right? I'll have to think about this carefully."

A lengthy pause. Showmanship.

Of course, he knew the question was likely to come. And, of course, he knew what he would say in response. But for a few moments during that interview, Celeste seemed to be genuinely mulling over whether he wanted to be president and whether he should share his innermost thoughts with us.

Then came the not-so-newsworthy response.

"You can't be governor of Ohio and not be interested in the national decisions that are going to be made in 1988, because it will have a profound impact on the state and this region. So who sits in the White House and how that person views this country is a concern I have."

His response wasn't memorable, but his style was. He responded to a very familiar question in a manner that sounded like he was addressing it for the very first time. A sign of a skilled politician.

Celeste needed all the skills he could muster in his race in 1986 against former Gov. James A. Rhodes. Suffering from the political wounds inflicted by the closing of savings and loans during the crisis of 1985, Celeste won the election with an impressive performance on the campaign trail. As a UPI reporter observed at the time, "Celeste outworked Rhodes, outhyped, outflanked him politically and out-lucked him."

Much of our discussion with Celeste centered on Ohio's economy, but his focus seemed to be as much on Tokyo and Taiwan as Sandusky or Toledo. He suggested that states need to worry less about competing with each other.

"In the past, we've been competing with people next door and people down the street. Now we need to find ways to cooperate with those folks so that we can compete with people from Singapore, Brazil, Japan and Taiwan."

A conversation with Gov. Richard F. Celeste.

You've called Lake Erie the state's most important asset. What is the state of the lake?

"There's been an enormous improvement in the quality of water in the lake. Unfortunately, there's also been an enormous rise in the level of the lake, which has caused problems for shoreline communities. But the first and foremost concern has to be with water quality."

How are you protecting the water quality?

"We're looking through the Great Lakes Governors' Conference at a system for investing in aggressive monitoring to protect that water quality. We've done a lot of investment, over a decade now, of upgrading sewer treatment facilities along the lake communities, which has made a major difference. As someone who goes up and fishes on the lake regularly, I could tell you there are thousands and thousands of boaters out on the lake."

What's happening to industrial workers who've lost their jobs?

"Part of the transition that's involved in staying competitive globally is that many of the 45- and 50-year-old workers who come out of those old plants have a very difficult time going into another job. But with their maturity and insight, if we can help them, many of them can become entrepreneurs in their own right. And there's been a very successful entrepreneurial training program in the Youngstown-Warren area, designed for former steelworkers."

In 1985 there was a major savings and loan crisis. A number of state-chartered thrifts were closed. Could that happen again?

"It certainly couldn't happen again the same way."

Why not?

"We faced as severe a crisis in financial institutions as anyone has faced around the country. Not only principal, but interest has been returned."

A major goal of your office has been to promote Ohio. What do you think Ohio's image is?

"Ohio is viewed as one of the states that has really been successful at fighting back. When I was in Texas, every public official I talked to, some of the community college people and all of the news media were saying, 'What can we learn from Ohio?' "

What can be learned from Ohio?

"We started a program four years ago called the Eminent Scholars Program. The state provides funding to universities who compete for this money so that they can bring to their university an outstanding nationally or internationally recognized scholar."

You've brought Ohio a lot of foreign investments. How is that received here?

"I don't think you'd get a unanimous vote in favor, but you would on the basic instinct toward hospitality. People want to make new visitors welcome, particularly when they invest in their community and bring jobs."

What impact is foreign investment having?

"One of my pet projects is to create a genuinely international high school in which we could have a Japanese curriculum that meets the standards of the ministry of education in Japan and the best kind of high school curriculum here in Ohio — and maybe a German or French curriculum side by side."

What would that accomplish?

"We could get a sense of what education around the globe is like. One of the things we need to do as a state and as a country is to overcome some of our sense of cultural isolation. One of the reasons our exports aren't more effective is we're one of the few countries left out of the metric system."

CELESTE PROFILE

PARTY: Democrat.

IN HIS WORDS: "Let's build on the best in each person. Vision and cooperation are the keys to successful public service."

BORN: Nov. 11, 1937, in Cleveland, to Frank Celeste, lawyer, ex-mayor of Lakewood, Ohio, and Peg Celeste, social worker and homemaker.

FAMILY: Married Dagmar Braun in 1962. Mrs. Celeste, 46, earned a master's degree in theology and counseling in 1987 and is the former director of an alcoholism-recovery program for women. Born and raised in Austria, she met Celeste at Oxford University. The Celestes have six children, Eric, 25; Christopher, 23; Gabriella, 21; Noelle, 18; Natalie, 17; and Stephen, 11.

EDUCATION: Bachelor of arts in history, Yale University; Rhodes Scholar, Oxford University.

TIMELINE

1963: Appointed executive assistant to the U.S. ambassador to India.

1967: Became a real estate developer, National Housing Corp., Cleveland; rejoined business in 1981.

1970: Elected to two-year term in state House of Representatives; re-elected in 1972.

1974: Elected to four-year term as lieutenant governor.

1978: Lost gubernatorial bid.

1979: Named director of Peace Corps during Carter administration.

1982: Elected to four-year term as governor with 59 percent of vote; re-elected in 1986 with 61 percent of vote.

1987: Elected chairman of Midwestern Governors Conference.

1991: Term expires in January; not eligible for third consecutive term.

NOTEWORTHY
Ohio's first Rhodes Scholar governor.

PERSONAL
Worked as garbage collector, radio disc jockey, assembly-line worker, cook in 1983 to learn about typical Ohioan's day. . . . Renovated homes in Cleveland and Sandusky, Ohio. . . . Likes to make pancakes for his family on Sundays. . . . Fan of Cleveland Browns. . . . Enjoys reading mysteries and novels by Elmore Leonard and Toni Morrison. . . . Collects first edition books by Ohio author Louis Bromfield.

THE FUTURE
Not eligible for re-election. "As a governor who has run a $17 billion industry with as much diversity as you find in state government, I believe I would be qualified to be a CEO in the private sector."

PRIORITIES

▶ Economic development: Initiated "Operation Jobs" program; established "Buy Ohio" program; initiated tourism campaign; established "Thomas Edison" program to promote technological innovation through university/industry partnership.

▶ Education: Established Eminent Scholars program; increased primary and secondary school funding by 55 percent; increased Selective Excellence programs.

▶ Human services: Signed missing-children legislation; established Children's Trust Fund for abused children and program to open clinics for women and children.

▶ Tax reform: Eliminated intangibles tax; provided $10,000 exemption on personal property; cut personal property tax for business.

GOV. HENRY BELLMON

IMPRESSIONS

There's no better evidence of how quickly and dramatically the world has changed than our interview with Oklahoma Gov. Henry Bellmon, in which Will Rogers and OPEC were both prime topics of conversation.

"The thing we're most proud of is our pioneer heritage," Bellmon told us. "We became a settled area as a result of land runs that gave us a kind of select population. The people who made those runs generally tended to be adventuresome people who were looking for a new challenge. So they came in on their own and vigorously competed to get a foothold. My father was one of those and my wife's grandfather, also."

Bellmon told us humorist Will Rogers was a "very representative" Oklahoman.

"Oklahomans tend to be a little laid-back, and I think they generally have a pretty good sense of humor."

Bellmon also made clear that Oklahoma can't afford to look too much to the past. They're too busy keeping both eyes on the Persian Gulf.

"The oil crisis largely depends on what OPEC does. The problems they've been having in the Persian Gulf have caused world oil prices to stabilize and get stronger."

Bellmon, a former Marine, was the only governor we met who spoke highly of Marine Lt. Col. Oliver North.

"I admire Ollie North. You may think I'm somewhat of a redneck — and maybe I am. But a nation as large and as powerful as ours has to be involved in some rather smelly international situations. I don't fault North for what he did, and he probably deserves some of the adulation that he's received."

Bellmon has a unique political perspective. He was first elected governor in 1962 and served the single term permitted by law. In 1968, he was elected to the U.S. Senate and was re-elected in 1974. He returned to the political spotlight with his 1986 campaign for governor.

A conversation with Gov. Henry Bellmon.

At one time, Oklahoma was to be exclusively Indian territory, and it still has one of the largest Indian populations. How are Indians in Oklahoma faring?

"Some Cherokees and a few of the Plains Indians still live exclusively in Indian communities and have not found ways of fitting into the total society. On balance, our Indians are better off than the Indians who live on reservations. They're well accepted in our state. William Keller, who was chief of the Cherokees, was head of Phillips Petroleum for many years. He was probably the highest-paid executive we had in our state. We have many Indians who have been government officials. So, Indians in Oklahoma do fairly well."

Humorist Will Rogers was a Cherokee, also. Was he representative of Oklahomans' style, or attitude, toward the government?

"I think he was very representative. Oklahomans tend to be a little laid-back, and I think they have generally a pretty good sense of humor. And even though our population has shifted a lot from the rural to the urban center since Will Rogers lived, most of us still have rural backgrounds within the last couple of generations. He was not atypical at all."

What's the long-range outlook for oil in Oklahoma?

"Natural gas is really more in our future than crude oil. We probably will not find any more large oil fields, but we have enormous natural gas potential, basically from the deeper horizons, those down around 20,000 feet, even beyond."

How does the future look for gas?

"Gas prices are so low that you can't afford to drill to those depths to find gas, so right now, the gas business is not good. But unlike crude oil, we produce most of the natural gas we use in our country. Our petroleum future is heavily tied to natural gas. We're probably within two years of a major gas shortage again, and when we do get a shortage of natural gas, then prices will obviously be better, and we'll see another expansion of drilling and developmental activities."

What do Oklahomans do to relax and have fun?

"When you're in Muskogee, you'll be in a fine recreational area, built mostly around water sports: fishing, skiing, swimming. In addition, we have some of the best quail hunting in the world in Oklahoma. We also have at least a few good recreational parks, one in Oklahoma City, and a pretty good one near Tulsa. The Cherokees operate it. We also have a lot of emphasis on athletics, not only on the college level but at high school as well."

You were a U.S. senator for more than a decade. What's the difference between being a senator and being governor?

"I like the governor's job much better. You're more in direct line of command and at least have the opportunity of being in charge of what goes on. In the Senate, particularly if you're in the minority party, you're always being jerked around by other people, and you never have any real voice in setting agendas, or you're never in charge of your own schedule. Governors can make things happen."

Is it easy to get things done in Oklahoma?

"It's tough. We have a weak governor by decision of our constitutional writers. We'd had a series of territorial governors before we became a state, and many of them had tended to be rather heavy-handed; so the constitution took a lot of the power away from the governors and gave it to boards made up of lay people."

BELLMON PROFILE

PARTY: Republican.

IN HIS WORDS: "I like to see things grow and I like to be the captain of my own ship. I really don't have any question I can do it. If people think you can get something done, then you've got a head start."

BORN: Sept. 3, 1921, on a farm near Tonkawa, Okla., to George and Edith Bellmon, farmers.

FAMILY: Married Shirley Osborn in 1947. Mrs. Bellmon, 60, is a homemaker. The Bellmons have three daughters, Patricia, 40; Gail, 37; and Ann, 35.

EDUCATION: Bachelor of science in agriculture, Oklahoma Agricultural and Mechanical College (now Oklahoma State University.)

TIMELINE

1942: Joined Marine Corps.

1945: Took over family wheat and cattle farm; owns oil wells on property.

1946: Elected to two-year term in state House of Representatives; founded soil conservation contracting business.

1960: Elected chairman, state Republican Party.

1962: Elected to four-year term as governor with 55.2 percent of vote; limited by law (changed in 1965) to one term.

1967: Returned to farm; co-founded Rush Metals in Billings, Okla.; national chairman, Nixon for President Committee.

1968: Elected to six-year term as U.S. senator; re-elected in 1974.

1980: Became news commentator, Oklahoma television station KOCO.

1981: Named adjunct professor, Oklahoma City University.

1983: Appointed director of state human services department; also was in-residence

---

NOTEWORTHY

In 1962, elected Oklahoma's first Republican governor. . . . First Oklahoma governor to serve in the U.S. Senate and then return to governor's office. . . . Oklahoma's second governor to serve second term.

PERSONAL

Enjoys quail hunting. . . . Fishes in pond on his farm. . . . Can nap at short notice and arise at 3 a.m. to read. . . . Favorite leisure activity is working on the farm. . . . Political hero is Dwight D. Eisenhower; personal heroine is his mother, Edith.

THE FUTURE

Expects to return to farming in 1991. "I really haven't looked beyond this term. I assume I have to approach it as the end of my political career. I'll be 69 years old — but anything's possible."

---

lecturer, Central State University; adjunct professor, Oklahoma State University.

1986: Re-elected governor with 47 percent of vote.

1991: Term expires in January; eligible for re-election.

PRIORITIES

▶ Economic development: Proposed establishment of business assistance center and energy marketing office.

▶ Tax reform: Proposed 6-cent gas tax hike, tort reform and 7 percent cut in income tax.

▶ Education: Proposed increase of more than $100 million in education budget; supports "no pass, no play" rule for extracurricular student activities.

▶ Criminal justice: Proposed delaying parole until inmates can read and write; proposed use of existing space to cut overcrowding.

GOV. NEIL GOLDSCHMIDT

IMPRESSIONS

Neil Goldschmidt was born to run. While voters in New Mexico elected as governor a man who had never held elected office, Oregon voters chose someone who has run for and won virtually every office he's come across.

Goldschmidt may well challenge George Bush for thickest resume of the 20th century.

As a high school junior, Goldschmidt was elected vice president of the student body. He went on to become student president at the University of Oregon. After a two-year term on the Portland City Commission, he was elected mayor of Portland.

In 1979, President Carter appointed him secretary of transportation. When Carter left office, Goldschmidt turned to another form of transportation: running shoes.

After serving as vice president of Nike Inc., Goldschmidt decided it was time to pursue the governorship. What appealed to him most about the job, he said, was that it could be a very flexible position.

"I found that it was possible, to some extent, to make up the job. What it is that you feel needs to be done. The thing that I like the best about public service — what I liked as mayor — is the ability to get to the microlevel to see what is going on, and to extract from that the information and the understanding that will allow you to change policies, or practices, or whatever, to be able to solve problems."

He has an interesting sense of public relations: During our interview, he permitted two young girls — roughly about 9 and 10 — to stand near the door and listen. At the close of the interview he even invited them over to have their photograph taken with the group.

What surprised us most was when he handed the gift we had just given him — a gold-plated paperweight bearing the USA TODAY logo — to one of the girls, saying she could take it to school with her if she promised to return it some day.

We left the office not knowing quite what to think. We had given similar gifts to more than 30 governors by that point, but this was the first time anyone had given it away before we could leave the office. A remarkably generous man? Or just a deep aversion to paperweights?

A conversation with Gov. Neil Goldschmidt.

Is the economy of your state sufficiently diversified?

"No, and I think that's really a function of whether we're willing to make investments in education. You go look at the national GNP list by states — we're now below the average income in the United States. Almost the total difference between us and the state of Washington is Boeing."

Federal lands comprise about 50 percent of the state. What are you looking for from the federal government?

"We need reforestation; 80 percent of the trees we're harvesting now are on federal land. The second concern for us is whether the United States government will invest in a major way in education."

What do you think the image of Oregon and its residents should be to those outside the state?

"This is a state where people are imbued with a tremendous feeling about the land they've inherited. People come here hauling their possessions behind them down the Columbia Gorge, and it impacts them the same way it has everybody since Lewis and Clark. You can't avoid it."

How do they show their love for the land?

"We have a statewide land use plan. Oswald West, who was governor way back, declared the beaches public highways and thereby protected them from anybody building on them."

How can you tell the difference between a native and someone who's come here from somewhere else?

"Oh, you can't. You know, it's a little bit like converts to Judaism, or Catholicism, or whatever religion they choose. The converts are much tougher than the natives. This is not a place that's easy for a transient to wander into. If you decide to come here, it's because you heard about it and you want to be here, or you've been here once and you want to come back."

How does someone become a convert?

"One of the major Japanese companies that invested in this state was the byproduct of its president coming to Portland for the Davis Cup tennis playoffs. He got out and drove around, went back to Tokyo, and essentially said to the management of the company, 'If we ever put a business in the United States, I want you to go to Oregon. Check it out.' They did, they liked it, and they put the business in."

The eastern part of the state and the western part of the state are very different. What challenge does that present?

"Today, we have 40 percent of the state's population and 50 percent of the state's economy in three counties around Portland. Twenty percent of the income growth in this state has been in one county for the past five years."

And the rest of the state?

"Central Oregon is almost its own state in the sense that its climate is so different, and its economy is so different. But it's also got assets that none of the rest of us have, the most important of which is that 300 days a year, you can be out and enjoy the weather."

How has modernization affected the timber industry?

"Changes have hammered the timber industry — very substantial increases in productivity. When I grew up in Eugene, in 1950, when I was 10, there was a mill that had over 1,000 employees. Today, there's a mill in Eugene that has about 160 employees turning out double the board footage. We have to do it to be competitive, but the labor base inside that industry, obviously, has shrunk."

GOLDSCHMIDT PROFILE

PARTY: Democrat.

IN HIS WORDS: "The power of the governor is a bully pulpit. It's a job where there's enormous potential to deliver a quality product."

BORN: June 16, 1940, in Eugene, Ore., to Lester Goldschmidt, accountant, and Annette Goldschmidt, homemaker.

FAMILY: Married Margie Wood in 1965. Mrs. Goldschmidt, 44, is a homemaker. The Goldschmidts have two children, Joshua, 18, and Rebecca, 15.

EDUCATION: Bachelor of arts in political science, University of Oregon; law degree, University of California at Berkeley.

TIMELINE

1967: Practiced law with Legal Aid Service.

1970: Elected to Portland, Ore., city commission.

1972: Elected to four-year term as mayor of Portland, Ore.; re-elected in 1976; established model mass transit system.

1979: Appointed secretary, U.S. Department of Transportation.

1981: Named vice president, Nike Inc.; named president, Nike Canada Ltd. in 1984; named board chairman, Nike Canada Ltd. in 1985.

1986: Elected to four-year term as governor with 52 percent of vote.

1991: Term expires in January; eligible for re-election.

PRIORITIES

▶ Economic development: Established Regional Strategies Program to provide funds and assistance for developing an economic strategy; reformed workers' compensation system to lower rates and maintain benefits.

NOTEWORTHY

Only USA governor to serve as mayor, cabinet secretary, corporate executive and governor. . . . Spent $2.6 million on 1986 campaign — record for Oregon governor's race.

PERSONAL

Enjoys walking and swimming, goes river rafting with family. "I like all kinds of sports." . . . Collects wine. . . . Heroes are John F. Kennedy, Winston Churchill and '60s anti-war activist Allard Lowenstein. . . . Prefers to read non-fiction, especially biographies and history books.

THE FUTURE

"I've made a number of promises to the people of Oregon and there still is a lot of work to be done. It's premature to think about future plans at this point."

▶ Criminal justice: Added 1,700 beds for jails and rehabilitation programs; proposed $54 million prison reform program.

▶ Education: Initiated School Finance Commission to develop school funding plan.

▶ Human services: Developed "children's agenda" by investigating issues around the state.

▶ Environment: Proposed Forest Practices Act to encourage public involvement in planning.

GOV. ROBERT P. CASEY

IMPRESSIONS

While running for the governor's office in 1986, Robert Casey said the job required "someone with guts, someone to lay it on the line, someone willing to take risks and fight for the families of Pennsylvania."

That statement from some politicians would be campaign rhetoric. For Casey, though, taking political risks has become a way of life.

This is a man who had been defeated in three attempts to reach the governor's office. He had lost campaigns for the Democratic nomination in 1966, 1970 and 1978. In two elections, other candidates with the same name siphoned off votes.

Although he had been elected auditor general in 1966 and again in 1972, it still took considerable courage for Casey to pursue yet another election for the top job in the state.

"My wife said to me, 'My God, are you prepared to lose a fourth time?' and I said, 'Yeah. Let me ask you a question. Are you prepared to win?' "

Casey said the earlier losses taught him some valuable lessons.

"It gives you a sense of where the power comes from, and as old Harry Truman used to say, 'You have to have a sense that you're a trustee for the power, you don't own it, you didn't create it, and it doesn't belong to you.' And I think you develop that sense after you've been kicked around a little bit."

Pennsylvania has faced tough times in recent years, particularly in the steel and coal industries. Still, Casey seems to personify the determination of the people of Pennsylvania.

"They've been knocked down themselves," Casey said. "They've had to pick themselves up, dust themselves off and keep going."

That's something Casey can identify with.

A conversation with Gov. Robert P. Casey.

You have several fine universities in this state. Are your young people staying here?

"They tend to move. That's been one of our major problems for a generation. We've been exporting talent to other states. We've got to reverse that trend by diversifying our economic base and jump-starting the economy in this state right across the board in manufacturing, and in the service economy and high tech."

Have you been able to offset the manufacturing loss?

"In recent years, it has been somewhat offset by gains in high tech and the service economy. But you cannot sustain the economy with high-tech and service jobs alone. You've got to have that undergirding of manufacturing support."

What changes could be made to attract businesses?

"One thing that's very important, and it doesn't cost 5 cents, is the personal commitment of the governor to be involved himself."

In what way?

"How many times have you heard the story of the chief executive officer who goes, for example, to South Carolina, has breakfast with the governor, and when the breakfast is over, the governor takes out his personal card, turns it over, writes his home phone number, hands it to the fellow, and says, 'If I can be of any help, please call me.' I've heard these kinds of stories about Lamar Alexander, Tennessee's former governor."

Did that help Tennessee get the Saturn auto plant?

"Saturn came about in significant measure because Alexander was a better salesman. There you have a national contract with the same work rules that would apply, no matter what state Saturn went to. So it wasn't any kind of competitive advantage in terms of working rules or hourly rates or anything like that. It was something else."

What should the federal government be doing to help states?

"We need a much more aggressive policy on steel, for example. If the national government's going to write off the steel industry, that's not my view of what should be occurring. Also we have communities in this state that can't treat their sewage water. And the money's being cut back. That's why our economic development plan has a component for investing in environmental infrastructure. But it doesn't begin to meet the overall need that's there."

What will it take to solve the problem?

"If the federal government thinks the principle of volunteerism will permit people to handle those problems by themselves, that's crazy."

You've got a remarkably diverse state. How many states of Pennsylvania are there?

"There's at least two when you analyze it in economic terms, the affluent Pennsylvania and the Pennsylvania that's not doing nearly as well. There was a story in *The New York Times* some years ago when presidential candidates descended on Pennsylvania and said, 'There's no way we can campaign in Pennsylvania or even understand it. It's really five states.' Look at the television markets. You've got the Ohio border, the Maryland border, the New York border and everything in between. It's really four or five states in that sense."

Do people still feel strongly about Three Mile Island?

"They're as concerned as they've ever been. The Chernobyl incident brings it all back again."

CASEY PROFILE

PARTY: Democrat.

IN HIS WORDS: "It's a great job and it's a great state. I'm enjoying it. It's a tough job, as tough as I expected it to be."

BORN: Jan. 9, 1932, in Jackson Heights, N.Y., to Alphonsus Casey, lawyer, and Marie Casey, homemaker.

FAMILY: Married Ellen Harding in 1953. Mrs. Casey, 56, is a homemaker. The Caseys have eight children, Margi, 34; Mary Ellen, 31; Kate, 30; Robert Jr., 28; Christopher, 27; Erin, 25; Patrick, 22; and Matthew, 17.

EDUCATION: Bachelor of arts in English, Holy Cross College, Indiana; law degree, George Washington University.

TIMELINE

1956: Practiced law with Covington and Burling; joined Nogi, O'Malley, and Harris in 1958; became partner in firm Casey, Haggerty and McDonnell in 1963; founded solo law practice in 1973; became senior partner in Dilworth, Paxson, Kalish and Kauffman in 1979.

1962: Elected to four-year term in state Senate.

1966: Lost bid for Democratic gubernatorial nomination; lost again in 1970 and 1978.

1968: Elected to four-year term as state auditor general; re-elected in 1972.

1986: Elected to four-year term as governor with 50.7 percent of vote.

1991: Term expires in January; eligible for re-election.

PRIORITIES

▶ Economic development: Reorganized state Department of Commerce; established Economic Development Partnership to set policy, develop jobs and establish a "response team" to advise businesses in trouble and attract new business.

NOTEWORTHY
Half of his Cabinet is run by women and minority department chiefs — a first in Pennsylvania.

PERSONAL
Enjoys playing golf. . . . Runs, walks a few miles a day around neighborhood. . . . Loves to read, especially newspapers. . . . Keeps a picture of his father — his hero — and a bust of John F. Kennedy in his office. . . . Loves all spectator sports, especially basketball.

THE FUTURE
Might try for second term in 1990. "I've run for governor four times so running a fifth time would not be a difficult decision to make."

▶ Education: Proposed $428 million funding increase, minimum starting salaries for teachers, tuition-loan waiver for students who agree to teach in rural areas and a program to encourage parental involvement in schools; increased scholarship funds 20 percent.

▶ Environment: Mandated $61 million fine against Texas Eastern Pipeline Co. for dumping toxic polychlorinated biphenyls; proposed mandatory recycling; established program to improve water and sewer systems; proposed state's first hazardous-waste cleanup program.

▶ Tax reform: Proposed program to reduce reliance on property taxes and to encourage economic growth and expansion.

GOV. EDWARD D. DiPRETE

IMPRESSIONS

If Norman Vincent Peale had not written *The Power of Positive Thinking*, Edward DiPrete might have.

The first Republican governor in Rhode Island in 18 years, DiPrete is accustomed to bucking the odds.

When DiPrete became governor in 1984, Rhode Island was struggling to overcome years of economic decline. Many now credit DiPrete with leading an economic revival.

DiPrete doesn't do much chest beating, but his pride is apparent.

"For years, Rhode Island has gone around with an inferiority complex. But I think the state is on a roll now," he said.

DiPrete, who once sold real estate for a living, now sells the state of Rhode Island.

"We had our 350th anniversary of the founding of Rhode Island in 1986," he said. "We had a poll taken in 1984 and one out of three people felt the state was headed in the right direction. That figure is now up to 70 percent."

DiPrete promised to run Rhode Island like a business, and he has improved the state's bottom line. He successfully pushed for a 16 percent reduction in the state income tax as well as the repeal of estate taxes. Still, the state enjoyed a surplus in 1987 of about $80 million.

DiPrete, the father of seven, said he turns to his Winnebago motorhome for relaxation.

"I usually drive down by the ocean. I find it very relaxing to go to Newport, down to Fort Adams, Beaver Tail or Jamestown, Narragansett, on the West Bay part of the state. I go frequently, even if it's only for a few hours."

We didn't have to hear any more. Clearly this was a governor who enjoyed the road as much as we did, and we invited him out to the bus.

He wasn't the only governor on our tour who asked to see our newsroom on wheels, but he was the first who looked as though he might seriously abandon his job to hit the open road. As he sat in the driver's seat of our BusCapade bus, we understood exactly how he felt.

A

conversation with Gov. Edward D. DiPrete.

Would you describe your management style as similar to that of a chief executive officer?

"Yes. As governor, I have stressed a management style of government which is evidenced by a spirit of cooperation between government and industry, state and local leaders, industry and our universities, and management and labor. In addition, I reinforce my management style by setting priorities, maintaining a state budget surplus, and by delegating authority to my staff and members of my cabinet."

Which welfare programs should be established at the federal level and which programs are best left to the state governments?

"Among the welfare programs that could be established at the national level are AFDC, food stamps and Medicaid. Those best left to state governments include programs dealing with shelters, homeless, teen-age pregnancy and child care."

Some critics of employment and training programs have stated that the best way to get people off welfare is to improve a state's overall economy. How do you respond to that criticism?

"Improving the state's economy is an important part of getting individuals to become self-sufficient. An improved economy creates job opportunities. However, because opportunities exist does not mean that people on welfare can access those jobs. Often they encounter barriers to their participation in the workforce such as a lack of adequate day care, the need for better transportation systems, and the lack of necessary educational and job skills. Employment and training programs are vital if we are to break down the barriers that welfare recipients encounter as they try to reach self-sufficiency."

Should public schools teach AIDS education?

"Yes. Following my direction and recommendation, the Department of Elementary and Secondary Education in Rhode Island implemented a program for students at the junior high school level to educate students about the disease. This action, in February 1987, I have been told, made Rhode Island the first state in the country to mandate AIDS education. At the same time, I proposed to my colleagues in the National Governors' Association that they approve a similar policy statement. I was pleased that at the NGA's annual meeting in July this statement was unanimously approved."

How have Rhode Island officials dealt with problems such as hunger and homelessness?

"We have our share of the homeless and people who need help, the same as any other state. I have tackled the problem head on, and I'm sure there are some people who probably rightfully will say we should do more. We established line-item appropriations in the state budget in '85 for the homeless and hungry. That has been increased substantially."

How important has the sea been to the well-being of the state?

"The sea is very important. Commercial fishing is prosperous in the state. The sea is also very important from a recreational point of view. Tourism now has become a major industry. The America's Cup has a lot to do with it."

Every state has hidden treasures. What is the most overlooked tourist attraction in your state?

"Rhode Island offers a tremendous number of tourist attractions throughout the state; however, I believe that our most overlooked attraction is the Blithwold Gardens and Arboretum which is located in Bristol, just a few miles north of Newport. This magnificent site includes a beautiful 45-room turn-of-the-century mansion and 33 acres of landscaped grounds, gardens and plants overlooking Newport."

DiPRETE PROFILE

PARTY: Republican.

IN HIS WORDS: "I like the executive branch of government. You can make things happen more quickly. The legislative branch is too deliberative for my style. I'm very happy that I'm governor."

BORN: July 8, 1934, in Cranston, R.I., to Frank DiPrete, immigrant carpenter and real estate salesman, and Mary DiPrete, homemaker.

FAMILY: Married Patricia Hines in 1956. Mrs. DiPrete, 53, is a homemaker and former nurse. The DiPretes have seven children, Edward Jr., 31; Dennis, 30; Nancy, 29; Patricia, 27; Mary Ellen, 25; Kathleen, 22; and Thomas, 21.

EDUCATION: Bachelor of science in business administration and philosophy, College of the Holy Cross in Massachusetts.

TIMELINE

1955: Joined Naval Reserve.

1959: Named vice president of father's firm, Frank A. DiPrete Realty Co.

1970: Elected to Cranston School Commission; re-elected in 1972; elected to four-year term on Cranston City Council in 1974.

1978: Elected to four-year term as mayor of Cranston; re-elected in 1982.

1984: Elected to two-year term as governor with 60 percent of vote; re-elected in 1986 with 65 percent of vote.

1987: Elected chairman, Coalition of Northeastern Governors; chairman, New England Governors' Conference.

1989: Term expires in January; eligible for re-election.

PRIORITIES

▶ Economic development: Created Rhode Island Partnership for Science and Technology; opened Business Action Center; orga-

NOTEWORTHY
In 1984 became Rhode Island's first Republican governor in 18 years.

PERSONAL
Loves to play Pac-Man. . . . Does family shopping in local supermarkets. . . . Family takes in strays so house is usually full of pets. . . . Likes to get away in Winnebago camper. "We like to drive down to the ocean and unwind."

THE FUTURE
Running for re-election in 1988. "In this state, you never stop running for office, whether it's governor or even mayor, if you happen to have a two-year term."

nized Governor's Small Business Advisory Council; proposed job training program.

▶ Education: Signed bill requiring mandatory AIDS education in schools; appointed task force to study state education; pushed through bill mandating that cities spend up to 5 percent of funding on dropout and literacy programs; proposed establishing preschools for disadvantaged children.

▶ Tax reform: Cut state income tax by over 20 percent since 1985; repealed state gift and estate taxes, gross-earnings taxes on oil companies and/or utilities and net worth tax.

▶ Environment: Signed mandatory recycling law; enacted $65 million bond issue to acquire land, recreation areas; proposed environmental trust fund for secondary waste treatment and establishing environmental quality department.

▶ Affordable housing: Created special governor's staff on housing and human services advisory committee; proposed rent-subsidy program and 15-year rental-housing program; established "Project Independence" to help mothers on welfare acquire homes.

GOV. CARROLL A. CAMPBELL JR.

IMPRESSIONS

Carroll Campbell and the state he serves have a lot in common. They both have changed — a lot — during the past few years. Yet, bits and pieces of the state's past still influence Campbell's and other South Carolinians' thinking. There's an ongoing effort to decide how much of the past should be preserved; how much should be forgotten.

Campbell spends his days in a Capitol that has the Confederate flag flying on top of it. Yet, the building sits in Columbia, the epitome of the New South, the Sun Belt South.

Campbell talked to us about the flag: "It's not a major issue. We poll it all the time. It flies by resolution of the General Assembly. They put it up and, by resolution, they can take it down. But essentially, it's not controversial. Unfortunately, it polarizes along racial lines, but it's not something that comes up very often."

In 1970, Campbell, a clean-cut, pleasant Southerner, spent most of the year fighting school desegregation. His activities earned him the wrath of civil rights groups but helped get him elected to the South Carolina House of Representatives.

Thirteen years later, he was mentioned by *U.S. News & World Report* as one of the USA's "up-and-coming" governors for his pre-school-education reform — reform expected to benefit all South Carolinians, black and white.

South Carolina and Campbell yesterday.

South Carolina and Campbell today.

Campbell was most enthusiastic when he was talking with us about economic development. More industry. More jobs. From Great Britain. From France. From Japan. From Germany. People and businesses from all over the world moving to the state.

We realized development was the South Carolina and Campbell of today — and of the future.

A conversation with Gov. Carroll A. Campbell Jr.

Who are your competitors in your recruiting efforts?

"It's regional, to some degree. All of the foreign people coming into the USA now — the Japanese, the Koreans, Germans, British — look at the United States objectively. They say, OK, where do we need to go in the marketplace to be competitive? If you use that as the single criterion for location, they all look to the Southeast first."

What do they see as the advantages?

"We don't have major labor problems; we don't have a harsh environment where you lose work days to the weather. We've got a lot of water. We attracted the Michelin Corp. a few years ago. Germany has just announced major expansions of its two facilities here."

Is there a conflict here between "Buy USA" and the push to attract foreign firms?

"No. They make it in the USA. Michelin tires are made right here in South Carolina. Companies come in with their headquarters because so many of our companies that we look upon as USA companies really aren't. They are part of international conglomerates. Companies like Electrolux AB of Sweden that own subsidiaries operating as American companies like White Consolidated Industries Inc. We're very careful in trying to recruit them. We've been very successful."

We've never seen quite so much "Buy USA" sentiment in a state — on radio and television, people on the street, in the factories. Why?

"The textile industry mounted a major campaign to encourage people to 'Buy USA,' to recognize that their jobs are affected by their neighbors' purchasing habits. It was just to let people be aware of how it impacts their lives and jobs."

Is the campaign working?

"There has been an increased awareness across the country. It worked fairly well."

Georgia is called the Peach State, yet South Carolina grows more peaches than Georgia does. Is Georgia stealing the show?

"We don't get real upset about that. We have a very strong peach and apple market in South Carolina. We are diversifying our agricultural base, just like we're trying to do our manufacturing base."

Segregated private clubs have been in the news here. What should the state's role be?

"First, I found out that the state was subsidizing employees' use of clubs, and I stopped that. All taxpayers pay into the government, and to support segregated clubs with taxpayers' funds is absolutely wrong. On the other side, from an issue of free choice where there's no government involved whatsoever, people have a right to associate any way they want to. So, I draw a clear distinction between people's rights of privacy and association and the government's rights in opening things up."

How is the economy in Columbia, the state capital, doing?

"Columbia has had essentially a recession-proof economy. It's an economy based in the government, in the university. We have Fort Jackson here and the University of South Carolina. Columbia is growing. It is becoming a true capital city. It is attracting a diversity to its economic base, and we're working hard on that economic development. It's our primary focus. In Greenville, we have the largest concentration of engineers per capita of any area in the country."

What has the Jim and Tammy Bakker episode done for religion in the Carolinas?

"It's done a lot to hurt the TV ministers. But it's probably done a lot to restore some of the support for mainstream beliefs."

CAMPBELL PROFILE

PARTY: Republican.

IN HIS WORDS: "I don't believe that you improve individuals by improving society. Instead, I believe you improve society by giving individuals the opportunity to improve themselves."

BORN: July 24, 1940, in Greenville, S.C., to textile mill superintendent Carroll Campbell Sr. and Anne Campbell, homemaker.

FAMILY: Married Iris Rhodes in 1959. Mrs. Campbell, 48, is a homemaker. The Campbells have two children, Carroll "Tumpy" III, 24, and Mike, 19.

EDUCATION: Master of arts in political science, American University.

TIMELINE

1959: Worked for real estate firm, L.A. Moseley.

1962: Co-founded Handee Park, parking business in Greenville, S.C..

1969: Lost bid for state House of Representatives; elected to four-year term in 1970.

1974: Lost bid for lieutenant governor; named executive assistant to South Carolina Gov. James B. Edwards in 1975.

1976: Elected to four-year term in state Senate.

1978: Elected to two-year term in U.S. House of Representatives; re-elected three times.

1986: Elected to four-year term as governor with 51.04 percent of vote.

1991: Term expires in January; eligible for re-election.

PRIORITIES

▶ Economic development: Set up a rural development initiative to develop infrastructure; pushed through fund to tie highway improvement to job creation; created state office to cut through red tape for small or new businesses; proposed regional airline hub.

▶ Education: Proposed increasing spending by more than $83 million; established Governor's School for Science and Mathematics; initiated program to fight illiteracy.

▶ Criminal justice: Signed bill including tougher penalties for drunken drivers and repeat offenders; proposed $4 million funding for youth services, including skills training as alternative to incarceration.

▶ Drug abuse and drug education: Opened drug information hot line; proposed $3 million in drug enforcement grants to target drug traffickers.

NOTEWORTHY

Elected South Carolina's second Republican governor this century.

PERSONAL

Worked from age 12 in grocery stores, for surveyors, cleaning cotton, cutting cloth. . . . Avid outdoorsman, loves hunting, deep sea fishing. . . . Enjoys watching college football. . . . Favorite music is rhythm and blues. . . . Runs, plays golf and rides exercycle. . . . Loves to read, especially periodicals.

THE FUTURE

"I've got a great job as governor of South Carolina. This state is moving ahead and I'm delighted to be able to play a role in this growth and progress. I'm not ready to announce specific plans, but I can certainly foresee running again for the office of governor in 1990."

GOV. GEORGE S. MICKELSON

IMPRESSIONS

Many young boys dream of being "just like dad" when they grow up. George Mickelson has come closer than most.

Mickelson's father was the 18th governor of South Dakota. Mickelson is the 28th. As he visited with us on a sunny June day, Mickelson reflected on the changing face of South Dakota.

"In 1947, when my dad was governor of this state, we were talking about a boom economy. We had come out of World War II with the world dependent on the industrialization of the United States, and South Dakota was in the heartland of the breadbasket."

Today, Mickelson notes, "It's a changing world. The economies that were no threat to us then — Japan, Germany and the European countries — are all countries that we are competing with."

That global perspective doesn't get in the way when Mickelson chooses to be a down-home, close-to-the-roots politician. He proved that while joining us on our bus ride to Eureka, population 1,300, where this author's hometown was celebrating its centennial.

Not only did Mickelson seem to get a genuine kick out of being interviewed aboard our 40-foot bus, but he also clearly was delighted to hit the streets of Eureka, shaking hands, exchanging small talk, addressing the crowd from a small wooden stage.

Mickelson might not be as colorful as predecessor Bill Janklow, but there's a warmth and genuineness about him, as well as an apparently heartfelt affection for his state.

"Being able to be involved and living some of the history of the state is very exciting to me. I pulled one of the first, if not the first, dynamite switches at Crazy Horse (monument) in June of 1947, when Korczak Ziolkowski began that project," Mickelson recalled.

Now, Mickelson takes his children to Crazy Horse and hopes they will one day take their children to see a completed monument.

Mickelson's family is clearly important to him. He seems determined not to allow his public life to damage his private life. He said he sets aside 10 days each month during which "I know I'm going to be home for supper."

A conversation with Gov. George S. Mickelson.

Does striving for diversification mean the family farm as we knew it is a thing of the past?

"No, but the definition of the family farm is changing. You can't buy a $70,000 tractor anymore and, with today's prices, make it pay off by farming a quarter section of land. So the size of the farms is increasing, but it's never going to be a thing of the past. I'm very aggressively seeking some markets for our agricultural producers in terms of processing and different ways of producing."

For example?

"I'm working with a company that wants to invest $50 million in this state in a hog-confinement unit. I'm being criticized by some who are saying we're taking the hog production away from the family farm. That's just simply not true. We kill over 3 million hogs a year in this state, and we produce only a million and a half. We have always been afraid to take some risks in this state, and I'm going to take some risks in the hope that we will be able to make progress."

Are South Dakota's small towns going to continue to shrink in size, or stay flat, or will some of this diversification and industry you're talking about change the situation?

"Diversification of our economy — and the excitement that even the small towns have in this state about playing a role in that — holds some hope for them maintaining a population base, and a business base. But yet, we have to be realistic. We aren't going to save all 314 incorporated communities in this state. There are some that are going to continue to shrink and will go by the wayside just as they have in the past."

In some of the small towns that you were talk- ing about, the population is 50 percent to 60 percent senior citizens. Is there a responsibility for the state to help them?

"The percentage of our population that is senior citizens is probably higher than most states. Yes, the state has a responsibility. As a society, we need to continue to look for alternatives, congregate housing, and those kinds of things, for our senior citizens. Small-town South Dakota is going to develop, to a large extent, around health-care facilities. That's big business in this state. I have directed our health department and our medical school to work cooperatively — traditionally they have worked on separate tracks. I have insisted that they work together to help us in a rural health-care delivery plan, which this state really doesn't have, and which also includes the reservations."

What would you like the image of South Dakota to be?

"Image and self-perception is something we're working very hard on. My goal is to diversify our economy. We're the most agricultural state in the nation. That's not necessarily bad, except that in the last several years, when the agricultural economy has been hurting, it has provided some real challenges for us."

Is that a continuation of what your predecessor, Gov. William Janklow, started?

"In many ways, he kicked the state in the pants to ensure we were flexible in legislation, which resulted in Citibank, and in putting South Dakota on the map, by being a very strong advocate for rural America. My approach is to continue that, but also to recognize that we need additional tools."

Such as?

"I am a big believer in developing higher education."

MICKELSON PROFILE

PARTY: Republican.

IN HIS WORDS: "I am really an optimist at heart. I have always had the attitude that I can do just about anything that I set my mind to if I prepare for it. But I'm learning that isn't necessarily true."

BORN: Jan. 31, 1941, in Walworth County, S.D., to George T. Mickelson, former South Dakota governor, and Madge Mickelson, homemaker.

FAMILY: Married Linda McCahren in 1963. Mrs. Mickelson, 46, is a homemaker, former teacher and bookkeeper. The Mickelsons have three children, Mark, 22; Amy, 19; and David, 16.

EDUCATION: Bachelor of science in business administration, law degree, University of South Dakota.

TIMELINE

1965: Joined the Army; served in Vietnam.

1968: Named assistant state attorney general; elected Brookings County state's attorney in 1970.

1974: Elected to two-year term in state House of Representatives; re-elected twice; rejected 1980 re-election bid to spend more time with family.

1980: Elected to state Board of Pardons and Parole.

1986: Elected to four-year term as governor with 52 percent of vote.

1991: Term expires in January; eligible for re-election.

PRIORITIES

▶ Economic development: Won a one-year, 1-cent hike in sales tax to create revolving, low-interest loan fund; raised minimum wage.

▶ Education: Established higher education

NOTEWORTHY
The only governor of South Dakota whose father was also governor of the state.

PERSONAL
Plays basketball. . . .Golf handicap is 15. . . . Likes to take his son David out in his 19-foot boat to fish. . . . Favorite author is James A. Michener.. . . Rides horses, loves to herd cattle. . . . Secret ambition — to be a cowboy or a jet pilot.

THE FUTURE
Term expires in 1991. "I made this career decision. Whether it be in three years or seven years there is going to have to be another career decision. I told my wife it's her turn to decide what we'll do next."

"future fund" for research and development.

▶ Health and human services: Declared moratorium on expanding nursing home facilities; mandated screening process to increase awareness of alternatives to nursing-home care.

▶ Tax reform: Created advisory commission to study state tax structure.

GOV. NED McWHERTER

IMPRESSIONS

Wknew Ned McWherter had an "open-door" policy, but we hadn't realized how wide open those doors could be.

Joining us for our interview on that April day in Nashville were more than a dozen local reporters and staffers and some local political hangers-on, including John Jay Hooker, who had run twice unsuccessfully for governor. McWherter's office was wall-to-wall people.

McWherter clearly enjoyed center stage.

While he's not known as a great public speaker, this setting was perfect for him. He answered our questions straightforwardly. He also seemed to play to the audience.

If the federal government decided to place the Supercollider atom smasher in Tennessee, where would he suggest putting it, McWherter was asked.

"It will be east of the Mississippi River and west of the Smoky Mountains," McWherter responded diplomatically. That meant all of Tennessee had a chance. The room filled with laughter.

This multimillionaire son of sharecroppers was among the most colorful governors we met.

And while we try not to succumb to stereotypes, we have to believe that most independent observers would pick McWherter as the Tennessean out of a lineup of the 50 governors.

260 pounds. An easy smile. A fondness for vanilla wafers. Cowboy boots. And country music.

"I started listening to the Grand Ole Opry on one of those Philco radios. They had one button on there you turned, and a very dim dial. So I was raised in a community where there'd be one of those radios, and everybody'd gather on Saturday night and go to their neighbor's house and listen to the Grand Ole Opry."

Tennessee is a vibrant and growing state, making progress on many fronts. But this country gentleman governor says he still has a soft spot in his heart for Hank Williams Jr. and Minnie Pearl.

A *conversation with Gov. Ned McWherter.*

A substantial percentage of Tennessee's black citizens supported your election. How is your administration going to respond to that kind of support?

"We've already responded. Our campaign rhetoric said that we could take the same dollars in Medicaid, and through innovative management, we could help pick up a lot of indigent care costs. That addresses itself directly to the black community and the Appalachian community. The new budget will have an increase of $76 million in available funds to pick up indigent care in the health care program."

What has the new Saturn plant meant to Tennessee's economy?

"It's important to us, and we're very proud that a corporate structure like General Motors would pick Tennessee. Spring Hill's an excellent location. Nissan is a very important ingredient of our economy here. They're working about 3,300 people."

Tennessee has a lot of industry that other people want, but there is also some — such as the proposed nuclear waste storage depot, known as the monitored retrievable storage facility or MRS — which many people don't want.

"That's true, including the governor."

What, if anything, can be done to enforce your opposition to it?

"We are doing everything legally we can do. Last year, the Legislature passed a resolution to voice our opposition. I've recently notified the federal government that we would veto MRS coming to Tennessee. The majority of the Legislature feels the same way."

Why are you opposed to an MRS?

"Some of us just can't understand why we need a temporary site in Tennessee, without a permanent site designated out West that was discussed. Temporary becomes permanent in many cases. I've just opposed Tennessee becoming a nuclear storage site, a dumping ground."

What are your major concerns?

"I worry about everything. And about transportation. That's more dangerous. I have to have confidence in my government. I would assume, with the technology available, that they can handle the material and repackage it safely. But the overall danger and the transportation, coming in and out of the site, create tremendous concern."

In light of Tennessee's history of debate over religion and the schools, should values and morals based on the Bible be taught in the classroom?

"Both should be taught. That's my belief."

Hank Williams Jr. is your favorite singer. Who else do you like?

"Waylon Jennings I like very, very much. Eddy Arnold's been a standby for a long time. Minnie Pearl tells everybody now she's my neighbor. I tell people I'm Minnie Pearl's neighbor."

Do you see a lot of Minnie Pearl?

"My mother's very ill, and Minnie Pearl comes over and checks on her every day."

Tennessee became known four years ago as a leader in education reform. Is education reform under attack?

"No, the attack we have is an attack to continue to improve education. Lamar Alexander, the former governor of Tennessee, pioneered some changes. For example, we pioneered a merit pay concept, including the career ladder. We established summer schools for our gifted students. We have a tremendously high dropout rate, as other states do. We're going to now incorporate the dropout rate and the adult illiteracy programs into our education reform."

McWHERTER PROFILE

PARTY: Democrat.

IN HIS WORDS: "I may not be a show horse but I am a workhorse."

BORN: Oct. 15, 1930, in Palmersville, Tenn., to Harmon Ray and Lucille McWherter, sharecroppers and family restaurant owners.

FAMILY: Widowed. Two children, Linda, 36, and Michael Ray, 31.

EDUCATION: Completed high school.

TIMELINE

1948: Joined Tennessee National Guard.

1957: Worked in Bay Bee Shoe Co. factory in Dresden.

1964: Opened Sturdy Steps Inc., children's shoe factory, in Martin, Tenn.; bought beer distributorship, Volunteer Distributing Co. Inc.; added investments in oil distributorship, nursing home, two banks, 1,200-acre ranch and truck line.

1968: Elected to two-year term in state House of Representatives; served seven terms.

1986: Elected to four-year term as governor with 54 percent of vote.

1991: Term expires in January; eligible for re-election.

PRIORITIES

▶ Economic development: Won $50 million in funding for infrastructure; appointed Economic Cabinet Council.

▶ Education: Increased pay for beginning teachers; established state drug education, rehabilitation and enforcement program; initiated program to eradicate illiteracy by the year 2000.

▶ Ethics in government: Established system of public integrity and disclosure requirements for state officials.

NOTEWORTHY

Served seven consecutive terms as speaker of the state House — a Tennessee record. ... In 1986, became Tennessee's first Democratic governor in eight years.

PERSONAL

In 1986, family gave him two black Labrador puppies, Nip and Tuck, to keep him company in governor's mansion. ... Ardent outdoorsman, loves to go bird hunting. ... Portrait of his hero, Andrew Jackson, hangs in his office.

THE FUTURE

"I don't have any plans for any other office. When I'm finished being governor of Tennessee I'm going to go back down the road to Dresden (Tenn.) and be a private businessman."

▶ Health and human services: Opened pilot day-care facility for state employees; proposed program to provide care for young children of working parents; established first statewide program to combat substance abuse.

▶ Criminal justice: Began construction of two maximum-security prisons; proposed reorganization of juvenile system.

▶ Fiscal conservatism: Reduced state budget by nearly $100 million; cut 1,900 state employees from payroll.

▶ Housing: Established statewide housing program for low-income families.

▶ Environment: Established state's first program to reduce generation of hazardous waste.

▶ Transportation: Initiated state's largest highway construction program, worth $450 million.

GOV. WILLIAM 'BILL' CLEMENTS JR.

Bill Clements doesn't suffer fools lightly.

Clements, 71, has two terms as governor under his belt and has heard more than enough ridiculous questions from the press, thank you.

So when one BusCapade reporter asked a lighthearted question about whether J.R. Ewing in any way resembled real Texas oilmen, Clements glared and responded: "Where are you from?"

"Boston, Mass.," came the reply. "That's what I thought," Clements said acidly. "I don't think that's a serious question."

Then again, Clements wasn't all that fond of some of our more serious questions. Shortly before our interview, it was revealed that while chairman of Southern Methodist University's board of trustees, he had approved payments to some of the school's football players.

We asked Clements about the impact on SMU. His response:

"I've clearly stated to the Texas press that I'm not going to discuss it anymore, except with the bishops and the committee that was appointed by the university to investigate it. And I don't intend to discuss it with the press anymore. Too much has already been said about it."

Clements' feistiness came as no surprise. He has a reputation as a tough politician and businessman who doesn't mince words. Not every governor has gone on the record calling the state legislature "a bunch of idiots."

Still, Clements' toughness has served him well. He was not politically prominent when he announced he was going to run for governor in 1978. He fought his way to election as the first Republican governor of Texas since 1874.

Although he lost his re-election bid in 1982, Clements bounced back in 1986, defeating incumbent Gov. Mark White by a healthy margin.

A *conversation with Gov. William "Bill" Clements Jr.*

The prison system is a major headache in Texas. Is private ownership of prisons a solution?

"I want to strongly emphasize that it's an option we should utilize, but it is not a solution. For all of the historical past, we have built what I would call conventional prisons in Texas. But we have changed our direction 180 degrees."

Why such a dramatic change?

"In a large measure, this is due to the federal court intervention. We should have more detention centers, more pre-parole centers, more probation centers where we take these minimum-risk inmates. We put them in urban areas where they can work in the daytime and come back to minimum security at night on a highly structured deal. At the same time, they pay restitution to their victims."

Hasn't this been tried in other states?

"Not in the degree that we're getting ready to try it. Between now and Sept. 1, we will put under contract four 500-bed facilities in the metropolitan areas, where this theory will be put into practice for low-risk, non-violent inmates."

You obviously believe a businessman can and should run the government. Is that true at the national level?

"I'd be the first to acknowledge that, historically, our national selection in either party has not been in the business community. I'm a little prejudiced, but that would be a good idea. Business backgrounds and business abilities lend themselves to government."

According to the Commerce Department, Texas ranks near the bottom in per capita spending for human services. Why?

"That is absolutely a myth that has been given a long life by the media. Texas has a different tax structure. We don't have an income tax, and we have depended upon the delegated responsibility to the local counties for property taxes. So these kinds of statistics do not include what is the most important revenue of taxation in the state of Texas, which is local taxes."

But even when local taxes are figured in, only eight states pay less taxes total than Texas.

"Again, that's a myth. When all taxes are considered, we rank 23. We're just about in the middle."

The nation has a new immigration law, which will have a dramatic effect on Texas and other states. How do you feel about it?

"I don't think the rest of the country understands the magnitude of the problem in just sheer numbers as to how many illegal aliens we have in Texas, and how many are in California, the two principal states. Most of the sources feel there are probably 5 million illegal aliens in California, plus or minus 3 million in Texas. Now, that immigration bill represents some real problems to us in Texas."

What will happen in Texas if all of the people who would be eligible under that law apply for and receive amnesty?

"We've got a horrible problem. And it's going to affect services of all kinds. It will affect the political scene, our economy, there is no question about it. Now having said all of that, I would anticipate that there will be a great number of amendments proposed to that bill. So I would not suggest to anyone that they start taking strenuous measures with regard to the bill as it is now written until we see what's going to happen."

CLEMENTS PROFILE

PARTY: Republican.

IN HIS WORDS: "There is nothing false about me. You get what you see — warts and all."

BORN: April 13, 1917, in Dallas, to William Clements Sr., farmer, and Evelyn Clements, homemaker.

FAMILY: Married second wife, Rita Crocker, in 1975. Mrs. Clements, 56, is a civic-work volunteer. Gov. Clements has two children from previous marriage, B. Gill, 46, and Nancy, 45. Mrs. Clements has four children from previous marriage, Dan, 32; twins Bonnie and Barbara, 30; and Jim, 29.

EDUCATION: Studied engineering at Southern Methodist University.

TIMELINE

1937: Began work on drilling rigs as roughneck and driller.

1947: Founded SEDCO Inc., world's largest oil-well offshore drilling company; later named chairman of board.

1965: Named board chairman of Southern Methodist University; served second term as board chairman, starting in 1983.

1969: Named to Blue Ribbon Defense Panel, Department of Defense.

1973: Named deputy secretary, U.S. Department of Defense.

1978: Elected to four-year term as governor with 49.9 percent of vote; lost 1982 gubernatorial re-election bid; re-elected governor in 1986 with 52.7 percent of vote.

1987: Apologized for approving payoffs to football players in Southern Methodist University scandal.

1991: Term expires in January; not running for re-election.

NOTEWORTHY
Became USA's oldest governor when he turned 70 in 1987.

PERSONAL
Had hip-replacement surgery in January 1983. . . . Labels reporters "wise owls." . . . Loves hamburgers, barbecue and pecan pie. . . . Enjoys hunting, fishing and golf — has been on several African safaris. . . . Favorite hymn is *The Battle Hymn of the Republic.*

THE FUTURE
Won't run for third term in 1990. Plans to travel.

PRIORITIES

▶ Education: Increased education budget; signed bill creating Texas Academy of Math and Science and accelerated secondary school program.

▶ Economic development: Established Department of Commerce to promote international trade and recruit business; supports tourism promotion program; supports cooperation with New Mexico to attract two-state manufacturing plants.

GOV. NORMAN H. BANGERTER

IMPRESSIONS

Mormonism is a demanding faith. Among other things, followers are taught that hard work is a virtue and that you have to take responsibility for your actions.

It came as no surprise that Utah's governor, Norman Bangerter, a Mormon, embodies those traits. We spent the better part of an hour with Bangerter, but one story that he told revealed a lot about the man who sits in Utah's governor's office.

We asked him if it is tough for a non-Mormon to live in Utah. He answered with an anecdote:

"I'll just tell you a story my father told. He was a Mormon bishop, and I've been a Mormon bishop and a Mormon stake president. He said that when he was a bishop, and this was back in the '20s, a family came to see him and said, 'We're looking at buying a house in your ward. We want to know what kind of ward this is.'

" 'What kind of ward did you come from?' my father asked. 'It was a terrible ward. The people were unfriendly, we didn't have any friends, nobody liked us, we hated it,' they said.

"My father replied: 'Well, that's kind of the way the people are here.'

"A few months later, another couple came with the same question. He replied with the same question. 'What kind of ward did you come from?' he asked. 'It was a wonderful ward. People were friendlier than anywhere we've ever lived. Just a great place to live,' they said.

"My father said: 'Well, that's kind of the way the people are here.' "

The moral of Bangerter's father's story: "I think we tend to make our own breaks. I don't think Mormons are any more friendly or unfriendly than the average person," Bangerter said.

Utah is a grand example of "making your own breaks." It is what relentlessly self-reliant people made it. And Bangerter is carrying on that tradition.

A *conversation with Gov. Norman H. Bangerter.*

Some people have suggested that state governments are most efficient when run as a corporation — with the governor acting as chief executive officer. Would you describe your management style as similar to that of a chief executive officer?

"Yes, a lot of responsibilities are given directly to department heads, and I expect that they will get the job done."

Governor, you're a Mormon; 90 percent of the state's legislators are Mormon. Is there less separation of church and state in Utah than other states?

"No, I don't think so. That's always a topic of discussion, with this being the headquarters of the Mormon Church. Obviously, it's hard to separate people's philosophies from their voting. That's hard for governors as well. You tend to reflect your upbringing and the culture in which you reside. Certainly, the church doesn't come in and say, 'You will do this,' or 'You won't do that.' "

One of your major concerns as governor is overcrowded schools. How do you handle that without raising taxes or limiting the number of children?

"I don't control the number of children who are being born, so I'll steer clear of that one. As I tell people, I've taken the pledge — I'm not having any more children. But I have six (and a foster son), so I guess I've contributed. While the overall school-age population in the nation has been going down, ours has been going up."

Will that continue?

"Our estimates are now that in 1993, we will peak in actual numbers in public school enrollment, and then for the next decade, we will have a numerical decline in public education. Our birthrate has dropped from something over 3 per woman to something like 2.7, which is still above the national average of 1.7. That gives us a challenge that we've always had."

How serious is the overcrowding?

"We do have about a 25 average class size, which is higher than the national average, probably the highest in the country. But we have above-average performance as measured by the ACT tests and other data. We graduate more of our kids than virtually any other state, and we complete more years of education than virtually any other state."

Drinking and gambling are frowned on in Utah. Would the state change to attract more tourists, or will it stay fairly conservative?

"Every place in the world is going to change. And they're going to change in Utah. We are no longer an isolated society. It used to be that the Mormon Church said, 'All people who join the church, come to Utah.' That doesn't happen anymore. Now they say, 'Stay where you're at.' That will continue. A Mormon population will be diversified more and more as years go on. And that will have an impact on the state."

Speaking of change, you've had some difficult decisions in your two years: the largest tax increase in recent history —

"You can play that one down, if you'd like!"

— was passed by the Legislature last year. Will you run for re-election, and what kind of value do you place on the polls that show that there isn't anybody you could beat?

"I don't worry about that. That's today. The polls are taken on Election Day. Are they unhappy because of the tax increase? Is my opponent going to be for lower taxes? No. Whether he'll articulate that will remain to be seen. I don't think that's the issue. You've got to have the issues."

Does that mean you're going to try again?

"Oh, we're planning to try again."

BANGERTER PROFILE

PARTY: Republican.

IN HIS WORDS: "I think we tend to make our own breaks."

BORN: Jan. 4, 1933, in Granger, Utah, to William, farmer and building contractor, and Isabelle Bangerter, farmer and homemaker.

FAMILY: Married Colleen Monson in 1953. Mrs. Bangerter, 52, is a homemaker. The Bangerters have seven children, Garret, 32; Erdman Jake, 32; Ann, 30; Jordan, 29; Blair, 27; Alayne, 23; and Adam, 19.

EDUCATION: Studied history and physical education at Brigham Young University and University of Utah.

TIMELINE

1953: Joined Army.

1961: Named Mormon ward bishop (equivalent to head of a congregation); named Mormon stake president (head of diocese) in 1967.

1964: Became partner in Bangerter and Hendrickson Co., general contracting firm.

1965: Founded NHB Construction.

1974: Elected to two-year term in state House of Representatives; re-elected four times.

1984: Elected to four-year term as governor with 55.9 percent of vote; elected chairman of Western Governors Association in 1986.

1989: Term expires in January; eligible for re-election.

PRIORITIES

▶ Economic development: Established program to help small businesses procure federal contracts; founded 17 "Centers of Excellence" to encourage university research with commercial potential.

▶ Education: Increased funding, cut administrative budgets; expanded programs for year-round and extended-day schools; proposed block grant program to allow local districts flexibility in developing curricula.

▶ Criminal justice: Set up high school drug education program; established reparations fund for crime victims; mandated double bunking to save prison construction costs.

▶ Streamlined state government: Cut state spending 10 percent in 1988; cut state regulatory burden by more than 60 percent.

▶ Welfare reform: Requires welfare recipients to work or receive job training.

NOTEWORTHY

In 1983 named one of USA's top 10 legislators by the Republican Party. . . . In 1984 elected Utah's first Republican governor in 20 years.

PERSONAL

Enjoys golfing, boating, water skiing. . . . Visits mountain cabin on summer weekends. . . . Hero is Winston Churchill, has read all his books. . . . Favorite food is chili. . . . Likes to sound the siren on his security car for his grandkids. . . . Nicknamed "Stormin' Norman" because every year his staff challenges legislature to basketball game — and wins.

THE FUTURE

Running for re-election in 1988. "Another term would allow me to complete what I started. I'm a builder. I would never leave a house half-built."

GOV. MADELEINE M. KUNIN

IMPRESSIONS

Shortly after we interviewed Madeleine Kunin at the State House in Montpelier, USA TODAY was the host of a town meeting in nearby Burlington. She arrived a few minutes before the meeting began and made her way to the back of the auditorium.

Kunin had no entourage, no assistants. Anyone glancing in her direction would have thought she was just another Burlington resident out to see the proceedings. If those at the meeting recognized her — and certainly many must have — no one made a fuss about her or disturbed her.

Later, it occurred to us that it might be an appropriate gesture to introduce the governor, but by that time, she had left on other business. Clearly, she had come by because she was interested in what we were doing, not because she wanted to be seen or to seize the spotlight.

Kunin was just as unassuming in our interview. She genuinely seemed as interested in our questions and viewpoints as she was in her answers.

She has a unique perspective. Not only is she Vermont's first female governor, but she's also a native of Zurich, Switzerland, who came to the USA in 1940.

Unlike former Kentucky Gov. Martha Layne Collins, who was criticized by women's groups for not promoting a more feminist agenda, Kunin's politics have been well received by women's groups.

"I have not had a set of issues that have exclusively been women's issues, but I've incorporated women's issues among my issues," she said. "I've been a strong supporter of the Equal Rights Amendment, of choice, of child care, of issues that are traditionally considered women's issues. It's also part of my being, part of my value system."

Over the years, she has embraced an agenda emphasizing education and environmental protection. She has taken some heat from the business community, but refuses to believe that there must be a trade-off between protecting the environment and attracting business.

"I don't see it as a choice of one or the other. I think you have to see them in tandem," she said.

A conversation with Gov. Madeleine M. Kunin.

What do you think are the nation's perceptions of Vermont?

"Vermont is seen as a green space, a place of beauty and escape, where life is still somewhat different, where values are more genuine and old-fashioned."

In what ways?

"There are more traditional values and work ethic and respect for individuality, but it is also a very modern place with high technology and good jobs and culture. People know more about the nostalgia part of Vermont than they do about the contemporary Vermont. But the nostalgia is also accurate. It may not be accurate in the way that it's caught in a time warp, almost, in the public mind, but we still are different."

Educational funding was a very important item on your agenda this year. Will it be on your agenda again next year?

"One specific project I asked the business people to consider getting involved in was redistricting, which is another way to create equity and quality. We have more school districts in the state of Vermont per capita than any state in the union. This leads to great inefficiencies as well as to different tax burdens."

Acid rain is a big issue here. What would you like to see the federal government doing?

"Supporting Vermont's U.S. Sen. Robert T. Stafford, basically, in his initiatives and really having some limitations with teeth on emissions. The knowledge is there. The call for delays in terms of further study just doesn't hold water anymore. We need someone in the White House, frankly, who will lead the charge in the Congress to not make this a regional tug-of-war,

but realize that this is in the national interest."

Does a woman have a chance to be nominated for vice president?

"I'd love to see it. I would urge a woman for president. It's interesting. Women do have to do more than pass the same tests that men do. One of the questions, for example, when Geraldine Ferraro was running was, 'Can someone from the House win the nomination?' With Rep. Richard Gephardt, that isn't asked in the same way."

What can be done to increase the number of women governors and to send more women to Congress?

"Two things. We're beginning to build support structures to make it more inviting. And traditional political men's groups are becoming more inviting to women. I finally concluded that there are also some internal barriers that women have that have to be overcome. They can only be overcome by seeing other women in those roles. So it becomes self-perpetuating."

What does a governor need to know in the '80s that governors of 15 years ago didn't?

"I think the more technical knowledge, or at least access to people who have scientific and technical knowledge, is very important. What do you do with low-level nuclear waste? How do you dispose of trash in an environmentally sound way? How do you deal with nuclear energy?"

What else do governors need to know?

"I think you have to have a much closer relationship to the federal government. I think even in the '60s, at least in Vermont, the federal government was a great resource of funds and if you wanted to start a new program you could find a federal grant to do it. Today we don't have that federal largesse, but we still are dependent on the federal government. We have to figure out how to do some of the things the federal government used to do."

KUNIN PROFILE

PARTY: Democrat.

IN HER WORDS: "I knew there was danger as a child, though I personally felt secure. That influences your thinking, your values. I always felt very strongly that you couldn't just live in a shell, that you had to live in a community and be part of that community."

BORN: Madeleine May, Sept. 28, 1933, in Zurich, Switzerland, to Swiss shoe importer Ferdinand May and Renee May, language tutor, who fled to USA in 1940 with her son, Edgar, and Madeleine to escape the Nazis.

FAMILY: Married Dr. Arthur Kunin in 1959. Dr. Kunin, 62, is a kidney specialist and university professor. The Kunins have four children, Julia, 27; Peter, 25; Adam, 22; and Daniel, 19.

EDUCATION: Bachelor of arts in history, University of Massachusetts; master of science in journalism, Columbia University; master of arts in English literature, University of Vermont.

TIMELINE

1957: Hired as general assignment reporter by The Burlington (Vt.) Free Press.

1960: Named assistant producer, WCAX-TV, Burlington, Vt.

1969: Free-lance writer, English instructor at Trinity College, Burlington.

1972: Elected to two-year term in state House of Representatives; re-elected twice.

1978: Elected to two-year term as lieutenant governor; re-elected in 1980; lost 1982 gubernatorial bid.

1982: Radio talk-show host, WJOY, Burlington.

1983: Taught at Harvard University's School of Government; taught at Middlebury College, St. Michael's College in 1984.

1984: Elected to two-year term as governor with 50 percent of vote.

NOTEWORTHY
In 1984, elected Vermont's first female governor and state's third Democratic governor since the Civil War. . . . Gubernatorial win was the closest margin in state history — 50.02 percent. . . . Record $250,000 was spent on the campaign by both candidates in 1984.

PERSONAL
Speaks German, French, English. . . . Nicknamed "Maddie" in college. . . . Adlai E. Stevenson is her hero. . . . Walks, swims, skis and plays tennis for exercise. . . . Reads fiction, but not as much as she used to. . . . Favorite author: Toni Morrison. . . . Likes impressionist paintings. . . . Enjoys sailing and canoeing.

THE FUTURE
Announced re-election bid in 1987. "Timing in politics is almost everything. I am not ready to move on. There is more to do here in Vermont."

1987: Re-elected by legislature after failing to win majority of vote; elected chair, New England Governors Conference.

1989: Term expires in January; eligible for re-election.

PRIORITIES

▶ Economic development: Headed trade missions to Japan and Europe.

▶ Education: Proposed equalizing distribution of education funding; increased state education funding 45 percent.

▶ Environment: Won passage of water quality measure; proposed trash disposal program, solid waste management bill.

▶ Budget: Erased $35.8 million deficit, finished 1987 with $60.8 million surplus.

GOV. GERALD L. 'JERRY' BALILES

IMPRESSIONS

Gerald Baliles seemed like the perfect Virginia governor. His state is a living history book, and he would fit right in at a convention of history teachers. It's not so much the way Baliles dresses, which is conservative. It's primarily the way he lets a serious interest in the past influence his understanding of the present and the changes that will shape the future.

History and reading were very much a part of our conversation with Baliles. We asked him about the effect of history on Virginia and he said:

"Two hundred years ago, Virginians led the nation. We were the writers, the fighters and the thinkers. And while we should never forget who they were, we should never let them forever dictate the course of our future. They were willing to face change, and to grapple with it, and we must do the same. As much as we like to read history, we ought to be more concerned about making it."

Then we asked him about change:

"I don't know whether you have read (Arthur) Schlesinger's *Cycles of American History*, but it is a very good book for capturing the climate of change that we are experiencing in this country. And he makes a great point of the acceleration. Change has always been with us, but it's the acceleration of change that has to be recognized.

"There's an old saying in Virginia that the race is won not merely by the swift, but by the far-seeing — those who anticipate change. The thing that I keep telling our folks is that we have lost our insularity. Our neighbors used to be North Carolina and Maryland. Today, our borders extend to Brussels and Beijing and Brazil. Our competition for economic development is no longer just South Carolina, it's also South Korea."

Gerald Baliles is not given to media-ready answers that easily can be chopped up into five-second radio bites. He doesn't think that way. Ask Baliles a question, and you've got to be ready for not only the answer, but the reason for it, too. And he has the knowledge of history to back up his reasons.

A *conversation with Gov. Gerald L. "Jerry" Baliles.*

What did the 1985 election of a black lieutenant governor and a female attorney general, along with yourself, say about the voters of this state?

"We won handsomely because we brought to the campaign credibility, a record of accomplishment, and a commitment to the future. We were successful in raising money, and we were successful in conveying to people that this ticket reflected a modern Virginia — recognizing change."

Were race and sex big factors in the election?

"People were willing to vote for the ticket regardless of the fact that a black and a woman were on the ticket."

Did that help it?

"I'm sure that in some cases it helped."

Is the country as a whole ready for a mix like that in the top two or three political offices?

"I hope so. It would say a lot about us as a country."

Do Virginians feel slighted by Massachusetts' claim that it originated the celebration of Thanksgiving?

"We had it first. To set the record straight, the Thanksgiving celebrated in 1619 in Virginia did predate the observance in Massachusetts. There's enough room in our history books for Plymouth Rock and Virginia's Thanksgiving — just as long as it's mentioned that Virginia was first."

Has Virginia provided you any personal heroes?

"In Virginia, everyone has a very healthy respect and affinity for all of our early leaders. Perhaps Thomas Jefferson is one who receives the most attention. When I was in Charlottesville, at the University of Virginia Law School, people spoke of him with such reverence it was almost as if he were just out of town for the weekend and would be back."

What should the rest of the USA know about Virginia?

"It is first in per capita income in the Southeast, 10th in the country, and climbing. If you look at one of our great resources, it's geography. Virginia's location, midway on the Atlantic Seaboard, provides us with great access to the American market within a day's drive of 60 percent of the nation's population."

What shape is the economy in?

"When you consider that Dulles International Airport is not only the fastest growing air facility in the country, but increasingly is the international gateway for travelers, and that the port of Hampton Roads is the fastest growing seaport, you recognize that we have the ingredients for a very successful economy. Unemployment is half the national average. The challenge is how to sustain that kind of prosperity in the future."

Are there plans to make Dulles a key international air center?

"Dulles and Washington National Airport both have been neglected over the years, partly because they were the only two airports in the country owned and operated by the federal government. It became clear several years ago that there was no reasonable expectation that the $700 million to $800 million required to modernize both facilities could ever be obtained from Congress. And so we began working with business and other leaders to create a regional authority for the operation of Dulles and National."

Where does it stand now?

"The commission is taking over the properties, the personnel, beginning to lay the groundwork for the bond issues that will be required to modernize both facilities."

BALILES PROFILE

PARTY: Democrat.

IN HIS WORDS: "I may be characterized as low-key and laid-back when I'm sitting around a table, but I can turn it on when I need to — and I will."

BORN: July 8, 1940, in Patrick County, Va., to Syrus Baliles, truck driver, and Lottie Baliles, homemaker. Raised by his paternal grandparents James and Emma Baliles, farmers, after his parents divorced.

FAMILY: Married Jeannie Patterson in 1964. Mrs. Baliles, 47, is a former high school teacher. The Balileses have two children, Laura, 19, and Jonathan, 17.

EDUCATION: Bachelor of science in government, Wesleyan University; law degree, University of Virginia.

TIMELINE

1967: Named assistant attorney general; named deputy attorney general in 1972.

1975: Elected to first of three two-year terms in state House of Delegates.

1981: Elected to four-year term as state attorney general; resigned to run for governor.

1985: Elected to four-year term as governor with 55 percent of vote.

1987: Elected vice chairman, National Governors' Association; took office as chairman in 1988.

1990: Term expires in January; not eligible for consecutive terms.

PRIORITIES

▶ Education: Opened foreign-language academies for secondary school students to enhance international education; proposed expanded budget to fight illiteracy.

▶ Environment: Signed Chesapeake Bay Agreement to control pollution; endorsed state Chesapeake Bay Preservation Act;

NOTEWORTHY

In 1985 became the first Virginia governor to run on a ticket including a black candidate for lieutenant governor and a woman for attorney general.

PERSONAL

Voracious reader. . . . Famous for ability to remember the names of "up to 200 people" at a time. . . . Dubbed "Boldly Cautious" by reporters. . . . Wears conservative, tailored suits, silver-rimmed glasses. . . . Enjoys fishing, always carries a fishing rod in the governor's limousine. . . . *M*A*S*H* and *MacNeil-Lehrer News Hour* are his favorite TV programs. . . . Describes himself as "intellectually curious" and "fascinated with concepts." . . . John F. Kennedy, Thomas Jefferson and grandfather James Baliles are his heroes.

THE FUTURE

Plans to do "whatever is on the horizon in 1990," when his term expires.

signed ban on phosphates.

▶ Economic development: Supports government reorganization to promote international trade; has made four trade missions overseas.

▶ Transportation: Called special legislative session on transportation; created 13-year infrastructure funding plan.

▶ Criminal justice: Won approval for construction of two new prisons; established "no read, no release" program for inmates.

GOV. BOOTH GARDNER

The first thing that struck us about Booth Gardner is that he's having fun. His 51-year-old face has a prankish, boyish beam to it. He likes being governor.

The morning the BusCateers arrived at his office, Gardner stepped out into the hallway, looked at one of us with a serious expression and dryly said: "I talked with your wife this morning. She told me you would be wearing khaki pants and a blue blazer." The BusCateer almost believed it — until Gardner gave it away with a smile.

The "take it easy" philosophy clearly threads it way through Gardner's approach to life.

"If you don't take some time out for yourself, you're crazy," he told us. "We had a professional coach who was interviewed in one of the daily papers in the Seattle area, and they interviewed his wife. And they said to her 'Is he taking good care of himself? Taking some time out to exercise?' And she said, 'No,' in such a way that the next question was, 'Why not? What would he do if he could?' She said, 'He loves to play tennis.'

"So I read that, thought about it for a couple of weeks, and called him. I said, 'I'm Booth Gardner, do you know who I am?' He said, 'Yes, sir.' I said, 'I want to play tennis with you.' There was a minute of silence. Then finally, he started to make excuses. And I said, 'Look, I've heard them all. I figure if I can find time to play tennis in my job, you can find time in yours.' " So, they played.

Is there a serious side to Booth Gardner? You bet. Just look at his list of priorities: economic development, environment, welfare reform, education, human services, criminal justice, comparable worth, tax reform, insurance.

Gardner is tackling them all — and whistling while he works.

A conversation with Gov. Booth Gardner.

Washington is the closest of the contiguous states to the Far East. How much are you involved in Pacific Rim trade?

"Tonnage out of our ports has increased significantly, and we're very competitive with other West Coast ports. We don't have the population base here, probably never will. I'm not sure that we want to be a major market. But in terms of being a financial center, being an end point for shipment to the Far East or for imports from the Far East, Washington is tremendously well located. We have in this state the highest income per capita on trade of any state in the country."

You've made tax reform a major push. Is Washington going to have an income tax?

"We have a dysfunctional tax system in this state. We're dependent on two taxes — the sales tax and the property tax. Everyone recognizes that we aren't generating the revenue required to meet the demands. So the attitude is out there to look at this issue. It's the people's issue. They want to get that issue resolved. If it passes, we've got a more balanced tax system. If it doesn't pass, the issue is laid to rest for the time being."

The state is legendary for its apples, but aren't some Washington residents now looking into seaweed farming?

"Aquaculture will be one of the rising industries in this state in the near future. We have environmental concerns, but if we can work our way through those, I'm very confident of aquaculture. That will be growing seaweed, and salmon, and shellfish. It will be a significant contributor to the state's economy in the not-too-distant future."

Washington has a rainy reputation. But people seem to love it anyway. Why?

"You're within an hour of some of the best skiing in the United States. You're within an hour of some of the best sailing. We have a tremendous cultural base. While we're constantly trying to improve our schools, they are considered excellent."

What do you think distinguishes Washington from other states?

"We're doing a lot more movie production in this state because you can virtually film as though you're in any other state. We've got mountains, mesas, desert, water, canals, and small, old communities to give you a New England flavor. In a lot of respects, we have two states here, and they're both beautiful: the West, which is made up of mountains, the Sound, numerous lakes, and tremendous beauty, and Eastern Washington, which is a desert state, but highly irrigated. So we have a tremendous range of agricultural products — next to California, probably the greatest diversity."

How are other sectors of your economy doing?

"One of the things we're striving for in this state is diversification. We've had historic dependence on aerospace, forest products, agriculture, and fishing. And we've had tremendous military presence. But our goal is to promote economic development in the sense that there are job opportunities for people. You can't have a strategy for economic development if you don't have a solid foundation. And that foundation in any state is its educational system and its human services system."

How do you assess your performance?

"Well, I took this job with the attitude that there's life after politics. My belief about a job like this is that there ought to be an eight-year commitment, with a four-year checkpoint for the public to make a decision. The job, in a lot of ways, is a killer. But my goal is to try to make sure that about 60 percent of the job is fun."

GARDNER PROFILE

PARTY: Democrat.

IN HIS WORDS: "I'm not the flashy, bend-arm type of governor. . . . I think the results are what measure our effectiveness."

BORN: Aug. 21, 1936, in Tacoma, Wash., to Bryson Ross Gardner, car dealer, and Evelyn Booth Gardner, homemaker.

FAMILY: Married Jean Forstrom in 1960. Mrs. Gardner, 49, is a homemaker and former business owner. The Gardners have two children, Doug, 26, and Gail, 24.

EDUCATION: Bachelor of arts in business, University of Washington; master's in business administration, Harvard University.

TIMELINE

1961: At 25, inherited mother's fortune; investments included a ski resort, professional soccer team, pie company, pastry plant, apple orchards, oil recycling business.

1966: Named assistant to dean, Harvard School of Business Administration; named director, School of Business and Economics, University of Puget Sound in 1967.

1970: Elected to two-year term in state Senate.

1972: Named president, Laird Norton Co.

1980: Elected to four-year term as Pierce County executive.

1984: Elected to four-year term as governor with 53.3 percent of vote.

1989: Term expires in January; eligible for re-election.

PRIORITIES

▶ Economic development: Led four trade missions to Asia; initiated "Team Washington" plan to promote economic development and international trade; proposed establishment of agricultural trade centers; established assistance center to cut red tape for new businesses.

NOTEWORTHY
Washington's millionaire governor.

PERSONAL
Jogs around Capitol Lake, works out at YMCA. . . . Nicknamed "Walk-around Booth" for his "management by wandering around." . . . Calls everyone by their first name. . . . Hero is his stepfather, Norton Clapp. . . . Self-described junk-food addict — loves cheeseburgers, milkshakes. . . . First thing he reads in newspaper is baseball box scores.

THE FUTURE
Running for re-election in 1988. No national ambitions, but: "It would be fun to be an ambassador to Norway or Sweden. . . . I'll probably go back to being a soccer coach."

▶ Environment: Proposed financing plan to clean up and protect water resources; proposed hazardous-waste cleanup legislation.

▶ Welfare reform: Established Family Independence Program, which provides incentives for job training, education.

▶ Education: Proposed programs for early childhood assistance and to combat adult illiteracy; funded expansion, upkeep of the state community college facilities.

▶ Human services: Pushed through nearly $4.8 million in AIDS prevention programs.

▶ Criminal justice: Established tougher penalties for sex crimes against children and tougher parole restrictions.

▶ Tax reform: Enacted sales tax deferral for new firms from out of state.

▶ Insurance: Signed USA's first state-subsidized health care insurance plan.

GOV. ARCH A. MOORE JR.

IMPRESSIONS

It would be easy to assume that Arch Moore is one of yesterday's "good-time Charlies." He's older than many of the '80s governors — born in 1923 — and first served as governor of West Virginia in 1969. Easy assumption, yes, but the BusCapade news team came away thinking that would be wrong. Moore appears attuned to — and ready to tackle — today's problems.

First, fiscal conservatism is crucial to his economically troubled state, and watching the dollars is something he's known for. In fact, we discovered it's not just something he's known for; he practices it personally. That immediately showed up when we interviewed him at the Grand Traverse Lodge in Michigan during the National Governors' Association convention.

Moore arrived for the interview early — before some of the members of the BusCapade news team — and spent the time picking through his hotel bill, occasionally mumbling about how expensive things can be. Every penny clearly counted with him.

Second, his answers to our questions pointed to the troubled West Virginia of today, not the smooth-sailing West Virginia of his first years in office.

We asked him how things have changed.

"If I had talked with you 12 years ago, Massachusetts Gov. Mike Dukakis would have had the highest unemployment in the country, and West Virginia would have had the next to the lowest. In 12 years, we've seen an absolute reversal. I came back to the governorship in West Virginia in 1985 after the state had led the nation in unemployment for six years."

He added: "We've got to diversify the economic base of the state to match what's happening in the country. For example, West Virginia trails the country in sharing in the distribution of defense spending dollars."

Arch Moore didn't spend any time talking about the past. This 65-year-old governor has his eyes on the future.

A
conversation with Gov. Arch A. Moore Jr.

What contributed to West Virginia's downturn?

"The demand for energy, the transition in the U.S. economy, has not been kind to West Virginia. The Rust Belt syndrome, even though we're a small state, had a tremendous impact upon us, because we were a heavy manufacturing state."

So it was a combination of factors?

"Bad economic days were compounded because we were furnishing the energy in the country to the manufacturing base, the steel complex, and so on down the line. So we got hit on both ends of the spectrum. We saw a great deterioration in the manufacturing industries and then in the energy base of our state, which still represents more than 50 percent of the total economy of West Virginia."

Coal production is down?

"Oddly enough, we've produced more coal in the last year than we've done at any time. But it's been at a lower price per ton because of world market conditions. That gives us a much smaller base to tax and to generate state revenues, and with a considerable leveling of the manpower that was used."

What has changed for the better?

"We have a modern highway system, which was one of our very inhibiting factors to development in the past. We maintain a high structure of cultural activities in the cities. I left the governorship in 1977, which is only 10 years back, with an annual budget of $700 million. I came back to a budget of $1.6 billion, so it was a significant escalation. But in order to generate those funds, we really made ourselves unattrac-tive. We had the highest personal income tax rate. We've now given that back to New York."

Is the job tougher this term than it was in your first two terms?

"To me, there isn't any difference. Public perception would perhaps suggest that it might be a little bit tougher, in that the economic times that I inherited, and the accumulated debt that I inherited, represent great challenges."

What's West Virginia's best kept secret?

"A lot of people do not realize we're a state. When you say you're from West Virginia and somebody says, 'Well, I have a cousin who lives in Richmond,' that's great, but Richmond is the capital of another state."

How do you describe the workforce?

"There is a work ethic here, that old, historic relationship of respect for employer. You'll get more out of a West Virginian, I don't care what you've got him doing. I can remember my years on Capitol Hill. The other congressmen wanted to know if I had any young West Virginian secretaries, because when they came to Capitol Hill, at 5 o'clock they didn't go out of the starting gate like they did at the Kentucky Derby. They were there till 10, 11, 12."

How would you describe the quality of life in West Virginia?

"We have the lowest crime rate of any in the country. Our system of state parks is the finest on the Eastern Seaboard. We've got more fresh water than any other state east of the Mississippi. There is a quality of life here that is perhaps a little lower key, less pressure."

Is there any one person who exemplifies the spirit of a West Virginian?

"Mary Lou Retton thrilled every American in the Olympics. And she still has that confidence that speaks to West Virginians. Also Chuck Yeager, who has not let his fame dilute his romance with his home state."

MOORE PROFILE

PARTY: Republican.

IN HIS WORDS: "What I've learned from losing is that you're not master of your own fate. . . . In winning I've got to be better than everybody else. I've got to do more than everybody else. I've got to do it faster than anybody else."

BORN: April 16, 1923, in Moundsville, W. Va., to Arch A. Moore Sr., stamping plant safety engineer, and Genevieve Moore, pianist and homemaker.

FAMILY: Married Shelley Riley in 1949. Mrs. Moore, 61, is a former teacher. The Moores have three children, Arch A. Moore III, 36; Shelley, 34; and Lucy, 31.

EDUCATION: Bachelor of arts, political science, law degree, West Virginia University.

TIMELINE

1943: Joined Army Infantry.

1952: Elected to two-year term in state House of Delegates.

1956: Elected to two-year term in U.S. House of Representatives; served five consecutive terms.

1964: Elected delegate to Republican National Convention; re-elected five times.

1968: Elected to four-year term as governor with 50.9 percent of vote; re-elected governor in 1972 with 54.7 percent of vote.

1971: Elected to chair National Governors' Association; elected to chair Republican Governors Association, 1976.

1972: Elected president of Council of State Governments.

1978: Lost bid for U.S. Senate.

1980: Lost bid for governor.

1984: Elected to third term as governor with 53.3 percent of vote.

1989: Term expires in January; eligible for re-election.

NOTEWORTHY

In 1972 became first West Virginia governor to win second consecutive term. . . . In 1984 became first West Virginia governor to win third term. . . . In 1988 became first West Virginia governor to seek fourth term.

PERSONAL

Large brass elephant welcomes visitors to Gov. Moore's office — part of his collection. . . . Avid bridge and hearts player. . . . Plays tennis. . . . Collection of presidential signatures includes those of Abraham Lincoln and Franklin Delano Roosevelt. . . . Loves to read, has library devoted to "the history of the Russian system."

THE FUTURE

Running for unprecedented fourth term in 1988. "My fundamental responsibilities are to the people of West Virginia."

PRIORITIES

▶ Economic development: Established community and industrial development office with international trade division; established fund for reclaiming abandoned mine lands; streamlined regulations on coal mining.

▶ Education: Unsuccessfully proposed $75 million bond sale for construction, 10 percent hike in teacher salaries.

▶ Fiscal conservatism: Proposed refinancing $225 million debt after reducing it from $350 million; cut state workforce by 4,200.

▶ Streamline government: Proposed creation of consolidated medical services fund.

▶ Tax reform: Cut personal income tax, corporate net income tax, workers' compensation premiums and bank surtax; repealed inheritance tax.

GOV. TOMMY G. THOMPSON

IMPRESSIONS

Before being elected governor, Tommy Thompson was known as "Dr. No," the minority leader in the state Assembly who consistently opposed what he viewed as excessive state spending.

That's why it was a bit of a surprise to find Thompson, just three months into his first term, so expansive and expressive about his own goals. Clearly, this was a man who had made up his mind to do much more than just hold the line.

Thompson might never be a free spender, but he was showing signs early in his term that he might be a free thinker — a leader who would explore new ways to do things rather than just increase expenditures for current programs.

One early proposal: Thompson's own brand of "workfare" for people on welfare:

"People will have to sign up for vocational training for high school equivalence or for college courses. The state will pay for that, as well as pay for job training and day-care services. The second part of it is 'learnfare.' That's going to require young mothers in school to continue getting their education, and the state will pay for their day-care services," Thompson explained.

During our interview, Thompson was particularly intent on trying on his new hat as chief salesman for the state of Wisconsin.

"Wisconsin is a beautiful state," he told us. "We have four seasons. We've got a diversified economy, a great educational system, and a lot of things to offer economic development, the entrepreneur."

Although there are more bars per capita in Wisconsin than anywhere in the USA, Thompson insisted that Wisconsin's image as a heavy beer-drinking state is a "misconception."

If Thompson doesn't subscribe to others' tall tales about Wisconsin's winters and beer drinking, there's one legend he wisely embraces.

We asked him the inevitable question about whether the Green Bay Packers could ever recapture their past glory.

"The Packers? They've got some internal problems. But as Vince Lombardi in 1966 was able to make the unsung and the unknown a world championship team, I'm sure the Pack will be back."

A *conversation with Gov. Tommy G. Thompson.*

Do you think a governor today has more of an obligation to go out and be a salesman for his or her state than his counterpart of 25 years ago?

"Well, there's no question about it. The things I'm doing right now would never have been the norm 25 years ago. I'm involved in economic development, I'm involved in attracting businesses to the state. I meet with business leaders to find out what I can do to improve the business image in Wisconsin. We're putting more money into promotion and into tourism attraction. Let's face it, the federal government has given us the opportunity. The leaders of our society are not those individuals that live in Disney World on the Potomac River. It's the individual governors and their respective states that have become the real national leaders. I'm not saying that because I'm one of them. It's just that this is where new ideas are coming from."

Many of your farms are in financial trouble. Have you considered a foreclosure moratorium?

"That is counterproductive. All you do there is hurt the individual farmer who's doing well and going in to get a loan from the bank. If you're going to have a moratorium on foreclosures, the bank is not going to loan money on agricultural pursuits; therefore, you hurt the same people you're trying to help."

When this crisis ends, how many farmers will you have lost?

"We're down to about 40,000 dairy farmers right now. In 1970, we had 95,000."

What is Wisconsin's biggest problem?

"The biggest problem we have is the fact that we have not been competitive. We have not sold ourselves as a state. We have not been able to increase our exports, and we need to do that."

Could you elaborate on campaign criticism of how the federal government handles welfare?

"I firmly believe that people do not want to be on welfare, but the system locks them into dependency. The federal government has passed national criteria that paralyze states. They aren't allowed the flexibility and innovation necessary to develop a program that's suitable for the people of their particular state."

A federal judge recently upheld treaties that give the Chippewa Indians the right to sell fish and game they catch. Can you make these treaties work?

"It's a very emotional subject, and it's probably one of the most difficult that I have to contend with as a new governor. We just negotiated the new fish-spearing season for the coming year. We also are asking Congress to review the treaty rights."

Before you were elected, you said fish spearing was "wrong." Have you changed your mind?

"No, I think spearing fish is wrong. That's my personal feeling. But as governor, you have got to uphold the law, and the law is such that the treaties are in place, and we have to enforce the treaties."

To many people, Wisconsin means dairy lands and beer drinking. Is that accurate?

"That is a misconception. Wisconsin University is the No. 1 public university receiving research grants. In the last several years, we have become the bio-tech capital of the world; we have over 100 small bio-tech companies that have started up."

Is the fun-loving, beer-garden part of Wisconsin's culture lost?

"I don't think the fun-loving part is going to be lost. It is part of the tradition. Where else but the University of Wisconsin-Madison can you find three-quarters of the football fans staying around after the team has lost in order to hear the band play the 'Bud' song?"

THOMPSON PROFILE

PARTY: Republican.

IN HIS WORDS: "You only get a chance to run for governor once. You really do, and you have to take the chances when they're there."

BORN: Nov. 19, 1941, in Elroy, Wis., to Alan and Julia Thompson, owners of small grocery store.

FAMILY: Married Sue Ann Marshak in 1967. Mrs. Thompson, 46, is a teacher. The Thompsons have three children, Kelli, 17; Tommi, 16; and Jason, 12.

EDUCATION: Bachelor of arts in political science and history, law degree, University of Wisconsin.

TIMELINE

1966: Served in the Army Reserves; associate with private law firm.

1970: Solo law practice; founded Thompson and Schuh in 1984.

1966: Elected to two-year term in state Assembly; re-elected to nine consecutive terms.

1986: Elected to four-year term as governor with 52.7 percent of vote.

1991: Term expires in January; eligible for re-election.

PRIORITIES

▶ Education: Proposed increased education funding; proposed college tuition waiver for disadvantaged Milwaukee students; proposed subsidizing college tuition for disadvantaged minority students who return to Milwaukee to teach in poor neighborhoods; established "learnfare" program requiring school-age mothers to continue going to school and providing day care; expanded literacy programs; proposed tighter truancy laws, awards for outstanding teachers; proposed Parental Choice pilot program to help low-income students attend private or public

NOTEWORTHY
In 1986 became only Republican governor to ever defeat a Democratic incumbent in Wisconsin.

PERSONAL
Nicknamed "Dr. No" by critics because of his pledges to control spending. . . . Loves to hunt deer. . . . Likes to walk on his family farm. . . . Enjoys Clint Eastwood movies, westerns. . . . Favors dark suits, red ties. . . . Likes to water ski, snow ski, lift weights. . . . Displays his elephant collection in his office. . . . Opera buff, also likes country music, rock and Irish music.

THE FUTURE
Rejected bid for Sen. William Proxmire's seat in 1987. "It wouldn't be fair to the people of Wisconsin. I ran for a four-year term."

school of their choice.

▶ Welfare reform: Implemented workfare program providing education or training and day care; launched transportation program to match van pools with new workers.

▶ Tax reform: Began phasing out inheritance and gift taxes; cut personal income tax rate; proposed property tax relief measures, government spending limits, expanding sales tax; supports creation of tax rate disparity credit.

▶ Health and human services: Expanded community options program to provide home care for elderly and handicapped people; doubled day-care funding.

GOV. MICHAEL J. 'MIKE' SULLIVAN

IMPRESSIONS

The front door to the unassuming ranch-style house opened, and there stood a guy wearing chewed-up cowboy boots, jeans, a belt with a big western buckle, and a simple button-down collar, blue oxford cloth shirt.

"Hi! I'm Mike Sullivan," he said. "Come on in."

This wasn't just any ranch-style house. No, this was the Wyoming governor's mansion. And this wasn't just any cowboy inviting the BusCapade news team into his home. Fact was, this wasn't a cowboy at all. This was the governor of Wyoming. And the news team was getting a short course in the way things are done in Wyoming: casual, no pretense, down to earth.

What the guy in the boots — the governor — said next was:

"We can do this interview anywhere you want to. We can sit around this coffee table in here. Or we can go outside, sit in the sun with the dog, and do it out there. Whatever you want to do is fine with me."

This was our 26th governor's interview on BusCapade, and by then we had been guided through so many ornate corridors and seated in so many stately, paneled offices, that we weren't quite sure how to respond. But, without too much hesitation, everybody decided that the dog and the sunshine were the way to go.

If we found any governor who personified his state, it was Mike Sullivan. He was a perfect fit, despite the fact that he said he had not ridden a horse since he was a child.

Sullivan makes it clear that he is proud of the Wild West image:

"It is part of our heritage and our tradition, makes not only the quality of life but the people, and the way we treat people, different as well. At least we like to think that we make people feel welcome."

He does.

Just as cordial was the first lady, Jane M. Sullivan. As we made our way out, we found her digging in the flower garden. She was clearly delighted to be wrist-deep in good Wyoming soil. "The guys were having a tough time getting started," she said. "I have a pretty good idea of where I want everything to go."

A conversation with Gov. Michael J. "Mike" Sullivan.

Your state has always had a boom-bust economy. Is there a way to escape that cycle?

"We're looking for ways. Any state that's as dependent upon natural resources and energy as we have been is going to go through a boom-bust cycle that we've seen nationwide in the energy business. That's the nature of our society. I don't think we learn our lessons too well."

How can you guard against the ups and downs?

"Our efforts are to try to diversify, to attract other industries, to increase and encourage the tourist industry. That is such an important part. We're hit with a double whammy, as are many of the Midwestern and Central states, because we have both the energy crisis and the agricultural problem."

What industries are you trying to attract?

"We're looking for service-oriented industries that look to be the wave of the future. We're not looking at high-tech quite as much as some have, because that seems to have its own boom-bust cycle. We're looking to bring in as much and as diversified industry as we can."

Young people are leaving Wyoming to look for jobs. Is that a problem?

"It is a problem. When you have the kinds of economic conditions that we have, it's going to continue to be a problem, because the job availability is simply not there. We not only have young people, we have other citizens who have to look elsewhere for jobs."

What are the biggest surprises for visitors to Wyoming?

"The wide-open spaces and the blue skies. They just can't believe how blue the sky is and that you really have a view of the horizons."

Montana calls itself "Big Sky Country." Your sky's just as big, isn't it?

"I can't imagine that you can get many places with a bigger sky, or a more beautiful one. One of the most beautiful parts about this end of the state is that every evening, the huge thunderheads develop. If you go from Casper to Laramie, there's the Shirley Basin area. You talk about open spaces, this time of year it's absolutely beautiful."

How would you rate Wyoming with some of the neighboring states, such as South Dakota, Montana, Colorado?

"What distinguishes Wyoming from any state is the sparse population and the wide-open spaces. Now, all of the states that you've mentioned have wide spaces, but they're not quite as sparsely populated as we are."

How do you feel about the MX missiles, which are based at Warren Air Force base in the southeastern part of the state?

"It's one of those issues that I'm still watching. I am concerned about the continuing defense escalation."

Wyoming residents have been more receptive to the MX than other states. What does that say about their attitude toward national defense?

"People in Wyoming basically are conservative. They're very supportive of the country and patriotic. I suspect to some degree that has lent itself to the receptivity. There was a demonstration recently at the air base by an anti-MX group, so we're certainly not without serious concerns about it."

Some critics of employment and training programs have said that the best way to get people off welfare is to improve a state's overall economy. How do you respond to that criticism?

"I agree — the best way to reduce welfare rolls is to improve a state's overall economy. But that does not negate the need for effective training programs, especially to prepare workers for new technology."

SULLIVAN PROFILE

PARTY: Democrat.

IN HIS WORDS: Referring to his private-sector experience, "There is an advantage in a fresh look, not burdened by prejudices you might develop in government."

BORN: Sept. 22, 1939, in Omaha, Neb., to Joseph "J.B." Sullivan, lawyer, and Margaret E. Sullivan, legal secretary who managed husband's law office.

FAMILY: Married Jane Metzler in 1961. Mrs. Sullivan, 49, is a homemaker. They met in college. The Sullivans have three children, Michelle, 24; Patrick, 22; and Theresa, 17.

EDUCATION: Bachelor of science in petroleum engineering, law degree, University of Wyoming.

TIMELINE

1964: Practiced law in Casper, Wyo., with Brown, Drew, Apostolos, Massey and Sullivan; specialized in trial work and defending medical malpractice cases.

1986: Elected to four-year term as governor with 54 percent of vote.

1991: Term expires in January; eligible for re-election.

PRIORITIES

▶ Economic development: Signed two bills to fund loan programs for new and expanding businesses; set up coalition of state agencies to coordinate tourism promotion; established Clean Coal Technical Program to research coal processing.

▶ Efficiency in government: Initiated studies of state spending and reorganization of state government.

▶ Improved crisis management: Requested crisis management plan from state agencies.

NOTEWORTHY
Never held elected office before becoming governor.

PERSONAL
Enjoys fly-fishing for trout. . . . Likes to go hiking. . . . Resumed golf, tennis, jogging after 1987 back surgery. . . . Heroes are John F. Kennedy and Mother Teresa. . . . Favorite author is Robert Ludlum, favorite poet is Robert Frost. . . . Showcases western art in his office.

THE FUTURE
Hasn't decided whether to run for re-election in 1990, "Wyoming has been very good to me and my family. Public service is an opportunity to repay the state."

Allen H. Neuharth, 64, is chairman of Gannett Co. Inc. and the founder of USA TODAY, The Nation's Newspaper. A native of South Dakota, Neuharth joined the Associated Press in 1950. Later he launched his first newspaper, a statewide South Dakota weekly called *So-Dak Sports*, which failed financially.

He then worked as a reporter, editor and news executive for Knight newspapers in Miami and Detroit for 10 years. He joined Gannett in 1963, became president in 1970, chief executive officer in 1973 and chairman in 1979.

He is also the author of *Plain Talk Across the USA*, published by USA TODAY Books.

Kenneth A. Paulson, 34, has been a reporter and editor with Gannett for 10 years. Paulson was the editor of the *Green Bay* (Wis.) *Press-Gazette*, managing editor of the *Bridgewater* (N.J.) *Courier-News*, and began his career as a reporter for the *Fort Myers* (Fla.) *News-Press*. He was also a member of USA TODAY's start-up staff.

An attorney and member of the Illinois and Florida bars, Paulson is chief of staff and special assistant to Neuharth.

Phil Pruitt, 37, has been a reporter and editor for 15 years. He has worked as deputy managing editor of USA TODAY's Money section and assistant managing editor of USA WEEKEND. He also has worked at *The Greenville* (S.C.) *News*, *The Columbia* (S.C.) *Record*, the *El Paso* (Texas) *Times* and *The* (Trenton, N.J.) *Times*. He currently is on special assignment with Gannett's corporate staff.

This book is based on extensive interviews conducted with the nation's governors during USA TODAY's 50-state, 34,905-mile BusCapade, from March 16 to Sept. 10, 1987. Some of the interviews published here were supplemented with follow-up interviews and responses to a questionnaire sent to all the governors.

The biographical data on the profile pages is current as of June 30, 1988.

Gannett President and Chief Executive Officer John Curley, USA TODAY Editor John Quinn, USA TODAY Executive Editor Ron Martin, USA TODAY Editorial Director John Seigenthaler, USA TODAY Publisher Cathleen Black, USA TODAY President Thomas Curley, Gannett Vice President/News Charles Overby and Gannett Vice President/Public Affairs and Government Relations Mimi Feller provided special support throughout BusCapade.

Research assistance on this book was provided by Theresa Barry, Elizabeth Sullivan, Melinda Carlson and the Gannett/USA TODAY library staff.

The Gannett New Media staff helped design, edit and publish this book: Nancy Woodhull, Gannett vice president/news services and president of Gannett New Media, and Phil Fuhrer, Emilie Davis, Robert C. Gabordi, J. Ford Huffman, Randy Kirk, Lark Borden, Theresa Klisz Harrah, Bill Beene, Rebecca Conroy, Mary Demby, Carolynne Miller, Shelley Beaudry, Anita Sama, Leslie Lapides, Bert Gustavson, Susan Lynch, Kent Travis and Beth Goodrich.

Graphics and photography assistance were provided by Darr Beiser, Kathleen Hennessy, Marcy Eckroth Mullins, Suzy Parker, Greg DeRuiter, Tim Dillon, Scott Maclay, Bob Roller, Dean Sensui, Kathleen Smith Barry, Rob Swanson, John Blanchard, Tom Snoreck, Maggie Somerville, Ann LaRose, Bill Librizzi and Robert Tony.

JoAn Moore, Gina Porretta and Ha Nguyen provided valuable technical assistance in producing the book.

Juanie Phinney and Barbara Dutchak assisted throughout.

The staffs of all the governors provided invaluable help.

We thank them all.

Al Neuharth, Ken Paulson, Phil Pruitt

OTHER TITLES AVAILABLE FROM USA TODAY BOOKS

USA TODAY Books is the imprint for books by Gannett New Media, a division of Gannett Co. Inc., with headquarters at 1000 Wilson Blvd., Arlington, Va. 22209.

For more information or to order, write to USA TODAY Books, P.O. Box 450, Washington, D.C. 20044, or phone 800-654-6931. In Virginia, phone 703-276-5985.

Plain Talk Across the USA

Allen H. Neuharth
Pages: 320. Hardbound.

Full color throughout with more than 500 photographs and interviews with people in all 50 states. Features details on all 50 states and conversations with notable personalities from each state. Retail price: $16.95, includes shipping. ISBN: 0-944347-00-2. Publisher: USA TODAY Books.

And Still We Rise:
Interviews with 50 Black Role Models

Barbara Reynolds
Epilogue by Coretta Scott King
Pages: 224. Paperback.

A celebration of success and accomplishment in the USA. Features conversations with 50 men and women who share their insights and offer examples for success. Retail price: $14.95, includes shipping. ISBN: 0-944347-02-9. Publisher: USA TODAY Books.

USA Citizens Abroad: A Handbook

American Citizens Abroad
Pages: 128. Paperback.

A usable guide to living or traveling outside the USA, written by U.S. citizens living overseas. Tips on taxes, voting, going to school, personal finance, customs and how to get help. Retail price: $9.95, includes domestic shipping. ISBN: 0-944347-13-4. Publisher: USA TODAY Books.

The Making of McPaper:
The Inside Story of USA TODAY

Peter Prichard
Pages: 384. Hardbound.

When USA TODAY was launched on September 15, 1982, many journalists laughed at it and called it "McPaper," the titan of "junk food journalism." Now it is called No. 1, the USA's most widely read newspaper. A candid look at the ups and downs along the way. Retail price: $19.95, shipping extra. ISBN:0-8362-7939-5. Publisher: Andrews & McMeel (Kansas City, Mo.).

The USA TODAY Cartoon Book

Charles Barsotti, Bruce Cochran, Dean Vietor
Paperback

Cartoons from the pages of USA TODAY's Life, Sports and Money sections. Funny, but filled with insight into our lives, our work and our play. Retail price: $6.95, shipping extra. ISBN: 0-8362-2077-3. Publisher: Andrews & McMeel (Kansas City, Mo.).

Portraits of the USA

Edited by Acey Harper & Richard Curtis
Pages: 144. Hardbound.

Glossy, high-quality coffee-table book. Features photos taken for USA TODAY, many of which are award winners. Photos are portraits of life in the USA, seen through the eyes of USA TODAY's photographers and selected by USA TODAY editors. Retail price: $29.95, shipping extra. ISBN: 87491-815-4. Publisher: Acropolis Books Ltd. (Washington, D.C.).

Tracking Tomorrow's Trends

Anthony Casale with Philip Lerman
Pages: 268. Paperback.

Features charts and information based on USA TODAY polls and news research. Information written in USA TODAY's light, easy-to-read style. Trends and what is likely through the 1990s. Retail price: $8.95, shipping extra. ISBN: 0-8362-7934-4. Publisher: Andrews & McMeel (Kansas City, Mo.). Audio cassette interview with the author: $8.98, shipping extra. Publisher: Listen USA (Greenwich, Conn.).

USA TODAY Crossword Puzzle Book
Volumes I, II, III and IV

Charles Preston
Paperback

A series of puzzles from USA TODAY's crossword puzzle editor. Each volume contains 60 puzzles never before published in book form. Retail price: $5.95 each, shipping extra. Publisher: Putnam (New York).